ARKANA

G000272325

The Historica

H. W. Schumann was born in 1928. He studied Indology, comparative religions and social anthropology at Bonn University and earned his Ph.D. degree in 1957 for a thesis on Buddhist Philosophy. From 1960 to 1963 he was lecturer at the Hindu University in Benares, India. In 1963 he joined the Foreign Service of the Federal Republic of Germany and served in consular and diplomatic capacities at the West German missions in Calcutta, Rangoon, Chicago and Colombo. For several years he was in charge of the India desk at the German Foreign Office. At present he is the Consul General of the Federal Republic of Germany in Bombay.

Dr Schumann who, during his seventeen years in Asia, visited all the places related to the life of the Buddha, lectured on Buddhism at Bonn University. His more recent books are *Buddhism: An Outline of its Teachings and Schools* (1973), which in its German version ran through five impressions, and an iconographical handbook on Mahāyāna- and Tantrayāna Buddhism, *Buddhist Imagery* (1986). *The Historical Buddha* combines profound erudition in the Pāli canon and in Indian history and familiarity with the Indian surrounding.

धम्मचक्कप्पवत्तनसुत्तं

एकं समयं भगवा बाराणसियं विहरति इसिपतने मिग-दाये । तत्र खो भगवा पञ्चवग्गियें भिक्खू आमन्तेसि – "द्वेमे, भिक्खवे, अन्ता पब्बजितेन न सेवितब्बा । कतमे द्वे ? यो चायं कामेसु कामसुखल्लिकानुयोगो हीनो गम्मो पोथुज्जनिको अनरियो अनत्थ-संहितो, यो चायं अत्तकिलमथानुयोगो दुक्खो अनरियो अनत्थसंहितो । एते खो , भिक्खवे, उभो अन्ते अनुपगम्म मज्झिमा पटिपदा तथागतेन अभिसम्बुद्धा चक्खुकरणी ञाणकरणी उपसमाय अभिञ्ञाय सम्बोधाय निब्बानाय संवत्तति ।

"कतमा च सा, भिक्खवे, मज्झिमा पटिपदा तथागतेन अभि-सम्बुद्धा चक्खुकरणी ञाणकरणी उपसमाय अभिञ्ञाय सम्बोधाय निब्बानाय संवत्तति ? अयमेव अरियो अट्ठङ्गिको मग्गो, सेय्यथीदं – सम्मादिट्ठि, सम्मासङ्कप्पो, सम्मावाचा, सम्माकम्मन्तो, सम्माआजीवो, सम्मावायामो, सम्मासति, सम्मासमाधि । अयं खो सा, भिक्खवे, मज्झिमा पटिपदा तथागतेन अभिसम्बुद्धा चक्खुकरणी ञाणकरणी उपसमाय अभिञ्ञाय सम्बोधाय निब्बानाय संवत्तति ।

"इदं खो पन, भिक्खवे, दुक्खं अरियसच्चं – जाति पि दुक्खा, जरा पि दुक्खा, व्याधि पि दुक्खो, मरणं पि दुक्खं , अप्पियेहि सम्पयोगो दुक्खो, पियेहि विप्पयोगो दुक्खो, यम्पिच्छं न लभति तं पि दुक्खं – सङ्खित्तेन पञ्चुपादानक्खन्धा दुक्खा । इदं खो पन, भिक्खवे, दुक्ख-समुदयं अरियसच्चं – यायं तण्हा पोनोब्भविका नन्दिरागसहगता तत्रतत्राभिनन्दिनी, सेय्यथीदं – कामतण्हा, भवतण्हा, विभवतण्हा । इदं खो पन, भिक्खवे, दुक्खनिरोधं अरियसच्चं – यो तस्सा येव तण्हाय असेसविरागनिरोधो चागो पटिनिस्सग्गो मुत्ति अनालयो । इदं खो पन, भिक्खवे, दुक्खनिरोधगामिनी पटिपदा अरियसच्चं – अयमेव अरियो अट्ठङ्गिको मग्गो, सेय्यथीदं – सम्मादिट्ठि ...पे०... सम्मासमाधि ।

"'इदं दुक्खं अरियसच्चं' ति मे, भिक्खवे, पुब्बे अननुस्सुतेसु धम्मेसु चक्खुं उदपादि, ञाणं उदपादि, पञ्ञा उदपादि, विज्जा उद-पादि, आलोको उदपादि । 'तं खो पनिदं दुक्खं अरियसच्चं परिञ्ञेय्यं' ति मे, भिक्खवे, पुब्बे ...पे०... उदपादि । 'तं खो पनिदं दुक्खं अरिय-सच्चं परिञ्ञातं' ति मे, भिक्खवे, पुब्बे अननुस्सुतेसु धम्मेसु चक्खुं उदपादि, ञाणं उदपादि, पञ्ञा उदपादि, विज्जा उदपादि, आलोको उदपादि ।

H. W. Schumann

The Historical Buddha

The Times, Life and Teachings of the Founder of Buddhism

Translated from the German by M. O'C. Walshe

ARKANA

ARKANA

Published by the Penguin Group
27 Wrights Lane, London W8 5TZ, England
Viking Penguin Inc., 40 West 23rd Street, New York, New York 10010, USA
Penguin Books Australia Ltd, Ringwood, Victoria, Australia
Penguin Books Canada Ltd, 2801 John Street, Markham, Ontario, Canada L3R 1B4
Penguin Books (NZ) Ltd, 182–190 Wairau Road, Auckland 10, New Zealand

Penguin Books Ltd, Registered Offices: Harmondsworth, Middlesex, England

First published in the Federal Republic of Germany, under the title *Der Historische Buddha*,
by Eugen Diederichs Verlag GmbH & Co. 1982
This English translation first published by Arkana 1989
1 3 5 7 9 10 8 6 4 2

Filmset in Monophoto Baskerville

Made and printed in Great Britain by
Richard Clay Ltd, Bungay, Suffolk

Frontispiece:
The beginning of the Buddha's first sermon in the Pāli language and in the Devanāgarī script. Pāli can be written in all the alphabets of south and south-east Asia and also in roman. The Devanāgarī script is used in North India and Nepal. European Indologists generally use the Pāli Canon in the transcriptions of the Pāli Text Society, London.

Contents

Illustrations

Preface

Few personalities in the history of human thought have had such a wide and lasting influence as Siddhattha Gotama, the 'Buddha', and none has left his mark more deeply on Asia. The religion founded by him has not only brought consolation to innumerable people, but has also provided the basis of a lofty humanism and a culture of great sensibility. The first sermon preached by the Buddha at Sārnāth near Benares in 528 BC was an event whose beneficent effects continue to this day.

The title *The Historical Buddha* indicates both the subject of the present work and the limits of its scope. It excludes any treatment of the non-historical Buddhas of the past and the future who are frequently mentioned in Buddhist scriptures; it also excludes all legends which developed around the person of the historical Buddha, except in so far as a historical kernel could be detected in them. The book deals with the demythologized person of the great sage, with the age in which he lived and with the political and social conditions which made his mission possible and permitted its success.

Since there are already a considerable number of biographies of the Buddha, a new biography needs some express justification. This lies in the fact that Indology as a discipline has in the past two decades finally descended from its ivory tower and has now come round to viewing the great thinkers of India in the context of the events of their time and their surroundings. The age of the Buddha, the sixth to fifth century BC, has been placed in a new light as a result of recent detailed investigations. The Buddha is viewed no longer as a holy man floating in the air, so to speak, but as a worldly-wise organizer who knew how to exploit political situations with tactical skill: as someone, in fact, comparable to the greatest Indian of modern times, Mahātma Gāndhi, who was able to fulfil his mission because he was not only a pious Hindu but also a brilliant advocate and a realistic political thinker. No period of history was really a 'good old time', and the age of the Buddha was no exception – as is proved by the great interest shown in new doctrines of emancipation.

We would do well to regard it as a period in which people differed from us neither in intelligence nor in moral standards, but only in possessing a different view of the world and less technical command over the forces of nature – as people who were moved by exactly the same desires and hopes as ourselves.

Buddhists sometimes maintain that the Buddha as a person is not important, that not the ephemeral events of his lifetime but only his timeless teachings are worthy of our attention. There is something to be said for this view, and in fact we can leave the Buddha out of his system without removing any essential element. On the other hand, every philosophical view is a rationalization of the mentality of the thinker who produced it. A different person, or the same person in different surroundings, would have developed a different mentality and accordingly would have rationalized somewhat differently: in other words, he would have thought differently. Accordingly, the creator of a system is worthy of interest as a person and in the context of his circumstances, especially for the westerner who thinks in historical terms, and for whom the How of an insight is just as interesting as the What.

The philosophical-religious system, aiming at emancipation, which the Buddha preached to his Indian contemporaries in the course of his forty-five years' mission, is here sketched in its earliest known form. Readers who wish to know about the subsequent developments of the Buddha's teaching are referred to my book *Buddhism: An Outline of its Teachings and Schools* (Rider, London, 1973).

Where, in the following account, we are concerned not with philosophical details but with biographical facts or relationships, it is permissible to give the Master's words in abridged form or in a paraphrase. In this way they possibly come to life better than when presented in the repetitive 'sacred' style which is the product of the revision of the Pāli Canon by several monastic councils.

This Canon in the Pāli language is the most important source for the biographer of the Buddha, and accordingly Buddhist names and terms are given here in their Pāli form (e.g. Pāli *nibbāna* instead of Sanskrit *nirvāṇa*). Other names and terms are given in whatever is the most usual form: Sanskrit, Prākrit or Hindī.

It would have been possible to illustrate this book with pictures of

Buddha images. I have refrained from doing so, because representations of the Buddha in art in India date only from some four and a half centuries after the death of the Master, not long before the beginning of the Christian era, and represent not the historical Gotama but the already legendary Superman (*mahāpurisa*) into which he had been turned. Thus the inclusion of illustrations from Buddhist art would have reintroduced the legendary elements which had been filtered out. The historical Buddha is a Buddha without images.

My heartfelt thanks go to all those who have made this book possible, first and foremost to my wife, who for five years had to spend silent evenings, first in Bonn and later in Colombo, and to sacrifice many joint enterprises. My son Harald Kim, too, has made sacrifices: although he was born in India at the full moon of May, on the Buddha's supposed birthday, he occasionally protested when Pa was more concerned with past times than with him. I am also most grateful to the most senior German Theravāda monk, the Venerable Nyāṇaponika Mahāthera of the Forest Hermitage, Kandy, for his unstinting help and strenuous efforts on my behalf. Despite his own literary work and the urgent editorial demands of the Buddhist Publication Society, he found the time to read the manuscript with care. His comments have contributed considerably in improving the exactness of several sections.

Last but not least I owe gratitude to Mr M. O'C. Walshe, who translated the book into English. As a former university reader in German, Vice-President of the Buddhist Society in London, translator of the Dīgha Nikāya and author of several books, no one could be better qualified for the task.

H. W. Schumann

Note on Chronology

A word of explanation is called for for the dating of the historical Buddha adopted in this book, according to which, following the widely recognized 'corrected Ceylonese chronology', the Buddha lived from 563 to 483 B C. The undeniable weakness of this chronology, which was recognized by some early Indologists, led Professor P. H. L. Eggermont to reopen the question in four articles in *Persica* between 1965 and 1979, and he has since been supported by Professor Heinz Bechert (*Indologia Taurinensia* X, 1982). Both scholars believe the Sinhalese chroniclers are wrong, and date the Buddha about 115 years later. Their arguments are noteworthy, but need to be further developed before they can be regarded as providing final proof, and yielding an acceptable alternative to the previously accepted chronology. Accordingly, I do not (yet) accept them, but it is open to the reader to subtract 115 years from the dates given for events in the life of the historical Buddha.

Guide to Pronunciation

Vowels have their 'continental' values:
a is like *u* in *cut*
ā is like *a* in *father*
i is like *i* in *bit*
ī is like *i* in *machine*
u is like *u* in *put*
ū is like *u* in *rule*
e is always long, as *eh*, except before a double consonant
o is always long, as *oh*, except before a double consonant
ai is as *ai* in *aisle*
au is as *ow* in *how*.

Consonants are approximately as in English. The following should be noted:
c is like *ch* in *church* but unaspirated
j is like *j* in *judge*
ñ is as in Spanish, or like *ni* in *onion*
v is like *v* or *w*
ś, *ṣ* are both like *sh* in *shoe*
ṛ is a syllabic *r* (now usually read like *ri* in *rid*)
Underdotted *ḍ ṭ ṇ* are pronounced with the tongue-tip turned back
Underdotted *ṃ* marks a nasalized vowel, but is usually read as *ng*.

In the aspirated consonants *kh gh ch jh th dh ph bh*, the *h* must be clearly sounded (note that *th*, *ph* are just aspirated *t*, *p*, and not as in *thing*, *phone*).

Stress. If the penultimate vowel or syllable is long, it takes the stress, otherwise this falls on the syllable before that, if any: e.g. *Gótama*, *vinaya*.

Abbreviations

AN	Aṅguttara Nikāya (PTS transl. 'Gradual Sayings')
BAU	Bṛhadāraṇyaka Upaniṣad
BPS	Buddhist Publication Society, Kandy
ChU	Chāndogya Upaniṣad
Cv	Cullavagga (of Vin)
Dhp	Dhammapada
DN	Dīgha Nikāya (PTS transl. 'Dialogues of the Buddha')
Dv	Dīpavaṁsa
Itiv	Itivuttaka (PTS transl. 'As it was Said')
Jāt	Jātaka
Khp	Khuddaka Pātha
Mhv	Mahāvaṁsa
MN	Majjhima Nikāya (PTS transl. 'Middle Length Sayings')
Mv	Mahāvagga (of Vin)
P	Pāli
Par	Parivāra (of Vin)
PTS	Pāli Text Society, London
Ṛv	Ṛgveda
ŚBr	Śatapatha-Brāhmaṇa
Skt	Sanskrit
SN	Saṃyutta Nikāya (PTS transl. 'Kindred Sayings')
SNip	Sutta Nipāta (PTS transl. 'Woven Cadences')
Sv	Suttavibhaṅga (of Vin)
TBr	Taittirīya Brāhmaṇa
Thag	Theragāthā (PTS transl. 'Psalms of the Brethren')
Thīg	Therīgāthā (PTS transl. 'Psalms of the Sisters')
Ud	Udāna (PTS transl. 'Verses of Uplift')
Vin	Vinaya Piṭaka (PTS transl. 'Book of Discipline')
VM	Visuddhimagga by Buddhaghosa (English transl. by Ven. Ñāṇamoli, 'Path of Purification')

Quotations are from the PTS editions, generally with *sutta* number and subdivisions. Where necessary the reference by volume and page of the PTS (Pāli) text is given as well. Parallel passages are not cited.

563–528 BC

I

Youth, quest and enlightenment

LANDSCAPE AND POLITICS IN NORTH INDIA IN THE SIXTH CENTURY BC

On the platform of the railway station in the North Indian university town of Gorakhpur can be seen, besides the Indian travellers, visitors from Japan, Sri Lanka, Thailand and Burma, as well as Tibetan exiles and westerners. They are pilgrims, on their way to visit the Buddha's birthplace at Lumbinī, and his deathplace at Kusināra. For this northern Indian plain between the foothills of the Himalayas and the banks of the Gangā (Ganges) is the sacred land of Buddhism. It was here that the Buddha proclaimed his insights between 528 and 483 BC, and where the first community of followers arose. From here his teaching began its peaceful conquest of much of Asia.

The landscape, which in the Buddha's time was thickly wooded, stretches from the Tarai on the edge of the Himalayas 300 kilometres to the south in a flat plain, patterned with fields and dotted with villages brooding under scattered trees in the hot sun, several times broken up by slow-flowing rivers on which wooden ships with grey sails make their leisurely way. The principal conurbations are Allāhabād, Vārāṇasī (Benares) and Patna.

That is how it is in May and June, when the temperature reaches over 40 °C, but the landscape and the towns look quite different when the monsoon breaks in mid-June, having arrived from the south-east in mighty cumulus clouds. Tremendous torrents of rain pour noisily over the land for several hours at a time, the soil turns into a quagmire, the previously gentle rivers burst their banks in spate. Soon the heat becomes oppressive, one's skin develops prickly heat and itches. But gradually the temperature drops and makes the months from October to March temperate (15 °C) and pleasant. In January it can even become quite cold (3 °C) at night, and the bazaar traders offer cotton-filled coverlets for sale. Gradually, the mercury rises again, and from April the hot period begins anew. The flame of the forest trees burst forth in brilliant ruby-red blossoms. The hotter it gets, the more often the brainfever bird, the falcon-cuckoo, utters its hysterical-sounding cry, thereby assisting the oppressive atmosphere in keeping the tired person from sleep.

Just as the landscape and climate dictate people's way of life, so too do the political and social conditions. Whereas India's history before the time of the Buddha is obscured by the haze of distance, the veil is lifted in the sixth century BC, allowing us to recognize the political set-up in the sub-continent. Events and persons become clearcut and individuals with the same capabilities, qualities and desires as those of our own time make their appearance. And it is the Buddhist scriptures that convey all this to us.

Not, though, for the sake of recording history, as the Indians of that time did not regard political events worthy of preserving in memory. The object of the monkish chroniclers was to pass on the teaching (*dhamma*) that the Blessed One had revealed in his sermons, and declared to be the sole authority for future seekers after salvation. Having been passed on orally for centuries, the canon was written down shortly before the Christian era. From the statements about the place, occasion and circumstances of the Buddha's discourses, and from the commentaries on them, the age of the Buddha comes to life for us.

If the oldest Indian literary works, the Vedas, reflect a rural way of life, in the Buddhist scriptures we find the picture of an urban culture. We hear too of villages and peasants, but it is above all the towns that form the background to the Buddha's mission; they are the focal points of a flourishing commercial and political life. Their social centre was the local ruler, the rāja, whose decisions were dependent on the council, and usually also on the necessity of loyalty to a mahārāja (king or 'great rāja').

According to the Buddhist scriptures, the political picture of the central Gangetic plain in the sixth century BC was determined by four kingdoms, a number of oligarchic republics and a group of tribes.

North of the Ganges lay the powerful kingdom of Kosala with its capital Sāvatthi (Skt Śrāvasti), which in the Buddha's lifetime was ruled successively by Kings Mahākosala, Pasenadi and Viḍūḍabha. Important cities of Kosala, besides Sāvatthi, were Sāketa (Ayojjha), the former capital, and the pilgrimage city of Vārāṇasī (Benares). The King of Kosala, apart from his central territory, was lord over two republics and three tribal areas.

South-west of Kosala, in the angle between the Ganges and the Yamunā, was the small kingdom of Vaṃsā (or Vaccha), with its capital Kosambī and the pilgrimage centre of Payāga (now Allāhabād). The King of Vaṃsā was Udena, the son of Parantapa.

The kingdom of Avanti stretched below Vaṃsā and Kosala to the south of the Ganges. Its king, Pajjota, resided in Ujjenī, but had in the southern part of his kingdom a second capital, Māhissati. Avanti lay outside the area visited by the Buddha, and was converted to his teaching by his disciple Mahākaccāna.

Finally there was the elongated kingdom of Magadha, which touched Avanti in the east and was bounded to the north by the Ganges. Its wealth was largely based on iron ore which was obtained by surface mining not far from the capital of Rājagaha, and which served both for export trade and for the local production of weapons. In Rājagaha ('Kingsbury') resided successively Kings Bhāti (or Bhātiya), Bimbisāra (who was married to a sister to King Pasenadi of Kosala), and Ajātasattu, who shifted the capital from Rājagaha to Pāṭaliputta (now Patna). Ajātasattu's son and successor was Udāyibhadda, who like his father gained the throne by parricide, and who suffered the same fate at the hands of his son Anuruddhaka.

Beside these four kingdoms there were in the Middle Country several republics, all of them to the east of Kosala and the north of Magadha. These were of aristocratic-oligarchic character and were each headed by a president or governor (rāja), who presided in the state council and, when this was not in session, carried on the business of government alone. Only members of the warrior caste (khattiya, Skt kṣatriya) were eligible for election as rāja, that is, the nobility, and the seats in the council were also reserved for men of this caste. However, the other castes were able to listen to the debates, as the council-chamber consisted merely of a roof supported on columns.

The republics were named after the ruling nobility, who formed a minority of the total population, though no figures have been preserved.

The republic of the Sakiyas (or Sakya, Sakka), whose capital was Kapilavatthu, and whose ancient territory is today divided by the Indian–Nepalese border, adjoined the kingdom of Kosala on the north-east and was a vassal-state of the latter. The Buddha was a member of the Sakiya nobility.

The very extensive Malla republic had two rājas, who resided in the towns of Pāvā and Kusināra. Kusināra is described as an insignificant place, but it was here that the Master passed away into absolute extinction (Parinibbāna).

The republic of the Licchavī with its capital Vesāli and the republic of the Videhas, with its capital Mithilā, had joined together in the so-called Vajjian federation, to which for a time certain tribes belonged as well.

Beside the monarchies and republics there were the tribes. We know little of their governmental set-up, but the difference between them and the republics seems to have been that in them the rāja was not elected but appointed by the elders of the tribe, and that neither the rāja nor the elders had to belong to the warrior caste. Among the most important tribes were: the Koliyas, who dwelt south-east of the Sakiya republic, the boundary being the little river Rohiṇī (now Rowaī). There were many marriage-links between the Sakiyas and the Koliyas. The Koliyan capital was Rāmagāma (or Koliyanagara). Further, there were the Moriyas, with their capital of Pipphalivana, whose tribal area adjoined that of the Koliyas, still further east. Finally, mention should be made of the tribe of the Kālāmas, whose capital was Kesaputta. Their home was in the westward-opening angle between the rivers Ghāgra and Ganges.

There were occasional differences of opinion between the kingdoms, republics and tribes – mainly over irrigation and pasture-rights – but the general attitude was of peaceful co-existence. Anyone could freely cross the borders between the different types of state. This was the geographic, climatic and political environment into which Siddhattha Gotama, the future Buddha, was born in 563 BC.

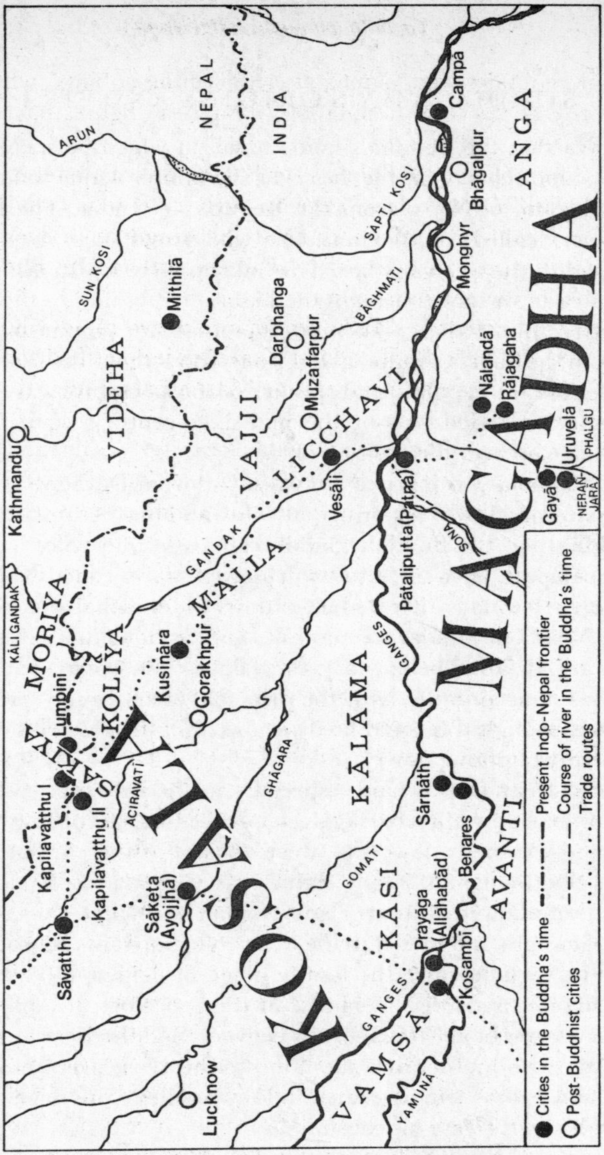

The area traversed by the Buddha in North India.

SIDDHATTHA'S ORIGINS AND BIRTH

Kapilavatthu, the Buddha's home town, in which he spent the first twenty-nine years of his life, lies near the border which today divides the Kingdom of Nepal from the Republic of India. The Buddha's father was called Suddhodana ('he who grows pure rice'), and he belonged to the Sakiyan clan. The Sakiyas were khattiyas: members of what was, at that time, still the highest caste, that of the warriors or, better, ministerials, who were responsible for administration and justice in the Sakiya republic, and from whose ranks the new rāja, the president of the republic and speaker of the assembly, was elected as occasion demanded. About the mid-sixth century BC it was Suddhodana who held the position of rāja.

Suddhodana was married to two sisters from Devadaha, the elder of whom, Māyā, was his principal wife and later became the mother of Siddhattha, the Buddha. Suddhodana's second wife, Pajāpati or Mahāpajāpati, gave birth to two children: a son called Nanda, who was born a few days after his half-brother Siddhattha, and a daughter called Nandā or Sundarīnandā. Like Suddhodana himself, the sisters Māyā and Pajāpati belonged to the Sakiya clan. Marriage within the clan was in accordance with the principle of endogamy practised at the time, though this could be disregarded in the case of love, or of a sufficiently tempting dowry.

More attention was paid, especially in the Brahmin caste, to the rules of exogamy directed against in-breeding, according to which marriage was not allowed between those bearing the same family name. Suddhodana's family name was Gotama, so he would not have been allowed to marry any woman with that name. That he obeyed custom and in fact made exogamic marriages is probable but not quite certain, since the family name of neither Devadahasakka nor Añjana is recorded. A glance at the genealogical table however reveals a close blood-relationship between Suddhodana and the two fair sisters: his mother and the father of his wives were brother and sister, and so too were his father and the mother of his wives. In other words, his wives were his cousins.

Kapilavatthu was Siddhattha's home town, but not his birthplace. As the *Nidānakathā*, the introductory narrative to the book of *Jātakas*

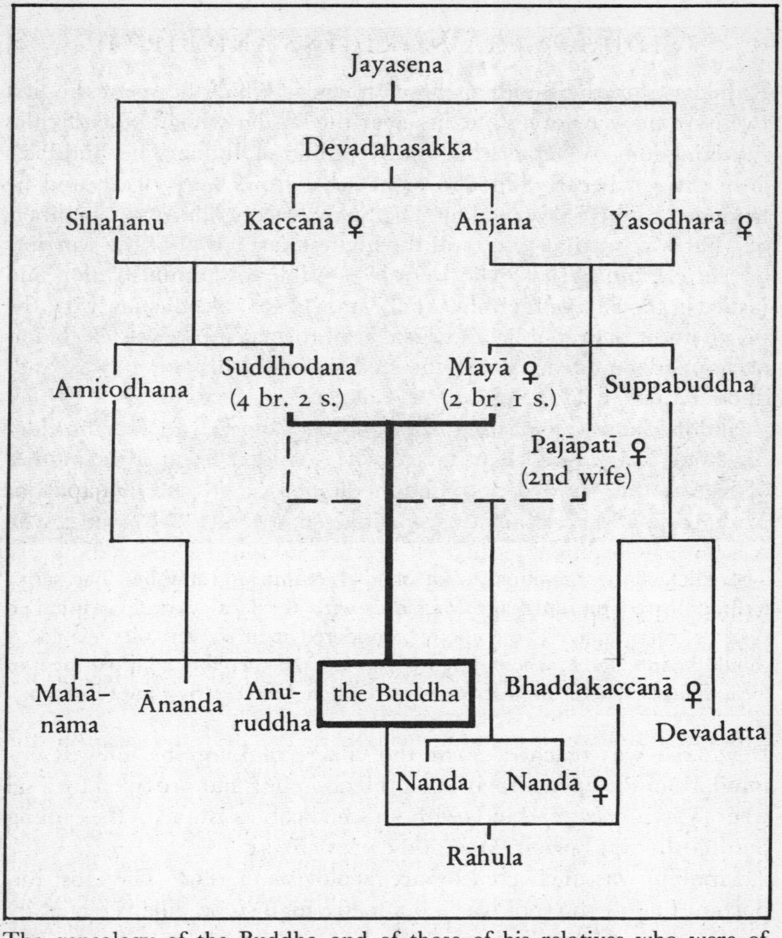

The genealogy of the Buddha and of those of his relatives who were of importance to the Order (simplified: some siblings and wives omitted).

('birth-stories') relates in legendary form, Māyā, who was already forty years old, had set out, shortly before the birth of her child, to go to the home of her parents in Devadaha, in order to have the child there, supported by her mother Yasodharā. The journey in bumpy horse- or ox-cart over hot and dusty roads brought the birth on before

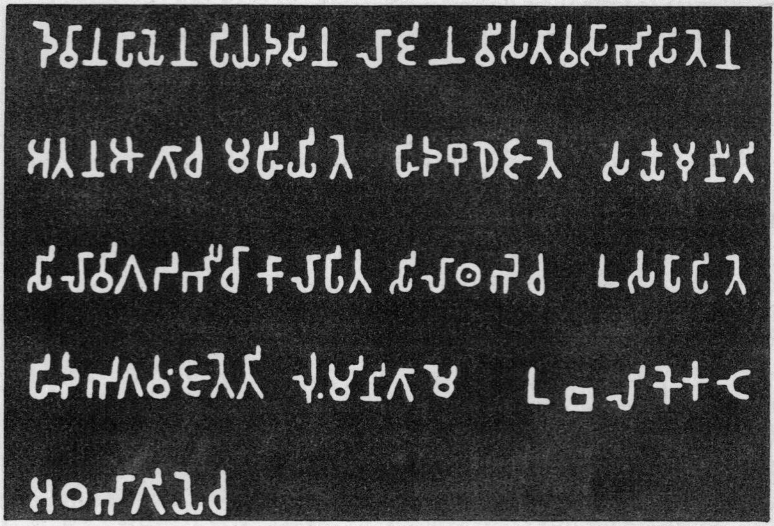

The edict of the Emperor Asoka on the column at Lumbinī. The script is Brāhmī and the language Māgadhī, with the local variations usual in Asoka's inscriptions. The emperor considered it important that his edicts should be intelligible where they were set up and therefore adapted them to local dialects. The Brāhmī script was deciphered in 1837 by James Prinsep.

Devadaha was reached. Near the village of Lumbinī (now Rummindai), in the open air with no protection but that provided by a sāl tree (*Shorea robusta*), and without medical assistance, the young Siddhattha was born in May of the year 563 BC.

Lumbinī was uncovered by archaeologists in 1896. The most important find at the spot was a 6.5 metre high stone pillar erected by the Emperor Asoka in 245 BC with the inscription:

> Twenty years after his coronation King Devānampiya Piyadasi (= Asoka) came here and paid homage, because the Buddha, the sage of the Sakyan clan, was born here. He ordered a stone relief (?) to be made and a stone pillar to be erected, to indicate that the Blessed One was born here. He exempted the village of Lumbinī from taxes and reduced its toll of produce (from the usual quarter) to one eighth.

Further, a stone tablet dating probably from the second century AD was found in Lumbinī, and is now preserved in a small temple on the spot. It shows Māyā giving birth to the child, standing and holding on to a branch of the sāl tree. Apparently, standing birth was a custom of the time.

After the rigours of the birth Māyā was unable to continue her journey to Devadaha, and her small retinue brought her back to Kapilavatthu exhausted. Joy over the birth of the newest member of the Gotama family was soon overshadowed by worry over the increasing weakness of the mother. Weakened by fever, she watched from her bed the preparations for Siddhattha's name-festival.

For divinatory purposes a wise man was called in, the aged Asita, an honoured friend of the Gotama family, whose name ('Not-White') refers to his dark skin, pointing to his descent from the pre-Aryan inhabitants of India. Asita had been the domestic priest of the Gotamas for many years – first under Sīhahanu, Suddhodana's father, and then under Suddhodana himself – before withdrawing into a hermitage. Asita inspected the three-day-old child and then prophesied, on the basis of certain bodily marks, that he was an extraordinary child, who would become a Buddha and would set the Wheel of the Law in motion (S Nip 693). With tears in his eyes because he himself would not live to see Siddhattha as Buddha, Asita impressed on his nephew Nālaka that he should in due course become a disciple of the Buddha.

Two days later, eight Brahmins performed the ceremony of naming Siddhattha. They too prophesied great things for him, either in the field of religion as a Buddha, or in the field of worldly fame as a mighty king. The youngest of this group of Brahmins was Kondañña, whom we shall meet again thirty years later.

But for Māyā the name-giving ceremony for her new-born son was the end. Seven days after giving birth, like so many mothers in tropical countries, she died, quietly and uncomplainingly.

However, the young Siddhattha did not grow up without a mother. Pajāpati, his mother's younger sister, and as Suddhodana's second wife his second mother, lovingly took charge of him: she had herself just given birth to Nanda, Siddhattha's half-brother. It is even said that she handed over Nanda to a wet-nurse and devoted herself especially to her sister's child.

PROBLEMS OF DATING

The majority of western historians of India consider the year 563 BC as being the birth-year of the Buddha and also the earliest assured date in Indian history. How is it calculated, and how great is the possibility of error?*

(a) Since the records of ancient India give only the intervals between events but do not, like later records, date the events themselves, it is necessary in order to establish dates in Indian history to call on Greek historians. Indo-Greek relations developed as a result of the Indian campaign of Alexander the Great (327 BC). About 303 BC the Indian Emperor Candragupta Maurya (P Candagutta Moriya) came to a territorial agreement and entered into diplomatic relations with Seleukos Nikator, Alexander's former general who ruled over Babylonia. Through the reports of the Greek ambassador Megasthenes, who was accredited to the imperial court of Pāṭaliputta (Patna), Candragupta (Gk Sandrokottos) became known to Greek historians, and through them we are able to date his accession to 321 BC.

This date further enables us to give precise dates to the sequence of events listed in the Singhalese chronicles *Dīpavaṁsa* and *Mahāvaṁsa* (fourth to sixth centuries AD). According to these (Dv 5.100; Mhv 5.18), Candragupta reigned for twenty-four years (until 297), his son and successor Bindusāra twenty-eight years (until 269), after which it took four years before Bindusāra's son Asoka succeeded in eliminating his brothers and anointing himself ruler (Dv 6.21; Mhv 5.22). This event would therefore have occurred in 265 BC.

The leap back to the birth of the Buddha is made possible by the statement made in both chronicles (Dv 6.1; Mhv 5.21) that Asoka became the ruler two hundred and eighteen years after the Parinibbāna (the final passing) of the Buddha. This event is therefore dated at 483 BC. Since the Teacher lived to be eighty, his date of birth comes out at 563 BC.

Although the figure of two hundred and eighteen years between the Buddha's passing and Asoka's coronation is regarded as dependable, this reckoning has its weaknesses. On the one hand it is

*See Note on Chronology, p. xii.

possible that the regnal years of the kings were rounded up to full years, and on the other, it should not be overlooked that in the *Purāṇas* Bindusāra is only supposed to have reigned for twenty-five years. So the reckoning based on the chronicles needs to be checked from other sources.

(b) One source of information is provided by the edicts which the Emperor Asoka (Devānampiya Piyadasi) caused to be carved on rocks and specially erected pillars throughout his vast empire. Rock Edict No. XIII, which dates Asoka's bloody conquest of Kalinga (Orissa) eight years after his coronation, and which was probably issued twelve years after that event, names five non-Indian rulers with whom the Emperor was in contact: Antiochus II of Syria, Ptolemy II of Egypt, Antigonus of Macedonia, Magas of Cyrene and Alexander of Epirus. The dates of all these are known, and the latest year in which they were all alive is 258, which is thus the latest possible date of the edict. Counting back twelve years to Asoka's coronation, together with the two hundred and eighteen years mentioned by the chronicles, we arrive at 488 BC for the death-year, and 568 for the birth-year of the Buddha. One possible source of error here is in the length of time that elapsed between Asoka's coronation and the issue of the edict, which may have been slightly less than twelve years.

(c) Chinese historians also provide some help through the 'Dotted Chronicle' of Canton, which shows one dot for every year after the Buddha's death. Down to the year AD 489 it presents 975 dots which would place the Buddha's Parinibbāna in the year 486, and his birth in 566 BC. With all respect for the historical accuracy of the Chinese, errors are not impossible here, too, especially since Buddhism reached China fairly late and the Chinese chroniclers did not start their chronicle immediately after the Indian master's death.

(d) We should also consider the Jain tradition. The founder of the Jain religion, the *Jina* ('Victor') or *Mahāvīra* ('Great Hero'), was a contemporary of the Buddha who lived to the age of seventy-two and is referred to in Buddhist sources as Nigaṇṭha Nātaputta.

European scholars usually date Mahāvīra's death at 476 BC, following the statement of the Jain monk Hemacandra (twelfth century AD) that the accession of Candragupta Maurya (321 BC) occurred 155 years after the Nirvāṇa of Mahāvīra. But Jain authors dispute the correctness of this figure and point to an alleged error of Hemacandra and to other passages in the Jain canon, which put 215 years between Candragupta's conquest of the kingdom of Avanti (312 BC) and Mahāvīra's death. This calculation would date Mahāvīra's Nirvāṇa at 527 BC. This is taken as the starting-point of Jain chronology (which was only introduced during the Christian era).

The attempt to deduce the Buddha's death-date from that of Mahāvīra is made more difficult because we have no unambiguous statements about the relative chronology of these two events. Despite the statement in one Jain Sūtra that Mahāvīra survived the Buddha by seven years (which, if we date Mahāvīra's death at 476, would confirm 483 BC for the Buddha's death-year), many Jains agree with the Buddhists that Mahāvīra died before the Buddha. Three times in the Pāli Canon (DN 29.2; DN 33.1, MN 104.1) the scene is described in which the Buddha is told of Mahāvīra's death, and the texts repeatedly indicate that Gotama was the youngest among the great religious teachers of his time.

Western biographers of the Buddha assume that the Teacher died two years after Mahāvīra, but the evidence for this is slight. If we were to accept the two years as a working hypothesis, we should arrive at either 474 (according to western scholars) or 525 BC (according to Jain tradition) for the Buddha's Parinibbāna, his birth-date being in each case eighty years previously.

(e) Still less credibility attaches to the chronology generally accepted in Asia today, according to which the Buddha died in 544 and was born in 624 BC. The Buddhist era ('BE') only came into existence in the eleventh century AD. Either the date subsequently worked out for the Teacher's death came to be mistaken for that of his birth, or else the monks, who presumably used a sixty-year cycle in their calculations, miscalculated by one whole cycle. This would give the Buddha's dates as 564–484 BC. But the hypothesis of such an error is naturally no proof.

Which of the dates calculated by these various methods can be regarded as historically the most probable? We can dismiss the dates based on either Jain or Buddhist tradition. They were calculated very late, and cannot stand up to historical criticism.

On the other hand, the dates deduced from the Singhalese and

Chinese chronicles, and Asoka's edicts, are well based and differ only minimally, so that according to them the Buddha's birth-date must lie between 568 and 544 BC. The date 563, which is supported by the Ceylon chronicles, is significant not merely as being in the middle but as being supported by two further, somewhat complicated calculations, based on South Indian and Singhalese king-lists, the date of the conversion of Ceylon, and also on scattered references to a very ancient system of dating, only fragmentarily preserved, which is based on 483 as the year of the Parinibbāna. We are thus justified in dating the Buddha's birth with the chronicles in 563 BC, admitting, however, on the basis of other historical evidence, the possibility of error of from plus five to minus nine years. The probability of an earlier date is slightly higher since it is supported by two methods (b and c), while a later date is supported by only one (d).

THE CITY OF KAPILAVATTHU AND ITS RĀJA

If young Siddhattha looked out northwards, he saw a jagged range of mountains on the horizon. This was, as he knew, about eight *yojanas* (80 kilometres) distant, but it was difficult to reach, for Kapilavatthu was separated from the mountains by a tract of reeds and jungle in which roamed tigers, elephants and rhinoceros, and many men who had ventured to cross this wild forest had died of fever. But if one succeeded in passing this obstacle the ground rose steadily, and one came to the wooded hills. Behind the foothills (today Śivalik or Churia) there was a green valley, and behind that again mountains (the Mahābhārata Range), some peaks of which could be seen from Kapilavatthu. Behind these, it was said, came still more and even higher mountains – the Himavat (Himālayas), whose mighty ice-peaks reached the sky, and there Jambudīpa, the Rose-Apple Continent, came to an end.

The prospect to the east was less forbidding. There lay Lumbinī, where he, Siddhattha, had been born under a tree, and beyond that lay Devadaha, where his mother, Māyā, whom he had never known, and Mother Pajāpatī, came from, and where grandfather Añjana had lived. From Devadaha one could travel a few days' journey towards sunrise, but then there was forest again and things became dangerous. There were dark-skinned hunters roaming there who spoke a language one could not understand.

To the west was quite different. There there was the road to Setavyā and Sāvatthi and beyond, and in Sāvatthi lived the king of whom father Suddhodana often spoke, and before whom one had to do *añjali* and a profound obeisance. The king had a large army, individual companies of which sometimes came to Kapilavatthu, where they were made welcome.

You could travel safely to Sāvatthi: the king's soldiers took good care to see that the caravans of ox-carts which carried all kinds of goods back and forth were not molested by robbers. Often columns of carts from Sāvatthi passed by, scarcely halting in Kapilavatthu, but continuing along the road to the south-east towards Kusināra and Vesāli and finally across the Ganges to Pāṭaligāma and on to Rājagaha, where there dwelt another mighty king. Siddhattha had heard that anyone who wanted to could get on a boat in Pāṭaligāma, and sail for several days up the Ganges to Vārāṇasī (Benares) and Payāga (Allāhabād). When he grew up he would visit all these and many other cities, in order to tell people about them. But whenever he described such plans to his father, Suddhodana only laughed and shook his head, saying a Sakiya was not supposed to wander about in the world like a homeless *paribbājaka*, or an oxherd or a merchant, but as a khattiya farmer he should till the land and practise the profession of arms, in order one day to be elected Rāja like he, Suddhodana, himself. And his father would point to the fields round about, between which stood groups of sāl trees, and to the city of Kapilavatthu standing there in the sun with its 'palace' and its clay houses and bamboo huts in the heat-shimmering air.

Which modern site corresponds to the original Kapilavatthu is still a matter of discussion by archaeologists. The Chinese pilgrim Fahsien, who visited the Buddhist sites in India between AD 399 and 414, makes statements which seem to point to the ruins by the modern Piprāvā, on Indian soil, 12 kilometres south of Lumbinī. His compatriot Hsüan-tsang, who visited the Buddha's lands some two centuries later (629–645) in search of the sacred scriptures, gives distances and indications of direction which point to the ruins at Tilaurakoṭ in the kingdom of Nepal, 24 kilometres north-west of

Lumbinī. The Indian–Nepalese border runs between these two points. They are 16 kilometres apart, but the landscape is similar in both.

The debate about the Buddha's home town is not entirely free from national prejudices. Nepalese scholars arguing for Tilaurakoṭ stress the extent of the ruins, and the existence of an ancient wall with a moat surrounding Tilaurakoṭ: features which only a rāja's capital city would possess. They point out that Tilaurakoṭ, like the Kapilavatthu of the Buddhist texts, lay on a river (the bed of which has since shifted 400 m to the north-west). In order to stress their claim to possess the historical Kapilavatthu, the Nepalese government in 1961 'renamed' Tilaurakoṭ and the entire surrounding district Kapilavastu (the Sanskrit form of *Kapilavatthu*), so that the place appears under this name on recent maps.

Indian archaeologists, on the other hand, maintain that Kapilavatthu is identical with the Indian Piprāvā, basing their claim on the following discoveries:

> In 1898, in a brick stūpa near Piprāvā, five vessels were discovered, one of which is described in an inscription in Brāhmī script, in the Māgadhī language, as the 'urn of the Exalted Buddha from the tribe of the Sakiyas'. The urn contained ashes and tiny votive offerings.
>
> In 1972, below this stūpa, at a level ascribed to the fifth century BC, a still older stūpa was found with two further urns, containing ten or twelve fragments of bones (of the Buddha?).
>
> In 1973–4, in a monastery ruin of the first or second century AD in Piprāvā were found various terracotta panels bearing a variety of inscriptions which make reference to the 'monastery of Kapilavatthu' or of 'Great Kapilavatthu', and a pot-lid found there bears similar wording.
>
> In 1975–6, finally, one kilometre south-west of Piprāvā, at a place called Ganwaria, the remains of an old building complex were found which could be interpreted as the 'palace' of the Sakiya Rāja.

Although the inscribed urn of Piprāvā found in 1898 – a 153 mm-

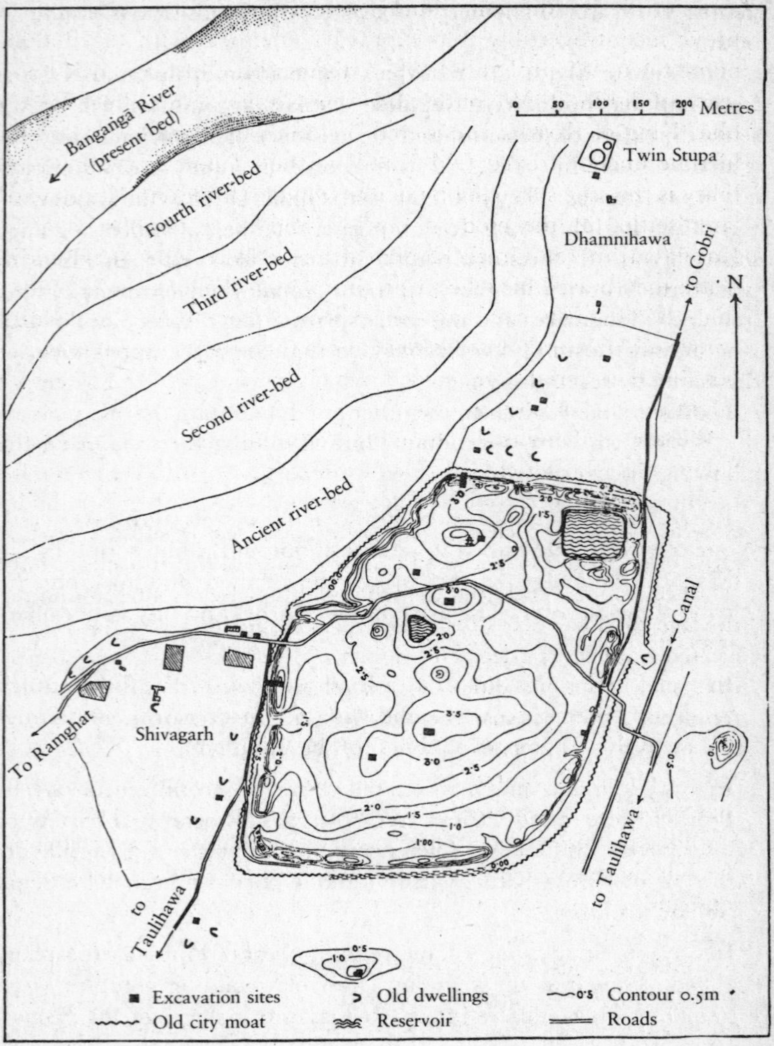

Tilaurakoṭ in Nepal, Old Kapilavatthu (= Kapilavatthu I).

high steatite vessel with an inscribed lid – really seems to contain ashes of the Buddha, the Piprāvā and Ganwaria discoveries do not prove incontrovertibly that Piprāvā is identical with the Buddha's home town. We probably have to distinguish Old Kapilavatthu, the scene of Siddhattha's youth, and New Kapilavatthu. Since Viḍūḍabha, King of Kosala, conquered the Sakiyans during the Buddha's lifetime and destroyed Old Kapilavatthu (Tilaurakoṭ), the probability is that the surviving Sakiyans who fled from Old Kapilavatthu later settled at the modern Piprāvā and there established a New Kapilavatthu (or Great Kapilavatthu), where after the Buddha's death they buried his relics. Certainty about the location of Siddhattha's home town can only be expected from future excavations. Above all, Tilaurakoṭ needs to be more thoroughly investigated. It is possible that aerial archaeology, which has not yet been attempted, might provide important clues.

We are well informed about the administrative structure of the Sakiya republic which was ruled from Kapilavatthu. When the half-brothers Siddhattha and Nanda were born, their father Suddhodana was, as stated, the elected rāja who ruled the republic's territory. How long he had held the office is not known, but it is clear that he retained it for several decades: when Siddhattha revisited his home at the age of thirty-six, his father was still in office. As the rāja was elected from the warrior and ministerial nobility, it is to be assumed that such elections did not take place at fixed intervals, but as required, either because the old rāja no longer performed his duties satisfactorily, or because the King of Kosala, the overlord of the Sakiya republic, wanted to put a new man in his place. It is certain that the rāja, once elected, could only take up his post if the King of Kosala gave his consent. Thus the Sakiyan rāja was always a man in the King's confidence – a factor which opened many doors for his sons and which was to play a part subsequently in the success of Siddhattha's mission.

Unlike in the Licchavī republic, where three rājas ruled jointly, Suddhodana ruled alone, but not autocratically, since all questions of consequence were debated in the council of the republic. The sessions in the council hall, which was open on all sides, could be listened to by all castes, though only male members of the warrior caste were allowed to speak, and, therefore, to take an active part in decision-making. They were therefore called 'rulers' (*rājana*). There was no voting in ancient India, because the idea that a majority could by mere numerical superiority bind a minority of different opinion to a decision had not yet occurred to people. Discussion simply continued until, whether through conviction or through exhaustion, the opposition gave in and a consensus was reached. In order to achieve such unanimity the rāja, as president of the council, had to possess considerable speaking ability and persuasive powers – characteristics which Suddhodana must have possessed to a high degree and which his son Siddhattha inherited.

We can gain an idea of the size of the area ruled over by Suddhodana from the Chinese Hsüan-tsang. He tells us that the Sakiya region had a circumference of 4,000 li (about 1880 km) and included ten cities – which the seventh-century traveller found destroyed and deserted. The city of Kapilavatthu, he says, was guarded by a wall, the brick foundations of which were still visible, of 15 li (about 7 km) in length. Apparently these ten cities must be largely identical with the nine that are described in Buddhist texts as Sakiyan cities: apart from Kapilavatthu itself, Devadaha, Cātumā, Sāmagāma, Khomadussa, Silāvatī, Medatalumpa, Uḷumpa and Sakkāra. They were probably regional capitals, each serving as a market and trading centre for a number of villages.

Hsüan-tsang's statements enable us, at least very roughly, to draw some conclusions about the area and population of the Sakiyan republic. Its area may have been about 2,000 square kilometres, of which a considerable part consisted of jungle and was unused for agriculture. If we assume for the fertile area of Central Tarai – working back from a higher figure at the present day – an average population density of 90 per square kilometre, this gives a total population of 180,000, of whom 8,000 will have lived in Kapilavatthu and 4,000 in each of the eight or nine provincial cities. Thus about 40,000 inhabitants of the Sakiyan republic were town-dwellers, and the remaining 140,000 villagers. The warrior nobility may have numbered about 10,000, most of whom lived in the cities but, like the majority of the population, practised agriculture.

The least popular of the rāja's duties was the collection of taxes, the extent of which is unknown. The peasants, who used barter among themselves and hardly knew money, had to pay their contribution in kind, mostly in rice, to special tax-gatherers who also had to provide storehouses and arrange for sale in the cities. The tax on the peasants depended on the success of the harvest, which was established by assessors: the later Indian theory of taxation, according to which all land belonged to the King who levied rent for its use by others, had not yet arisen.

Wherever possible, taxes were collected not in kind but in money. As there were no state-minted coins yet, the currency consisted of square silver, bronze or copper pieces valued at subdivisions of the *kahāpaṇa*. A milch-cow was worth eight to twelve *kahāpaṇas*. The *kahāpaṇa* was divided into 4 *pādas* = 20 *māsakas*. Smaller sums were reckoned in cowrie-shells. The coins bore the hallmark of a private banker who, as issuer, guaranteed the correct weight and promised to repay the face value in goods. He also did more business as a moneylender. No wonder the bankers became the most influential men in the community.

We do not know what share of the taxes Suddhodana had to pay over to his overlord in Sāvatthi, the King of Kosala. Since the income from taxation varied with the harvest, it was probably not a fixed amount. It is also possible that the King of Kosala was satisfied with presents which the Sakiya republic sent him from time to time as a mark of subservience.

Other duties of the rāja included public works such as the building of roads, caravan-stations, water-tanks, and the provision of dams and wells. As there were no volunteers for such work, all able-bodied men, and especially the artisans with their useful qualifications, were compelled to give labour (*rājakariya*). These public works were planned and directed by engineers who were paid a salary by the rāja out of taxes. The establishment of parks, dams and cisterns was later included by the Buddha in the list of ethically meritorious activities which would lead to a good rebirth (SN 1.47).

In addition to these internal activities, Rāja Suddhodana had to be active in the diplomatic field on two fronts. In particular he had to maintain contact with the King of Kosala in Sāvatthi, the overlord over the Sakiya republic. It was necessary to retain the king's goodwill and trust towards the small republic while at the same time keeping him at a distance so that the semi-independence enjoyed by the republic was preserved. Suddhodana must often have travelled to Sāvatthi, where sometimes conferences of rājas took place.

While the state policy of Kosala, the concluding of alliances and the waging of wars, was in the hands of the king, the rājas of the republics and tribes were in charge of 'good neighbour' policy. This was the second branch of Suddhodana's diplomatic activity. The object was to come to arrangements with the immediate neighbours without sacrificing their own essential interests. The most common problems were the regulation of pasture and irrigation rights along the frontiers. The rāja's skill was tested by his ability to effect satisfactory agreed solutions.

Warfare was not among the functions of the rāja. He had to maintain peace, but if he failed in this and armed conflict broke out, this was conducted by the military commander or general (*senāpati*), who held a post independent of the rāja. In the kingdom of Kosala all the generals, the commander of the central forces as well as those in the republics and tribes, were under the direct command of the king. In this way the king prevented any of his subject rājas combining with 'their' generals to play power-politics on their own.

For the rājas this separation of political and military power had two aspects. On the one hand they knew that the king had, in the person of the general, an ever-present means of compelling them to do his bidding. On the other hand, they were also protected against any attempts at a *Putsch* on the part of the general, because the king would never have tolerated the deposition of a rāja he had appointed and the seizure of political power by the general.

Another field of activity for Rāja Suddhodana was that of justice, in both criminal and important civil actions. We have no direct information about how criminals were seized and what form a trial took among the Sakiyas, but we can draw conclusions from the republics of the Koliyas and the Mallas, which adjoined the Sakiyan republic to the south-east. These had a police force whose members were distinguished by a special way of wearing their hair, and who were notorious for arbitrary brutality and corruption.

The process of law among the Sakiyas was probably little different from that customary in the Vajjian federation. Here, the basis of jurisdiction was a (written?) code, which presumably consisted of maxims or exemplary case decisions. Legal experts attended every trial and made sure the proceedings were in accordance with this code. The interests of the parties, or of the accused, were taken care of by advocates or defence counsel, and the case was decided by one or more judges. Appeals were lodged with the parliament, the general, the vice-rāja (who does not seem to have existed among the Sakiyas), and the rāja. It is assumed that the entire process took place in a single session, and that the rāja, as the highest local resort, pronounced the final judgement. The rāja could not pass a death sentence: this was reserved to the overlord in Sāvatthi.

SIDDHATTHA, THE RĀJA'S SON

That the sons of Rāja Suddhodana enjoyed a privileged position in Kapilavatthu because of their father's position, goes without saying. Whereas the majority of the population lived in houses of clay or huts of bamboo and reeds, which in the lower-lying parts of the city were built on piles to avoid flooding in the monsoon and the invasion of rats, snakes and scorpions, the rāja's sons lived in their father's house which, because it was of several storeys, was called 'the Palace'. It was probably built of brick, stood on a slight eminence and was surrounded by a low wall of earth which denoted the rāja's private defensive zone. Nearby was a pond with blue, red and white lotuses.

In Suddhodana's house the variations of climate due to the three Indian seasons (winter, summer, rainy season) were met by the seasonal change of sleeping-quarters: in the summer they slept on the roof-terrace. Even the numerous servants in the rāja's house had quite a good life. Instead of the usual servants' food of broken rice and rice soup they got full-grained rice and even meat (AN 3.39).

Among the children of Kapilavatthu the young Siddhattha stood out: he was better cared for and turned out than the others. His clothes were of Benares cloth, and at least in his early days he was continually surrounded by servants and by a nurse. In his own words he was 'spoilt, very spoilt'.

The Pāli Canon provides (DN 1.1.14) a list of ancient Indian children's games. We can picture the young Siddhattha playing with his half-brother Nanda at the eight- or ten-square game (chess? draughts?), or jumping with other boys over squares marked on the ground. Other favourite games were jackstraws, hitting sticks, and playing with toy ploughs, carriages and bows. Older boys could also amuse themselves with guessing thoughts and recognizing letters written in the air or on the guesser's back: this of course meant that the player in question knew how to read.

Whether Siddhattha could read is uncertain. A later legend indeed tells how he astonished his teacher by the ease with which he mastered the Indian alphabets, but in fact the Pāli Canon gives no indication that the Buddha was literate. The ability to read was in his day considered a useful accomplishment, but not one that formed part of elementary education. This was especially the case because, owing to the lack of suitable writing material, there were no written books, the only written documents being notices and agreements carved on stone or wood. Writing, literally scratching (*lekhā*) was considered an art (Sv 2.2.1) which was almost always practised as a profession. The attitude of the grown-up Siddhattha appears from his declaration (Ud 3.9) that the acquisition of skills such as writing was not suitable for a monk, who should be solely concerned with liberation.

On the basis of Siddhattha's lifelong interest in matters intellectual and spiritual, we can assume that the acquisition of such learning as was required for a youthful khattiya came easily to him. His education was greatly aided by his frequent presence at council meetings and court cases, at which his father presided. The council chamber helped to train his intelligence and teach him skill and accuracy in expression.

However, his intellectual development was accompanied by that of other qualities which probably worried his 'realistic' father as being apparent signs of weakness. These included sensitivity and a leaning towards reflection, perhaps even brooding. The realization that life was not always pleasant, and that behind all happiness (*sukha*) there lurk transitoriness and sorrow (*dukkha*) did not strike Siddhattha for the first time just before he adopted the homeless life (as legend would have it), but befell him already as a youth, while he was still living, free from outward sorrows, in the bosom of the family:

'I lived a spoilt, a very spoilt life, monks (in my parents' home). And, monks, in the midst of that happy life the thought came to me: "Truly, the simple worldling, who is himself subject to old age, is disgusted when he sees an old man. But I too am subject to old age and cannot escape it." At this thought, monks, all delight in my youth left me.

"Truly, the simple worldling, who is himself subject to disease, is disgusted when he sees a sick man. But I too am subject to disease and cannot escape it." At this thought, monks, all delight in my health left me.

"Truly, the simple worldling, who is himself subject to death, is disgusted when he sees a dead man. But I too am subject to death and cannot escape it." At this thought, monks, all delight in my life left me.' (AN 3.38)

Even in the formal language of the Canon the power of the initial experience can be genuinely and strongly felt. In a sub-tropical world in which a friend with whom one has just been happily chatting may be suddenly carried off by a fever, killed by the bite of a krait, or torn in pieces by a tiger, thoughts like those of the young Siddhattha are never far distant. And in principle they are valid always and everywhere.

Another characteristic of Siddhattha's appears from the records: his lack of interest in things military. Every khattiya boy was expected to be keen on riding, chariot-driving, archery, fencing, wrestling and handling elephants, and no doubt Siddhattha too must have been instructed in these things. But to the disappointment of all the Gotamas he seems to have been only averagely good at such activities, which for the son of the Rāja was rather shameful. Suddhodana must have been quite concerned at his son's unworldly and unmilitary ways.

When Siddhattha reached the age of sixteen (in 547 BC), Suddhodana decided to bind his over-thoughtful son more firmly to the world by marrying him. Of course it was an arranged marriage in which the partners were not consulted, but the texts do give an indication that they were drawn to each other. In accordance with the customs of endogamy and exogamy, a girl from the wider family was chosen, a niece of Gotama's dead mother and stepmother, the daughter of his uncle Suppabuddha (or, according to later sources, of an uncle called Daṇḍapāni) – in other words, Siddhattha's cousin. Her name was Bhaddakaccānā, but in the Pāli texts she is also called Bimbadevī, Yasodharā (like Siddhattha's grandmother) and Gopā. Some texts simply call her Rāhulamātā ('Mother of Rāhula'). She was the same age as Siddhattha.

His prospective father-in-law made difficulties, not wishing to see his daughter married to such an unmilitary, pensive young man. Siddhattha had to prove that he could stand his ground in skill at arms and sports before he could be trusted to support a family. The legend tells of a contest which was arranged so that Siddhattha might give proof of his qualities as a warrior. He passed the test by, allegedly, putting all his opponents in the shade. Thereupon Suppabuddha (or Daṇḍapāni) overcame his misgivings and agreed to the wedding.

It should not be supposed that the young husband was insensible of the attractions of his beautiful wife: he speaks with too much knowledge when, later, he says that there is nothing in the world that binds the spirit of a man as much as a woman (AN 1.1). But he did not allow sensual pleasures to draw him away, in the long run, from his contemplation. For whatever reason, the marriage remained childless for thirteen years.

According to Indian custom, the young couple will have lived in the house of the husband's father, in Rāja Suddhodana's 'palace'. The sources do not tell us how he passed his time at this period. Probably Siddhattha assisted his father in his political activities, and took turns with Nanda in overseeing the cultivation of the family fields; he may even have cultivated land of his own or had this done. In ancient India 75 per cent of the population lived from agriculture, including the nobility and most of the Brahmins.

AN ANCIENT INDIAN CITY

Siddhattha was probably not very drawn to agricultural activity, being by nature a thinker. With him, periods of retirement alternated with those in which he sought contact with people. The young Siddhattha must often have wandered around Kapilavatthu with his eyes open, exchanging a few words with a dyer, making a remark to an elephant trainer, or greeting a moneylender. The parables drawn from various trades that we find in his discourses show how sharply and consciously he must have observed the varied activities of the city.

Although we know little about Kapilavatthu, we can reconstruct something of what it looked like. Literary sources and numerous works of art, especially the reliefs of the Bharahat (Bhārhut) stūpa give us an impression of Indian cities in the sixth century BC.

The cities of that time generally lay on rivers and had, when the ground permitted, a rectangular form: circular city plans were unusual in ancient India. The city was surrounded by a moat of often considerable breadth and depth, which was fed from the river, and which the male youths used for sports and bathing. On the inner side of the moat the excavated earth was built up to form a rampart, often surmounted by a palisade or a stone wall with a footpath. Every 50 metres, i.e. within bowshot reach of the next, was a bastion, so that a neighbouring bastion could be cleared by archery of hostile escalading parties. At the four quarters the wall was pierced by fortified gates.

At the centre of the area enclosed by the wall, which was in principle divided up by a network of streets at right angles, stood the rāja's 'palace'. The palaces of some rājas – though not, it seems, that of Suddhodana – consisted of five individual houses, three standing parallel to each other, with two long-houses at right angles to them, closing the ends, so that the whole complex formed a divided rectangle. Of the two inner courts, one served as a utility yard, while the other was used for pleasure and relaxation. This one was usually planted with trees, and contained a swing with a large seat, suspended from four brass chains, for swinging was a favourite occupation of Indian ladies.

The main building was the central structure between the two courtyards. This was usually of two or even three storeys, each storey being smaller than the one below, so that there were open terraces. The roof was usually barrel-shaped.

Opposite the 'palace' was the council hall, open on all sides, actually only a roof supported by columns, and the mayor's house. Next came the houses of the officials, i.e. the serving nobility, which mostly consisted of four buildings in a square round an inner courtyard. The front portion was used as living-room and sleeping quarters, while the other structures housed the kitchen, servants' quarters and stables. Each of these houses, which strongly resembled the farmhouse it often still was, was separated from its neighbour by a narrow alley. This arrangement whereby the officials (who were nearly all of the warrior caste) lived close together, created a regular khattiya quarter, naturally interspersed with servants from other castes.

The cult centre for sacrifices – a meadow by a town pond with a raised platform as a feeding-place for the gods, and three fire-hearths – lay within the city wall, as did the dwellings of the Brahmins, who lived partly on the sacrificial ritual, but mainly from agriculture. In the Middle Land, they did not yet enjoy the exaggerated social prestige of later times, and as a caste ranked second to the warrior nobles. This was different further west (approximately to the west of Payāga (Allāhabād)), where the Brahmins had already gained the position of first caste.

Around the bazaar, not far from the better residential quarters, were concentrated the shops and workshops of the more luxurious and elegant trades, each in its own street: bankers and gold merchants, ivory carvers, clothiers and perfumers, brass and iron merchants, dealers in rice, condiments and sweetmeats. Every branch of industry, and every trade, was formed into a guild (*seṇi*), which exercised extensive regulatory functions. The guild decided questions of production and sale, fixed prices, which even the local rāja accepted, took part in the training of apprentices and even interfered in the domestic differences of members; if necessary the guild also looked after the widows of deceased members. Their pride showed itself in guild insignia which were carried on the occasion of public festivities, and also in the fact that the guild banned unworthy members from plying their trade – which often amounted to a sentence of beggary. All decisions were taken by a guild council, at the head of which was a guild chairman (*jeṭṭhaka*, *pamukha*). Above him was the guild president (*seṭṭhi*), who represented the interests of the particular branch of trade externally. He was usually purveyor to the court, and frequented the rāja's palace.

The richest guild was that of the bankers. Their main source of income came from moneylending, for which there were fixed rates of interest. A fully secured credit, as for the marriage and dowry of a daughter, cost 15 per cent, an only partially secured credit cost 60 per cent per annum. Commercial credits were especially dear owing to the high risks involved. Charges for financing a caravan were up to 120 per cent per annum, and for sea trading up to 240 per cent. The moneylenders, who belonged almost exclusively to the merchant caste (*vessa*), were not very high in the social scale, but in point of influence they were the leaders. Their president usually acted as doyen (*mahāseṭṭhi*) of the local heads of guilds, and was thus the most important man in the local commercial community.

A large house in the city was occupied by a certain lady who is often mentioned in the texts. Prostitutes were common enough in ancient India, and were contemptuously tolerated. But the artistic city courtesan (*gaṇikā*) was viewed with pride. She was not only beautiful and elegant, but also a witty if intriguing woman who enticed men chiefly through her artistic and literary culture. She was generally kept by one rich lover, who occasionally changed and sometimes ended up less rich, and she received other gentlemen of society at her song and dance performances, which were accompanied by a professional orchestra, or at her poetic contests and conversation parties. Young men of the better-off classes learnt good manners and life-style in her salon. No conventionally educated woman of the time had her command of the various forms of music, and none was able to converse in the elegant language as she could. Her appearances at weddings and other festivities gave the city a cultural tone. The forms of Indian dancing which have now become classical were partly developed by the town courtesans.

We do not know whether Kapilavatthu had a town courtesan, but it is probable. The names of the courtesans of other North Indian cities are known, together with accounts of some of their escapades, but also of their religious foundations. A courtesan could always adopt a bourgeois way of life through marriage.

The houses in the central area were solid and well cared for, frequently painted with figures and ornaments, but the further away from the centre, the more this impression changed. In the outer suburbs the workers and servants lived in clay huts and stilted bamboo shelters. They too were grouped according to their trade. There were streets of carpenters, joiners, carriage-makers, wood-carvers and instrument-makers, metal founders and stonemasons, weavers, dyers, tailors, potters, leather-workers and painters, florists and garland-makers, cattle-dealers and butchers, fishermen and cooks, barbers, bathmen, washermen, and town attendants. Each of the more respectable trades formed a sub-caste (*jāti*) within the system of the four castes (*vaṇṇa*). Outside the caste system were the casteless, with whom members of a caste had no social contact. But the idea of the 'untouchability' of such people had not yet arisen. This is only referred to in the (centuries later) *Jātakas* (e.g. Jāt 377).

It would be a historical error to interpret the caste system of the sixth century BC in the rigorous terms of later 'Hinduism'. The Buddha's contemporaries, especially in the Middle Land, where the process of Brahminization had advanced less than in the west, generally regarded the caste system as a secular hierarchy of trades, ranks and professions, and of education, which could be broken through. Change of profession, involving the transfer from one sub-caste to another, was difficult but possible, and even the ascent into a higher caste was not out of the question, for example if the rāja took a competent man of lowly descent into his service, or made a rich banker his finance minister.

If one left the city by one of the city gates, which were shut and guarded at night, one came, beyond the moat, to the leafy burrows that served as homes for the very poorest, who probably earned a fraction of a *māsaka* as fuel-gatherers or dung-brick makers, or perhaps found occasional employment cutting the grass in the parks of the rich. Parks of this kind were to be found in the neighbourhood of every Indian city, and one of the pleasures of the wealthy was to picnic there, and in summer to enjoy there the relative cool of evening.

For the young Siddhattha, these parks had a particular attraction, because it was here in the shade of the banyan trees that the wandering mendicants camped. Unkempt and with matted locks, they were often intelligent and subtle adventurers of the spirit, who scorned the sacred hymns of the Veda and the Brahmin sacrificial cults, and who had adopted the homeless life in the search for enlightenment. It was these free-thinking *samaṇas* and *paribbājakas*, who sought for mystical experience outside traditional forms, that Siddhattha liked to listen to as they philosophized, but the Gotama family, observing with anxiety his unworldliness and his curiosity about the transcendental, tried as far as possible to put a stop to this. When the legend tells us that Suddhodana guarded his son from contact with the world in order to keep the sight of suffering from him, the real reason may have been to keep him from ideas of renouncing the world.

THE VEDIC SACRIFICIAL CULT

No doubt the sacrificial religion of the sixth century BC disappointed anyone with serious religious aspirations. The divinatory enthusiasm that, a thousand years earlier, had enabled the Indo-Aryan seers to hear the wisdom (*veda*) of the gods in their own hearts and to turn that which they heard (*śruti*) into hymns; the literary pride with which they had collected their hymns to form the Veda, the 'sacred science', and to chant them in solemn rhythms at the sacrifice – all this had gone. The hymns were still chanted at the sacrifice as before, but in Gotama's time they were regarded merely as mechanically operating magic spells. The sacrifices had become more and more complicated and prolonged, and the sacrificial offerings and the fees for the priests had become more and more expensive for the sacrificer. The weight of mechanical 'good works' had almost suffocated the numinous.

The development from the inspired cults of early times to the ritualistic sacrificial religion of the sixth century can be followed in broad outline in the texts. Apart from the 1028 hymns of the *Ṛgveda*, the oldest document of Indian culture (*ca.* 1500 BC), we have the *Yajurveda*, the *Sāmaveda* and the later canonized *Atharvaveda*, also the prose *Brāhmaṇas* (*ca.* 1000 BC) which elucidate the ritual, the *Āranyakas* and the oldest *Upaniṣads* (*ca.* 700 BC). The *Upaniṣads* breathe the spirit of a spiritual renewal, and can already be reckoned as part of that movement for religious independence into which Siddhattha Gotama, the later Buddha, was to be drawn.

For people of our time many of the god-figures of the Vedic heaven are scarcely imaginable, because they combine theistic features with the conceptions of natural phenomena in a manner that defies logic. Very often, the characteristics ascribed to a certain god belong to contradictory categories which cannot be combined in thought. Thus, a large number of Vedic gods remain beyond definition in a semi-darkness, or three-quarter-darkness of inconceivability.

The first place in the Vedic pantheon was occupied by Indra, the Lord of the Gods, Master of a Thousand Powers and guardian-deity of the Indo-Aryans who had entered the Ganges plain from the west about 1200 BC. He was a mighty warrior and had once slain the drought-demon Vṛtra with his club, thus releasing the waters sealed up in his snake body as rivers. Brandishing the rainbow as his bow, sending forth lightnings from his sceptre (*vajra*), he rushed in his divine chariot from one battle to another with the demons who tried to prevent him from sending the fertility-bringing rain to the thirsty earth. His drink was soma, the sacred intoxicating potion which, mixed with honey and milk, his adherents offered to him in generous libations, in order to gain his good-will. For Indra was not only the embodiment of strength and manhood, and the stimulator of ideas and deeds, he was also the provider of wealth in the form of cattle, the fulfiller of material wishes. Whoever had Indra on his side lacked nothing. With native impudicity one worshipper of the great god appeals to his conscience:

If I, oh Indra, were like you,
Provider of all earthly goods,
Then he who sings my praises here
Would soon obtain the finest herds.

I would help him, Lord of Power,
In his honour I would give
And give, who gave me praise and thanks,
If only *I* were Lord of Herds!

(Ṛv 8.14.1–2)

Next to Indra came Varuṇa and Mitra. Varuṇa, the personification of the all-embracing sky, was revered as the guardian of truth (*ṛta*) and the cosmic order. His task was to preserve the regularity that underlies the course of the sun, the alternation of day and night, the phases of the moon and the seasons. He was also responsible for contracts and oaths, for a broken promise is a lie, and infringes the sacredness of truth which it is Varuṇa's task to protect. Since Varuṇa is regarded in the late Vedic period also as the lord of oceans and waters, he punished oath-breakers with dropsy: the diseases so common in India, oedema and filaria. A victim of such a disease implores Varuṇa:

Let me not go to the House of Clay, O Varuṇa!
  Forgive, O gracious Lord, forgive!
When I go tottering, like a blown-up bladder,
  Forgive, O gracious Lord, forgive!

Holy One, in want of wisdom I have opposed you.
  Forgive, O gracious Lord, forgive!
Though in the midst of waters, thirst has seized your
    worshipper.
  Forgive, O gracious Lord, forgive!

Whatever sin we mortals have committed
  Against the people of the gods,
If, foolish, we have thwarted your decrees,
  Oh god, do not destroy us in your anger!

(Ṛv 7.89, transl. A. L. Basham)

Varuṇa is frequently accompanied by Mitra, and in this combination Varuṇa denotes the night sky, and Mitra the day sky and the sun. Elsewhere Varuṇa is addressed as the strict pursuer (of lawbreakers), and Mitra ('Friend') as the uniter of mankind.

The heavenly bodies and natural phenomena played a predominant role in the Vedic pantheon. Uṣas, the dawn, was represented as a tender young maiden. The sun-god was called Savitar or Sūrya; he was worshipped as the originator of vegetable and animal life, and also as the dispeller of ignorance. The Maruts were the storm-gods of monsoon and rain-bearing winds, friends of Indra. Vāyu was the name of the wind-god, who was credited with purifying power and the ability to blow misfortune away. Parjanya, the rain-god, created the germ of life in plants and other beings. Pṛthivī was the earth-goddess, big-bosomed, broad-hipped and fruitful.

But how could one have sacrificed to the gods without Agni, the god of fire, who carried the sacrifices up to heaven with his tongues of flame and smoke, and persuaded the heavenly ones to visit the sacrificers on earth?

> Agni, the sacrifice that you
> Surrounding it, upwards bear,
> That alone reaches heaven.
>
> Agni, powerful with prayer,
> Faithful, bright in glory,
> O God, bring the gods to us!
>
> (Ṛv 1.1.4–5)

Agni was the god of the sacrificing Brahmins, and also the sacrificial priest of the gods. As bodily warmth he was a condition of life, but he was also a destroyer. The last sacrifice a man lays on Agni's altar is himself on the flaming funeral pyre. And then the grim god of death, Yama, carries the deceased off to his realm in the sky.

In early Vedic times the sacrifice had been understood as a ritual feasting of the gods. The word *ārya*, with which the Indo-Aryans described themselves, means 'hospitable' and is – since the gods are included in their hospitality – also a name for their religion. Invisible to profane eyes, the gods visited the sacrificer, descending on the open-air altar-like sacrificial seat. They were solemnly entertained by him to food and soma drink, and showed their gratitude with counter-sacrifices, such as causing the sun to rise every day, sending rain and assuring victory and wellbeing, and granting the sacrificer success, progeny, plentiful cattle and long life and strength. This counter-sacrifice of the gods could be depended on, provided no mistake had been made in the invocation and entertainment of the 'radiant ones'.

It was just this fear of ritual error which led to a fundamental change in attitude towards the sacrifice. For if it was no longer the intention of the sacrificer, but the observation of the correct forms that was of decisive importance, it was advisable for the lord of the sacrifice to entrust the feeding of the gods to an expert. The men who, on the basis of their command of the formalities and their knowledge of the magic word (*brahman*), undertook the carrying out of sacrifices on commission, and who in course of time came to be regarded as the sacrificial technicians and cultic experts, received the designation, first as an occupational term, later as a caste-title, of Brahmins (*brāhmaṇas*). And because people believed that the Brahmin celebrant could cause harm to his employer by wrongly performing the ritual, or distorting the hymns, everyone who wanted a sacrifice performed took good care to put the appointed Brahmin in a good mood by promising him a large fee and giving him a sumptuous meal.

As the cult-practices became more complicated, the sacrificial Brahmins became very arrogant, not only towards the sacrificers, but even towards the gods. Statements like, 'The gods depend on the sacrifice' (ŚBr 14.6,8,9) are frequent in the *Brāhmaṇa* texts, in fact the idea that the gods depend on the skill of the sacrificial Brahmin and could do nothing without the strength they obtain from the sacrifice runs right through the *Brāhmaṇa* literature. In fact: 'The [cultic] homage maintains earth and heaven, the homage is for the gods, the homage is lord over them' (TBr 6,51,8). The sacred sacrificial word (*brahman*) is a mechanical piece of magic which compels the gods to do the will of the Brahmin celebrant. The Brahman is almighty, and he who knows it and can utter it properly is superior to all others.

It is to the Brahmins' credit that, despite the unheard-of arrogance which they derived from their command of the magically effective word, they did make efforts to discover the reasons for its magic power. It was, as they recognized, the indwelling truth (*ṛta*, *satya*) which constituted the effective power of Brahman. *Ṛta*, 'truth', here means not so much logical truth in the sense of congruence between fact and statement, as *absolute* truth, truth as reality. Since Brahman, the 'true' sacrificial word, contains all reality within itself, since it includes whatever exists or is conceivable, it can perform anything.

Naturally, the cult centre of Kapilavatthu was laid out in accordance with the *Brāhmaṇa* texts. To the west of the elevated altar platform which served as a feeding-place for the gods, and which before each sacrifice was covered with cut grass, there burnt the fire which served for the preparation of the sacrificial food. It symbolized the sun, which causes life to come to fruition, and was therefore in a circular hearth.

To the east of the altar of the gods was a square hearth, in the shape of the world, which was imagined as a rectangular plate. The sacrificial food was poured into the flame that burnt there, so that Agni could carry it aloft.

Finally, to the south was the third fire which represented the moon, and was therefore in semi-circular form. It was meant to keep away the demons and prevent them from interfering with the sacrifice. A full sacrificial ritual required three celebrants and a supervising priest. At the end of each sacrificial act came the cry of *svāhā!*, 'hail!'

In addition to the great commissioned sacrifices, there were many smaller ones and all sorts of rituals to which the term 'sacrifice' is not applicable. There was sympathetic magic (such as causing rain by pouring water), adoptive magic (such as eating a tiger's heart to become brave), and there were rituals associated with the calendar and with domestic events of all kinds: weddings, births, name-givings, on the occasion of deaths, and so on. These too received their effectiveness through the magic word (*brahman*), which only a professional celebrant could pronounce with the proper intonation. The rank of ceremonial Brahmin was only gained by one who had lived for twelve years as a pupil in the house of a Brahmin guru, tending the fire, learning the hymns, mantras and rituals and leading a life of abstinence to develop superiority over the world. Only at the conclusion of this training was the young Brahmin allowed to wear the distinctive hair-style of the professional Brahmin, consisting of a knot of hair on the right side of the head, or in some places of three knots. If we consider the long and difficult course of training required to become a sacrificial Brahmin, we can understand why it was that only a small proportion of those men who belonged by inheritance to the Brahmin caste became professional priests.

THE RELIGIOUS LIBERATION MOVEMENT

With a nation as deeply religious as the Indians, and so eager for spiritual experience, a reaction against the Vedic-Brahmin sacrificial cult in its degenerate, mechanistic form was inevitable. This began in the seventh century BC, caught on among sections of the youth and, in the sixth century, developed into a powerful spiritual movement. It was not a revolution, because it remained tolerant, opposing the sacrificial religion only in public disputations. It was an unorganized spiritual movement, which left the established religion aside and in the quest for new spiritual goals adopted new paths. Some of these turned out to be false paths which led nowhere, others led to previously undreamed-of heights. In the sixth century BC the Indian mind attained to philosophical and religious heights which are still valid today.

The variety of emancipated groups can be reduced to four basic types of seekers after salvation: (1) the *Aupaniṣadas*, (2) the materialists, (3) the self-mortifiers, and (4) the wandering mendicants. Gotama came into contact with all of these for a longer or shorter period, and each group contributed something, if only negatively, to his system.

1 Those closest to the Vedic tradition were the *Aupaniṣadas*, the followers of the Upaniṣads, which had come into being from 700 BC onwards. Their doctrine was derived from the Vedas and *Brāhmaṇas*, but represented such an original development that their authors expected to meet with opposition from the orthodox. The *Aupaniṣadas* therefore kept their discoveries secret, as the name of their texts indicates: *upa-ni-ṣad* means 'to sit down with (someone)' – in order to convey the doctrine privately to him.

However, the texts did not remain secret for long. Their central message reached the ears of the Brahmin ritualists, who adopted a very skilful tactic: recognizing that an idea that has entered circulation can no longer be suppressed, they boldly adopted the Upaniṣads, making them into the superstructure of their own philosophy of sacrifice, and then added the 'secret' texts to the Vedic canon as an appendix (*vedānta*, 'end of the Vedas'). In this way the Upanishadic doctrine of all-unity became a part of the Brahmin tradition.

Only five Upaniṣads are pre-Buddhist in origin: the earliest of all is the *Bṛhadāraṇyaka*, and the *Chāndogya* is nearly as old. Then follow, somewhat later, the *Taittirīya*, *Aitareya* and the *Kauśītaki*. Since these texts are largely the record of experimentally based fabulation, and contain long passages of speculation about identity in the style of the *Brāhmaṇas*, they are not altogether enlightening. But in places, particularly in the narrative passages, sudden flashes of joyous recognition appear, intuitive insights that cast a brilliant light on a problem. No single one of these Upaniṣads presents a complete philosophy: each one only provides partial contributions. It is only the combination of the relevant statements of all the Upaniṣads together that constitutes the system that, under the name of Vedānta, forms a peak of Hindu thought. The system was worked into a precise philosophy by Śankara about AD 800, and, in a renewed form, by Rāmānuja about AD 1100.

From the *Ṛgveda* to the Upaniṣads we can follow the historical development of the word *brahman*, and its shift of meaning. In the Veda *brahman* denoted the sacrificial word which is effective owing to the indwelling truth (*ṛta*, *satya*) in it. In the Upaniṣads it comes to be a full embodiment, a synonym of truth itself: 'The name (i.e. the essence) of this Brahman is Truth' (ChU 8.3,4), 'Brahman *is* Truth' (BAU 5.5). More than this: *Brahman* came to mean in the Upaniṣads the Absolute, 'Ultimate Reality', and the Upaṇishadic thinkers make great efforts to make this Absolute, which embraces totality and is immanent in everything, intelligible in words. They use the typical method of mysticism, the symbol, the identity of opposites, and negative description.

Brahman is the cause of everything (BAU 1.4.21); just as everything that exists in the world is included in space, so space is included in the imperishable, which is Brahman (BAU 3.8.8). Since it pervades everything as spirit, it is also at home in man: the body is the castle of Brahman. It dwells in a tiny empty space in the heart, minute, and yet as great as the cosmos. In it lies the All, everything that exists and all latent possibilities. When the body grows old and dies, Brahman does not grow old and die (ChU 8.1, 1–5). Whoever knows the imperishable Brahman is assured of deliverance after death (BAU 3.8.11). The task of whoever seeks liberation is to become a knower of Brahman.

The knowing subject is the *ātman*, the self, and it is this that performs the tasks of seeing, hearing, thinking and knowing (BAU 3.5.1). The *ātman* creates the worlds, the gods, and earthly beings (BAU 2.1.23), and is ruler over everything (BAU 4.4.24). It dwells in the heart, smaller than a grain of rice or barley, but greater than the earth, greater than heaven and these worlds (ChU 3.14.2–3). The body is the dwelling-place of the eternal, non-physical *ātman*

(ChU 8.12.1), and dies as soon as the *ātman* leaves it (ChU 6,11,3). But the *ātman* is unborn (because eternal), not subject to ageing or death, invulnerable, immortal (BAU 4.4.30). It can only be spoken of in negations (BAU 4.4.27).

The *ātman*, it is true, is the self, the soul, but it is not confined to the individual, being identical with all *ātmans*: 'This *ātman* of yours is the *ātman* present in all' (BAU 3.4.1). There is no difference between the souls of beings; they are all one. Every 'other' is in essence 'myself'.

The parallelism of the statements about Brahman and the *ātman* is obvious, and suggests to us that the Brahman, the Absolute, the World-Soul, and the *ātman*, the individual soul, are to be regarded as identical. And in fact this is the great recognition and central message of the Upaniṣads, thus making them the basic texts of the Indian doctrine of all-unity. The relation between the multiplicity of the empirical world and the unity of the Absolute is a problem with which all subsequent Indian philosophy has been concerned.

Over and over again, in the Upaniṣads, the identity of Brahman and *ātman* is stressed: 'Truly, this great unborn *ātman*, the unageing, deathless, invulnerable, immortal *is* Brahman' (BAU 4.4.25). 'Just as a snake-skin, dead and cast-off, might lie upon an anthill, so the body lies after death. But this non-physical, bodiless *ātman*, consisting of knowledge, is Brahman (and lives on)' (BAU 4.4.7). 'This *ātman* is Brahman' (ChU 3.14,4). The unity of *ātman* and Brahman is most readily perceptible in dreamless deep sleep. In the withdrawal of such sleep, when the *ātman* temporarily rests, inactive, in Brahman, it becomes clear: 'That is the *ātman*, that is the deathless, the invulnerable, that is Brahman' (ChU 8.11.1).

If this mystic monism was one great discovery of the *Aupaniṣadas*, the doctrine of transmigration was the other. The idea that the individual survives death in one form or another had already made its appearance in the *Ṛgveda* and the *Brāhmaṇas*. But it was the *Aupaniṣadas* who recognized the compulsion and regularity of rebirth, and the decisive function of one's deeds in determining the outcome. He who is unliberated circles round in the cycle of metempsychosis (BAU 6.2.16), driven on by lust (*kāmayamana*: BAU 4.4.6) and ignorance (*avidyā*), i.e. ignorance of the *ātman* (BAU 4.4.10–13). If he performs good deeds (*karman*), he will have pleaseant rebirth, if evil deeds, an unpleasant one:

> According as one acts and behaves, so he will be (re)born. He who does good, will be born as a good man, he who does evil, will be reborn as an evil being . . . Therefore it is said: Man is entirely composed of desire (*kāma*). As his desire is so is his understanding. As his understanding, so is his action. And according to his action, so he will fare. (BAU 4.4.5)

> Those who are here of pleasing behaviour may expect to enter a pleasing womb: the womb (of the wife) of a Brahmin, a Kṣatriya or a Vaiśya. But those who have been of stinking behaviour may expect to enter a stinking womb: the womb of a bitch, a sow or of a casteless woman. (ChU 5.10.7)

Liberation from this frightening cycle of transmigration which is determined by a mechanically operating natural law on the basis of one's deeds, is to be achieved by the person who has destroyed lust (*kāma*) and ignorance (*avidyā*). Such a perfected one enters into Brahman and his *ātman* is dissolved in Brahman. Through this extinction in Brahman he is liberated.

There is no doubt that this recognition of all-unity, and the conception of rebirth as the product of natural necessity conditioned by one's deeds, are among the profoundest religious discoveries of mankind, but they also gave rise to a host of new philosophical questions. The doctrine of unity had overcome the division between individuals, but it had drawn a new dividing-line between the eternal, self-sufficient Brahman/*ātman* and physical nature (*prakṛti*); the vertical dichotomy was replaced by a horizontal. At once the problem of reality presented itself: Is the material world, as opposed to Brahman as the Absolute, *real* or is it illusion (*māyā*)? Then, too, questions arose as to the relation between Brahman and *prakṛti*: What leads the self-sufficient Brahman to become embodied in the world of transmigration? And how can the actions of a man bind the *ātman*, which is possessed of freedom in itself, to a physical body? The post-Upanishadic systems of India are largely attempts to answer these questions.

2 The Materialists scornfully rejected all doctrines of emancipation,

regarding anything beyond the visible world as mere fantasy. Their name, *Lokāyata*, 'directed towards the (visible) world', gives expression to this attitude. Another name for them, *Cārvāka*, is derived from one of their thinkers. Their opponents mockingly called them 'deniers' or 'negators' (*nāstika*).

As Indian thinking likes to codify its contents – there are guide-books even on thieving and love-making – the Materialists too had their anti-ideology systematized, namely in the sixth century *Barhaspatisūtra*. This work is only known from a few quotations, but we can gain some idea of the view of the Materialists from the efforts of their opponents to refute them. The following summary of the *Lokāyata* position is based on Haribhadra's 'Compendium of the Six Systems' (*Ṣaddarśanasamuccay*) (eighth century AD) and Mādhava's 'Summary of All Systems' (*Sarvadarśanasaṃgraha*) (fourteenth century).

Consistently with their conviction that direct sense-perception is the only source of knowledge, and that there is therefore no knowledge based on deduction, intuition, experience, teaching or divine revelation, the *Lokāyatas* deny the existence of another world. Whatever cannot be perceived by the senses does not exist. There is no God, no salvation, no soul (*ātman*). Right and wrong (*dharma/adharma*) do not exist nor do good and evil deeds lead to a result in another birth. Once the body has been burnt on the funeral pyre, it (i.e. the individual) does not arise again.

The existence of a soul cannot be deduced from the vital functions of living beings. All things, including our bodies, are conglomerates of the four elements, earth, water, fire and air, which combine, on the basis of their own nature – their indwelling tendencies – to form that particular structure. All psychic activity is merely the result of the interplay of the four elements, and develops, just as out of the harmless ingredients rice and molasses, intoxicating alcohol arises through fermentation.

Whoever renounces sense-pleasures because they are bound up with pain, acts like a fool. Do we throw a rice-grain away because it is surrounded by spelt? Therefore there can only be one sensible course: Live happily as long as life remains in you, and eat ghee, even if you get into debt. The only thing of value in life is what increases happiness.

Turning to the unseen and rejecting the seen –
Cārvākas know: That's the folly of the world!
(*Ṣaddarśanasamuccaya* 9.6)

In the anti-materialistic polemics of Indian philosophical literature it is noticeable that the *Lokāyatas* are by no means spurned as immoral or anti-social. Their nonconformity was confined to matters of the spirit. They were sceptics, secularists and hedonists, but they fitted in to the community of city or village without difficulty. And at times, when the Brahmins took themselves too seriously, it may well be that even pious believers gave vent to their feelings by quoting a disrespectful *Lokāyata* saying.

The philosophical influence of the *Lokāyatas* was considerable. By using their sharp-tongued criticism and earthy cynicism to mock the claims of the idealist schools, they worked against philosophical flights of fancy and acted as a valuable corrective.

3 The Sanskrit word *tapasvin*, 'ascetic', is often translated 'penitent', but wrongly. Penance is the attempt to make amends for a sin that has been committed, but asceticism in the Indian sense is the attempt to shape the future. It is based on the belief that self-mortification (*tapas* as means) produces heat (*tapas* as result), i.e. psychic-magic power which can be stored up and used for emancipation. A precondition of success is absolute sexual restraint. If the ascetic yields to the sexual drive, the stored-up *tapas* is at once and totally lost.

According to a widespread belief the ascetic acquired supernatural powers by storing up more and more *tapas*. Already in the *Ṛgveda* we learn that the god Indra owed his position in heaven to *tapas*, but it was only in the seventh/sixth century BC that the *tapas* theory became really popular. In the (post-Buddhist) Hindu literature it plays a large part, and we repeatedly hear of ascetics who became dangerous competitors of the gods by their stored-up *tapas*. The gods, not lost for a solution, sent the ascetic a beautiful nymph who seduced him and thus ruined his *tapas*.

That the Vedic-Brahmin sacrificial priests were opposed to the ascetic movement is understandable. Not only did the ascetic, by leaving his family, home and village, reduce the number of their customers, he also demonstrated, by replacing the material sacrifice with the sacrifice of his own pleasures, that there was a way of self-emancipation, thereby reducing the value of the old sacrificial religion. In the eyes of the Brahmins, adopting the life of an ascetic or wandering mendicant could only be justified in the case of a man of advanced years, who had looked after his family, observed his caste duties, and whose son had taken over his functions in domestic and social life.

The outward signs of an ascetic were the rejection of possessions and family, wild hair, and, frequently, total nakedness. Ascetics lodged as hermits alone in the jungle, or in small groups in 'ascetic-groves', in any case far from villages and towns in order not to be disturbed by householders or inflamed by their daughters. If an ascetic practised his observances rigorously for a long time, he was regarded as holy, and the nearest village was proud to supply him with the little he needed.

The aims of some of those who imposed severe ascetic observances on themselves were sometimes not very elevated. There was a proverb, 'What you do without, will be repaid tenfold', and many an ascetic may have aimed, as the final goal of his efforts, at precisely those joys he renounced for the present. For others, a half-way goal provided the motive, the development, by the accumulation of *tapas*, of paranormal powers such as flying like a bird, walking on water, passing through walls, and gaining knowledge of distant or concealed objects, or of past and future. The power to overcome natural laws and physical limitations was assumed by the populace with any advanced ascetic, and admired even without proof. But for those with insight, the real and only worthy goal of asceticism was emancipation, whether this was thought of as acceptance among the gods, as unification with one particular god, or as understanding of the Absolute, and absorption in it.

The goals of the ascetics were more or less conventional, but not their methods. The scale reaches from subtle meditation exercises, through various peculiar practices right down to revolting forms of self-torture, in which a form of exhibitionist vanity is apparent.

Among the odder forms may be reckoned the cow- and dog-ascetics mentioned in MN 57. The former, according to the commentary, had put horns on his head and fastened a cow's tail to his body, and lived for preference among the cattle, while the naked dog-ascetic ate off the ground, barked and slept curled up like a dog.

The most elementary form of ascetic observance was fasting, sometimes till death. Some ascetics ate only fruit or whatever grows beneath the earth's surface; others took only liquid nourishment. An original idea was fasting according to the moon: the ascetic ate nothing at new moon, and from then on till full moon he ate one mouthful more each day, and then reduced his intake in the same way till the next new moon.

Posture could also be made an ascetic practice. Some stood all day up to the hips in water, while the 'bat-ascetics' preferred to spend several hours each day hanging by their knees downwards from a tree. There were ever-sitters and ever-bent ascetics who never straightened out, and there were others who spent their time standing, often on one leg, till creepers grew round them. Some ascetics never slept, or lay on beds of nails or heaps of thorns. There were occasionally 'five-fire ascetics' who sat in the lotus posture between four fires with their face, the eyes long since blind, turned towards the fifth fire, the sun.

The number of self-mutilators was great. Some had cut off a limb, others had broken it and allowed it to grow at a strange angle. Quite frequently some deliberately allowed one arm to rot away by holding it aloft, while others bored a hole through their penis, generally attaching a heavy stone to it and thereby simultaneously demonstrating chastity and painful asceticism. Often ascetic practices were accompanied by a vow of silence, sometimes so strictly observed that the ascetic would not answer even by a gesture or a nod.

More important, however, than all these physical practices were the exercises in spiritual self-mastery. Practisers of breathing exercises used an artificial rhythm for in- and out-breaths, thereby inducing states of exaltation. In meditation the ascetic plunged deep into his own mind. The deepest stage of meditation consisted of a trance-state, which was regarded as a temporary emancipation.

4 More numerous than the *Aupaniṣadas*, *Lokāyatas* and self-mortifying ascetics were the fourth group of seekers after salvation, that of the wandering mendicants. Buddhist sources speak of them as

paribbājakas (Skt *parivrājaka*) and *samaṇas* (Skt *śramaṇa*), i.e. 'wanderers' and 'strivers'. *Paribbājakas* were wandering mendicants of Brahmin origin, whether their practice was orthodox or not, while the term *samaṇa* was reserved for those of other castes who followed various heterodox ways. Towards the end of his life the Buddha tried to narrow down the term *samaṇa* to wandering mendicants whose doctrine included an eightfold path (DN 16.5.27), in other words to apply it only to bhikkhus of his discipline (*vinaya*).

It is hard today to understand what made the homeless life appear so attractive to people in ancient India, and what made the life of the wandering religious mendicant such an important movement. We must realize that about 600 BC, in the agrarian society of northern India with its polytheistic sacrificial religion, a movement arose which sought a way out of the narrow framework of ritualism and of the social group. A psychosis of freedom-seeking and seeking after knowledge, an urge towards spiritual maturity had seized on men, and induced thousands of them of all castes to abandon their employment, entrust their wives and children to the care of the great family, and to leave their bamboo hut, their village or city, in order to adopt a monastically celibate wandering life in the hope of gaining liberating wisdom.

The break with tradition, and the wandering, mendicant life were the only things these ascetics had in common: ideologically they followed very different ways. Some were sophists, who specialized in refutation without propagating any positive doctrine of their own. Some were *Ājīvikas*, who as fatalists and determinists held the view that everything, including their own emancipation, was predetermined unalterably. But the majority of the wanderers were experimenters in religion, joining now this, now that guru. Perhaps they sought the goal for a time with the *Aupaniṣadas* or in the practice of asceticism, or else tried some method of their own for the gaining of wisdom. Their debates with those holding other views, which were generally held in groves on the edge of a village or town, were the intellectual amusement of the time and attracted many people, including the elder son of the Sakiyan Rāja of Kapilavatthu.

SIDDHATTHA'S PATH TO THE HOMELESS LIFE

These philosophical disputations must have made a deep impression on the young Siddhattha Gotama. He felt the powerful pull of the anti-Vedic movement, and the strong temptation to join the *samaṇas*. As he put it more than once later: 'The household life, this place of impurity, is narrow – the *samaṇa* life is the free open air.'

We possess a description of his departure for the homeless life in the *Nidānakathā* already mentioned, which dates from the fifth century AD at the earliest. Despite its legendary character, it contains statements which could well be derived from a genuine tradition. If we place this text side by side with the scanty but reliable autobiographical statements of Siddhattha after he had become the Buddha, we can gain some impression of how his abandonment of worldly life may have occurred.

The *Nidānakathā* has adopted a narrative from the *Dīgha Nikāya* (DN 14.2), which tells of the four excursions of the (unhistorical) Vipassi, a previous Buddha, and applies them to the historical Siddhattha Gotama. It tells how Siddhattha, who was living a life of luxury in Kapilavatthu, desired to visit a park outside the city. Riding in his four-horse chariot, driven by a charioteer, he saw an aged man by the wayside, bent, trembling, grey-haired and with rotting teeth. Dismayed at this sight, he asked the charioteer what kind of a man this was, and was told he was one whose life-span was approaching its end. Deeply shaken by the realization that he too would one day be old, the Rāja's son returned home.

On three further outings, the legend declares, Siddhattha saw a sick man, a dead man, and a monk. This last meeting made him wish to become a monk, so that he decided to renounce the world that very night. Just in that night his wife Bhaddakaccānā (or Yasodharā) gave birth to a son, who was called Rāhula.

When the time to renounce the world had come, Siddhattha had a horse bridled by his servant Channa, but he wanted to see his newborn son before his departure. When he entered the room of the sleeping Bhaddakaccānā the oil lamp went out, and as the young mother held her hand protectively over her child's head, it was impossible for Siddhattha to have a look at his son. Without having seen him, he left the city of Kapilavatthu at midnight riding his horse Kanthaka and accompanied by Channa: the (east) gate of the city, which was closed and guarded, was opened for him by the magical aid of the gods.

Touching the territories of three rājas, Siddhattha reached the river Anomā in the same night, and on the other bank he cut off his hair in monkish fashion and put on the robe of a *samaṇa*. He entrusted his horse and ornaments to Channa, who brought them back to Kapilavatthu. Siddhattha spent the first week of his new life in a mango-grove near the village of Anupiyā, and then made his way towards Rājagaha.

Thus far the legend, told here in somewhat demythologized form. The probably historical features are that Siddhattha's renunciation of the world took place immediately after the birth of his son Rāhula, and that he spent the first days of his open-air life near Anupiyā. The Anomā river is probably the modern Aumī, a tributary of the Gandak in what was then the Malla republic, but the Malla village of Anupiyā cannot be identified. That he touched the territories of three rājas to get there is correct, because in order to reach the Malla republic to the south-east of the Sakyan republic, he had to pass through the territory of the Koliyas.

The midnight departure and Siddhattha's cutting off his hair on the banks of the Anomā, are features of the legendary narrative, but not of the Buddha's own account. This makes it clear that at least his father Suddhodana and his foster-mother Pajāpatī knew of his intentions, but were unable to hold him back:

> 'When I was still a Bodhisatta (one bound for Buddhahood), the thought came to me: "The household life, this place of impurity, is narrow – the *samaṇa* life is the free open air. It is not easy for a householder to lead the perfected, utterly pure and perfect holy life. What if I were now to cut off my hair and beard, don yellow (*samaṇa*) robes, and go forth from the household into homelessness?"
>
> And I, being young, a youth with black hair, in the prime of my youth, in the first stage of manhood, cut off my hair and beard, although my father and (foster) mother opposed this and wept

with tearful faces, donned the yellow robes and went forth from the household life into homelessness.' (MN 26.16 = MN 36.10)

If we put this simple narrative beside the statement in the *Nidānakathā* that Siddhattha's renunciation (*pabbajā*) followed immediately on the birth of Rāhula, the assumption seems plausible that he had long been urging his parents to agree to this step, and that they had made their consent dependent on the birth of a grandson. This might even explain Siddhattha's belated fatherhood – after thirteen years of marriage, when both he and Bhaddakaccānā were twenty-nine: perhaps Bhaddakaccānā, in order not to lose her husband, had long refused to have children. At any rate, once the son demanded by Suddhodana and Pajāpatī was born, Siddhattha lost no time in realizing his intention to renounce the world. Thus this spoilt young man who, as the son of the Sakiya Rāja, could have had a political career in front of him, adopted, in 534 BC at the age of twenty-nine, the hard life of a wandering mendicant.

Where he went first is not made clear by the sources, though they are not contradictory. According to the summary account he gave many years later (in MN 26 and 36), he went immediately after leaving Kapilavatthu to Āḷāra Kālāma's hermitage, but according to the *Nidānakathā* he first spent a week at Anupiyā, and then went on to Rājagaha. This visit to Rājagaha, during which Siddhattha met the young King Bimbisāra of Magadha, is confirmed by the *Sutta Nipāta* (SNip 3.1). The king was then twenty-four and had already ruled for nine years.

The story goes that while the ascetic Gotama was going on his alms-round in Giribbaja, the old fortress kernel of Rājagaha ('Kingsbury'), King Bimbisāra saw him from the terrace of his palace. Rendered curious by the mendicant's noble appearance, the king had inquiries made, and then went to meet him at the Paṇḍava hill – the north-easterly of the five hills surrounding Rājagaha. On being asked about his origins, Siddhattha replied that he had come from the Kingdom of Kosala in the foothills of the Himālayas, and belonged to the Sakiya clan. He had renounced sensual pleasures and become a wandering mendicant in order to gain self-conquest. With that, the narrative breaks off. It is precisely its paucity of content that points to a historical incident, for life seldom provides us with a rounded-off story.

That the king should have gone to meet the young *samaṇa*, and not the other way round, is plausible. It was a pastime of many people to wait on the religious, especially because it was believed that the sight of one who was spiritually advanced shed something of the latter's magical potency on the onlooker. But we do not yet find any indication of the friendship which was later to develop between Bimbisāra and Siddhattha.

Siddhattha does not seem to have stayed long in Rājagaha. Impatient for liberation, he left the royal capital and placed himself under the tutelage of a teacher called Āḷāra Kālāma. Āḷāra did not belong to the leading heads of schools of his time: we only hear of him from Buddhist sources and in connection with Siddhattha's quest for enlightenment.

Siddhattha describes his studies under Āḷāra as follows:

'Having gone forth in order to seek for the good, for the incomparable peace, I went to Āḷāra Kālāma and said to him: "Reverend Kālāma, I wish to lead the religious life according to your discipline and teaching." He replied: "Please stay, your reverence. This teaching is such that an intelligent man can, in a short time, attain to understanding equal to that of his teacher, and dwell in it." And indeed I quickly learnt this teaching. But I was only paying lip-service and reciting a doctrine I had picked up from the older (pupils), and as others did also, I maintained I had known and understood the teaching.

'Then it occurred to me that Āḷāra Kālāma must have proclaimed his teaching not out of mere faith, but because of having realized it himself by direct knowledge. I said to him: "Reverend Kālāma, how far have you yourself realized this teaching by direct knowledge?" And he declared to me the Sphere of No-thingness.

'I thought: "Not only Āḷāra has faith, strength of will, mindfulness, concentration and wisdom. I have these things too." And before long I had realized the teaching and abode in that state. I told Āḷāra Kālāma, and he said: "It is a gain for us, it is profitable for us to have the reverend one as our companion in the holy life.

This doctrine which I have realized, you too have realized. As I am, so you are; as you are, so am I. Come, your reverence, we will lead this company of pupils together!"

'In this way the teacher treated me as an equal and honoured me. But I thought: "This teaching does not lead to revulsion, to dispassion, to cessation, to calm, to knowledge, to awakening, to Nibbāna, but only to the Sphere of No-thingness." So then I had had enough of this teaching, rejected it and turned away.'

(MN 26.16f., abridged)

Our curiosity as to what Āḷāra really taught remains unsatisfied, because Siddhattha did not consider it worth reporting. The expression 'Sphere of No-thingness' denotes a condition of trance-like meditation in which the meditator is awake but inturned. This kind of meditation was Āḷāra Kālāma's speciality. His pupil Pukkusa, who subsequently became a disciple of the Buddha's (DN 16.2.27) told how Āḷāra had once sat, fully conscious, under a tree without noticing five hundred carts passing close beside him (because his concentration was so strongly turned inward). These scanty indications might point to Āḷāra's system having been an early form of yoga.

Āḷāra's business ability is easier to recognize. The fact that he offered a joint share in the running of his school to Siddhattha can have only one explanation: he considered that this son of a rāja, who had recently had a conversation with King Bimbisāra, must have close connections at the Magadhan court, and hoped through him to gain the king's patronage for his school, thereby gaining more pupils.

Siddhattha reacted in accordance with his upright character and his genuine striving for emancipation: he turned the offer down. He had not gone forth into homelessness in order to be corrupted by a mediocre head of a school. He would doubtless have considered his stay with Āḷāra as time wasted if he had not picked up a few hints from him, about the technique of meditation, and about the organization of an order of *samaṇas*. That is probably the reason why he thought of Āḷāra again years later.

Despite his disappointing experience with Āḷāra, Siddhattha's belief in spiritual teachers was unshaken. Confident of having this time found the right guru, he went to the head of another school,

Uddaka Rāmaputta. In the *Majjhima Nikāya* (MN 26 and 36) he describes his experiences with Uddaka in almost the same words as those for Āḷāra. All we are told about Uddaka's teaching is that he had not discovered it himself but learnt it from his father Rāma, and that it led to the Sphere of Neither Perception nor Non-Perception. We can, however, deduce something of its content from a remark made by Siddhattha many decades later to the novice Cunda (Mahā-cunda) (DN 29.16), to the effect that according to Uddaka (ordinary) people see and yet do not see, instancing a well-sharpened razor, of which one can see the blade but not the operative part, the edge, on account of its fineness. Those who know the Upaniṣads will at once be reminded of the parallel with the *Chāndogya Upaniṣad* (6.12), where Uddālaka Āruṇi bids his son Śvetaketu split one of the tiny seeds of the fig, and then reveals to him in its imperceptible subtlety the essence of the Universe and of the Self. The assumption is therefore justified that Uddaka taught Upanishadic ideas, i.e. the doctrine of Brahman as the Absolute present in all things. Whatever the Buddha knew of Upanishadic philosophy and adopted, partly unchanged and partly in antithetic reversal, into his own teaching, he probably learnt from Uddaka.

When Siddhattha had attained to the stage of knowledge reached by Uddaka's father Rāma, Uddaka offered him, not partnership, like Āḷāra, but the sole leadership of his school. He recognized in his pupil one with religious gifts greater than his own. But Siddhattha rejected this offer too, flattering though it was. His quest was for emancipation from suffering, not the leadership of a school. So, since Uddaka's teachings did not satisfy him and he was put off by Uddaka's self-praise (SN 35.103), he left him and continued his wanderings. His studies with these two teachers had lasted for less than a year, perhaps only six months.

SIDDHATTHA THE ASCETIC

Leaving behind Uddaka Rāmaputta's hut and school, which were probably somewhere near Rājagaha, Siddhattha journeyed south-westward till, near Uruvelā, a garrison city for the troops of the King of Magadha, he found 'a charming plot of land, a lovely wood and a clear-flowing river which was good for bathing and quite delightful, with villages all about for gathering alms' (MN 26). At this spot on the bank of the Nerañjarā (today Nīlājanā), which combines with the Mohanā to form the Phalgu, he settled down to practise asceticism. Yoga and Upanishadic teachings had proved unsuitable to him to gain the emancipatory vision; perhaps asceticism was the proper way. Later, he gave his monks a full description of his adventures of those six years, because we do not like to speak of anything so much as of hardships surmounted.

The passage quoted describes the forest chosen by Siddhattha as 'lovely' – however, it would be wrong to form too idyllic an impression of an Indian forest. The tree coverage which, in the Buddha's time spread over the greater part of the sub-continent, varies from zone to zone. In the region of present-day Bihār it took and takes the form of scattered dry deciduous forest, which sheds its leaves in the summer and is only green in the rainy season. The predominant type of tree is the sāl (*Shorea robusta*), some specimens of which reach a height of 30 metres. The clearings are full of undergrowth and clumps of bamboo line the river banks.

There is a rich fauna. Bats and flying foxes hang in dozens like soft velvet bags from their favourite trees. Red-brown and black monkeys chase each other through the branches, and a family of light brown gazelles stalks gracefully past. Predators are scarcer than is often supposed, but there are enough to cause one alarm. It is not for nothing that the Indian peasant is deeply suspicious of the forest, which he peoples with spirits and whose semi-darkness he penetrates only to collect firewood or to look for a runaway goat or cow.

The first period in the forest was very hard for the thirty-year-old nobleman from Kapilavatthu. 'The loneliness of the forest is hard to bear, it is hard to take pleasure in being alone . . . When at night I stayed in such frightening and fearful places, and an animal passed by, or a peacock broke a twig, or the wind rustled among the leaves, I was filled with terror and panic.' It took time, as he told the Brahmin Jāṇussoṇi (MN 4), before he succeeded in overcoming this fear through mental self-discipline.

We can clearly perceive various stages in the course of Siddhattha's ascetic practices. He made several different starts, and he was not always alone. Descriptions of that period which the Buddha gave to the Jain lay follower Saccaka Aggivessana and his own disciple Sāriputta are given in the *Majjhima Nikāya* (MN 36 and 12).

The young ascetic began his quest for truth by trying to compel understanding with his mind: 'With teeth clenched, my tongue pressed against the palate, my mind subdued, (I endeavoured to) restrain and subjugate my thinking.' The result was sweat pouring from the armpits, and the realization that though the mind, as an instrument, can be disciplined, conclusions and insights cannot be obtained by force and without intuition.

Equally fruitless was the 'non-breathing meditation', i.e. holding the breath for as long as possible. The result was not any ecstatic state or higher insight, but a roaring in the ears, sharp pains in the skull, headache, stomach-cramps and a burning sensation in the entire body.

The double failure of such 'internal' methods led Siddhattha to go on to 'external' methods. If we are to believe the text (MN 12), he tried out practically the entire list of ascetic self-tortures. He went naked and accepted no food brought to him, but begged his own food, which had to be vegetable. At each house he would accept only a hollow hand's full, and at times limited himself to an alms-round only every seven days. At other times he ate only what grew wild. When, in the cool season, he wore clothing, it consisted only of rags, shrouds from corpses, old skins, grass and bark. He did not cut his hair and beard, but pulled out the hairs. He refused to sit down, standing, leaning or squatting on his heels. If he had to lie down, he did so on thorns. He gave up washing, trusting that the thickest dirt would fall off by itself. At the same time he exercised extreme compassion, tried to harm no creature and felt compassion even for a drop of water: 'If only I can avoid harming the little creatures (in it)!' He fled away from the cowherds, grass-cutters or firewood-gatherers who entered the forest, and hid himself.

As for his lodging, he spent the days of the Indian winter (December–January) in the woods and the nights, when the temperature was only a little above freezing-point, in the open air, while in the summer (May–June) he did the opposite, spending the night in the suffocating atmosphere of the forest, and the days outside in the hot sun. Here, he used to camp out in a charnel-ground, where cowherds' children spat at him or made water over him, threw dirt at him or tickled his ears with blades of grass. For some time he fed on things that were not even part of the normal food of ascetics. When the cowherds left their beasts alone, he fetched the dung of the calves, and sometimes he would eat his own excrement 'when it was not fully digested'.

How far we are to take these descriptions literally, we cannot be sure, but they are not mere inventions. His practice of self-starvation, in particular, can be regarded as factual. In fact he reduced his intake to the point of taking only a handful of grain or a single fruit in the day, so that he seemed on the point of death by starvation. He gives a vivid description of this state of affairs:

> 'Since I took so little each time, my body reached a state of extreme emaciation. My limbs became like the dry and knotted joints of bamboo. My buttocks became like a buffalo's hoof, and my spine with its protruding vertebrae became like beads on a string. My ribs were visible like the exposed rafters of a dilapidated house. Just as in a deep well the surface of the water gleams far below, so my pupils, sunk deep in their sockets, gleamed far below. Just as a bitter gourd, when it is cut, quickly dries up and shrivels in the sun, so my scalp dried up and shrivelled. If I wanted to touch my belly-skin, I encountered my backbone, because the two had come so close together. If I wanted to pass excrement or urine, I fell over on my face. If I rubbed my limbs, the hair, rotted at the roots, came away in my hand.' (MN 12.52 = MN 36.21)

It is natural that such a rigid observance of asceticism attracts admirers. In addition to a following of householders from Uruvelā, Siddhattha also had a group of five admiring ascetics from his home district in the foothills of the Himālayas. Koṇḍañña from Doṇavatthu had been one of the eight Brahmins who, thirty years before, had performed the name-giving ceremony for the new-born Siddhattha Gotama: he was therefore at least fifteen years older than Gotama. Bhaddiya, Vappa, Mahānāma and Assaji were the sons of four other Brahmins from that group. Together with Koṇḍañña, they had followed the young Gotama into the homeless life some time after his departure, and, fascinated by the honest rigour of his endeavours, had joined in his observances. They had agreed that the first one of them to come to an understanding of the truth (*Dhamma*) should tell the others. None of the five doubted that Siddhattha would be the first.

SIDDHATTHA THE BUDDHA

But the five ascetics were disillusioned, shocked and angry: Siddhattha, their model and hero, had become unfaithful to his quest, he had broken off his ascetic practice and accepted adequate nourishment – a whole bowl of rice. It seemed that the rāja's son wanted to live a life of luxury. Shaken, the five turned from him and left him alone. Siddhattha was no longer their guide, and should no longer be their companion. What had happened? We have an explanation from his own mouth:

> 'By this method, on this path, by this severe asceticism I did not attain to the highest goal of human striving, the true Ariyan knowledge and wisdom. Why not? Because I had not gained that wisdom (*paññā*) which, when one has it, is the noble guide (out of the circle of rebirth), leading the practiser to the total destruction of suffering.' (MN 12.56)

> 'Whatever ascetics and Brahmins have ever felt feelings that were painful, sharp and severe, it cannot exceed this. And yet even with this extreme asceticism I did not gain the highest goal of human striving, the true Ariyan knowledge and wisdom. Might there not be another way to awakening?' (MN 36.22)

Pondering on this other way, he remembered an incident from his youth. Many years ago, when his father the Rāja had ploughed the field with his own hand, he, Siddhattha, had been sitting at the edge of the field in the cool shade of a rose-apple tree, and had unexpectedly entered a state of aloofness from unwholesome states of mind, into a state of absorption (*jhāna*) accompanied by thinking and pondering, delightful and happy. Could it be that this type of contemplation was the way to enlightenment? And, since an emaciated body showing every sign of deprivation is not the best equipment for a spiritual search, Siddhattha had, shortly after recalling that youthful experience, abandoned asceticism and fasting and returned to a more balanced way of life. But the group of five ascetics, who could only see his abandonment of asceticism and not his adoption of a new method of seeking, thereupon deserted him.

Left alone in the forest of Uruvelā, Siddhattha, now no longer an ascetic but a *samaṇa*, started on the new path. In this he was helped by the meditation experience he had gained under Āḷāra Kālāma.

The meditation which prepared the ground for his break-through to enlightenment consisted of the fourfold absorption (*jhāna*) frequently mentioned in the Canon. This practice does not necessarily lead to enlightenment, but like all meditation is purely a preparatory practice. It makes the mind capable of enlightenment, but enlightenment itself is a rare event, depending on favourable karmic conditioning and a serious striving after wisdom. The four stages of absorption are described (e.g. in MN 36.25) as follows:

Stage 1 Cessation of sense-desires and unwholesome states of mind, accompanied by thinking and pondering; well-being resulting from detachment.

Stage 2 Cessation of thinking and pondering, development of tranquillity and one-pointedness; well-being resulting from concentration.

Stage 3 Cessation of delight in favour of freedom from affects; equanimity and mindfulness with bodily ease.

Stage 4 Cessation of feelings of pleasure and pain; development of equanimity free from joy and sorrow in mindfulness and purity.

When Siddhattha had thus made his mind (*citta*), 'collected and purified, without blemish, free of defilements, grown soft, workable, fixed and immovable' (MN 36.26), he turned his attention to the recollection of previous existences:

'I recalled many a former existence I had passed through: one birth, two births, three, four, five, ten, twenty, thirty, forty, fifty, a hundred, a thousand, a hundred thousand births, in various world-periods. (I knew:) "I was there, such was my name, such my family, such my

caste, my way of life. I experienced such and such good and bad fortune, and such was my end. Having died, I came to life again there, such was my name . . . and such was my end." In this way I recalled many previous existences with their various characteristic features and circumstances. This knowledge (*vijjā*) I gained in the first watch of the night' (i.e. between 9 p.m. and midnight).
(MN 36.26)

In the middle watch of the night, Siddhattha gained the second kind of knowledge: the natural law of ethical causality (*kamma*), in accordance with which good (i.e. wholesome) deeds are followed by good rebirth, and bad (i.e. unwholesome) deeds by evil rebirth:

'With the heavenly eye, purified and beyond the range of human vision, I saw how beings vanish and come to be again. I saw high and low, brilliant and insignificant, and how each obtained according to his *kamma* a favourable or painful rebirth. I recognized: "Those beings who make evil use of body, speech and thought will obtain after the breaking-up of the body at death a painful rebirth, they will sink down, perish, and (go to) hell. But those who make good use of body, speech and thought will obtain a favourable rebirth, and (go to) heaven."'
(MN 36.27)

Finally, in the last watch, when the horizon was already becoming visible in the east as a white line of light, Siddhattha broke through to the third knowledge, the understanding of suffering and the 'Four Noble Truths' which form the framework of his doctrine:

'I directed my mind to the knowledge of the destruction of the influences (*āsava*) and knew as it really is: "This is suffering (*dukkha*), this is its cause, this is its cessation, and this is the path that leads to its cessation." And as I recognized this, my mind was free from the influences of sense-desire, of becoming and of ignorance. And the knowledge arose in me: "Rebirth (for me) is destroyed, I have completed the holy life, done is what had to be done, there is no more of being for me!"' (MN 36.28)

And he uttered the cry of jubilation:

'My emancipation is assured,
This is my last birth,
There will be no more re-becoming!'

(MN 26.21)

In this night of the year 528 BC Siddhattha Gotama, the thirty-five-year-old son of the Rāja of Kapilavatthu, had gained enlightenment (*bodhi*). He had become a *Buddha*, an 'enlightened' or 'awakened' one, and was thus freed from the cycle of rebirths. Tradition dates this event (like Gotama's birth) in the first full-moon night of the month Vesākha (April–May), and locates it near Uruvelā (today Bodh-Gayā) under a particular *assattha* or pipal tree (*Ficus religiosa*). The full moon of Vesākha is accordingly the most important festival of the Buddhist world, and the *assattha* is the sacred tree.

As an event which originated a new school of thinking and a new religion, the enlightenment of the Buddha deserves psychological analysis. Under the influence of Zen Buddhism modern writers have – wrongly – described this enlightenment as like a lightning-flash. From Gotama's account in MN 36 we learn that the enlightenment was spread over three night-watches (about nine hours), and was thus a gradual process. This agrees with his statement that in his doctrine progress is gradual and there is no sudden, spontaneous understanding (*aññā*), just as the seashore does not lead abruptly into deep water, but slopes away gradually (Ud 5.5 p. 54). In addition, the process of enlightenment was guided by reason, as appears clearly from the words, three times repeated: 'I directed my mind to the understanding of . . .' We must therefore picture Gotama's enlightenment as a happy condition, lasting several hours, of extreme mental clarity, which activated all the intellectual abilities and focused them, like a burning glass, on one point at a time. There was nothing ecstatic about this *bodhi*, it was not an out-of-the-body state or a trance.

Nor was Gotama's search at this point a blind fumbling in the dark. He knew precisely on what objects to direct his attention. Since he had been familiar with Upanishadic ideas of rebirth from his stay with Uddaka, he was able to direct his mind to the profounder penetration of this theme. The same applies to the system of four truths, which he will have known from the well-developed medical theory which already existed in the India of the sixth century BC. According to this one asked first about the disease, then about its cause, then about the possibility of annihilating that cause, and finally about the medicine. Gotama's enlightenment consisted largely in the analytical understanding of pre-existing thought.

But it went further, because it was also synthetic, i.e. an understanding which opened up new areas of knowledge. The 'aha' experience of analytical penetration was accompanied by the 'oh' experience of joyous creative intuition, in which accepted opinions and fresh insights combined in Gotama's mind like crystals to form a new truth and doctrine (*dhamma*). In the glorious clarity of *bodhi* a new system of thought was formed out of elements old and new, which explained the world 'as it is' (*yathābhūtaṃ*), pointed out a way from suffering to deliverance, and finally transcended all previous insights into one all-comprising truth. It is just this overriding element of illumination which points to beyond the visible and gives the Buddha's teaching that magical fascination that still moves mankind and leads people towards the good. There is no contradiction between Gotama's statement on the one hand that his doctrine is like an old, overgrown path that he has rediscovered, leading through the jungle to a forgotten city (SN 12.65.19ff.), and his insistence elsewhere that it is something new, 'never heard before' (Mv 1.6.23).

We must distinguish the rational element of the enlightenment, which forms the content of the doctrine (*dhamma*) from its psychological effect on himself. It has always been a basic conviction of Indian religions that knowledge, understanding or wisdom could remove the factors that bind us to suffering and rebirth. The Buddha, too, never doubted this. How did he justify breaking off his ascetic practices? Because, he says, they do not lead to 'that wisdom which, when one has it . . . leads the practitioner to the total destruction of suffering' (MN 12.56). Lack of knowledge (*avijjā*) binds us to the cycle of rebirths, while understanding (*ñāṇa*), knowledge (*vijjā*) or wisdom (*paññā*) liberate us from it: They are the means of emancipation. And therefore it was clear to the Buddha that his enlightenment had definitely freed him of the burden of rebirth and delivered him: 'There will be no more re-becoming (for me)!' was his cry after attaining Buddhahood.

Further, the experience of enlightenment gave him the feeling of belonging, as a Buddha, to a different category of being, having only the outward appearance in common with unliberated beings. The knowledge that pain could still indeed touch him physically, but could no longer affect him mentally, and that nothing could reverse his liberation, conferred on him that detached superiority to existence which he always displayed in the forty-five years of his ministry towards kings and beggars, friends and opponents.

Orthodox tradition regards the enlightenment (*bodhi*) as an experience of understanding which revealed to the Buddha all the elements of his teaching in complete and final form. In other words, orthodox tradition assumes that gaining buddhahood turned Siddhattha from a thinker into a possessor of the truth. Fortunately it can be proved that Gotama's creative thought continued even after his *bodhi*. For him as a person the enlightenment was the end of his search for emancipation, but for his teaching it was the beginning of a course of development.

This can be seen from the fact that the complete teaching which emerges from the Master's discourses contains elements which were not present in the original enlightenment. Precisely the most striking point in his whole system, and one which contradicts the philosophy of the Upaniṣads, namely the doctrine of non-self (*an-attā*), according to which a permanent soul (*attā*, Skt ātman), an ego that survives the death of the body cannot be found in the empirical personality and that rebirth takes place without a transmigrating soul as a conditioned process – precisely this teaching belongs to the period *after* the enlightenment, when the young Buddha was making his still broad-meshed insights more precise and filling out the details of his teaching.

THE 'SACRED' TREE

In the Buddha's accounts of his enlightenment (MN 26 and 36) it is nowhere mentioned that this event occurred under a tree. Some scholars therefore consider the tree as the location of his enlightenment to be unhistorical, and suggest that pre-Buddhist tree-cults have found their way into Buddhism at this point. But is it not

The *assattha* or pipal tree (*Ficus religiosa*) is easily recognized by its leaves. In Buddhist countries it is generally known as the *bo*(*dhi*) tree.

natural that a homeless wanderer, wherever he is, would sit down under a tree that would shield him from the dew by night, and from the sub-tropical sun by day? We can take it as a matter of course that Siddhattha pursued his speculations leading to enlightenment at the foot of a tree. And the fact that the tree was an *assattha* tree, easily recognizable by its heart-shaped leaves with the long curved point, is something that the Buddha could so easily have mentioned to his monks in passing that we can readily regard it as a historical fact.

The *bodhi* tree behind the 51 m-tall Mahābodhi temple at Bodh-Gayā (the ancient Uruvelā), which was erected in the first century AD, is visited daily by some dozens of pilgrims. But only the very credulous believe that it is the original *assattha* under which Gotama gained his enlightenment 2,500 years ago. It can be shown that the tree was replaced several times in the course of time, though always with descendants of the original tree. Thus the present tree is descended from the original one in a direct line.

The *bodhi* tree was placed under special protection by the Buddhist Emperor Asoka, who reigned over India as a peaceful ruler from 265 to 232 BC. He not only had a stone fence (no longer existing) built round the tree, and marked the sacred spot with a (likewise vanished) edict-pillar with a lion capital; he also arranged for King Devānampiyatissa of Ceylon (Laṅkā), who had been converted to Buddhism about 242, to receive a shoot of the *bodhi* tree to plant at his capital of Anurādhapura. The tree that grew from this shoot, and its successors, have repeatedly furnished the shoots or seeds with which the Indian tree was replaced after being destroyed.

The destruction of the original *bodhi* tree of Bodh-Gayā is supposed to have been caused by Tissarakkhā, Asoka's beautiful second wife, whom the emperor married four years before his death. Because His Majesty devoted more attention to the tree than to her, we are told (Mhv 20.4f.), she pierced the tree (which she probably believed contained a nymph) with a *maṇḍu* thorn. This is a thorn which is believed in India to possess the power of destroying the life centre of plants and causing them to wither. This story apparently aims at providing an explanation for the death of the tree towards the end of Asoka's reign.

The destruction of the replacement tree on religious grounds is ascribed to the Gauḍa (Bengal) king Śaśānka. Śaśānka, a fanatical Śivaite and enemy of Buddhism, passed through Bodh-Gayā in the beginning of the seventh century AD on a campaign against Kānyakubja (Kanauj). Filled with hatred, as Hsüan-tsang tells us, he not only had the sacred tree felled, but in order to complete its destruction, he had the roots dug out and burnt. The second replacement tree was planted by Pūrṇavarman, Asoka's last successor on the throne of Magadha.

In 1876 the *bodhi* tree of Bodh-Gayā was uprooted by a storm. Whether this was Pūrṇavarman's tree, or yet another replacement, is unknown.

There are conflicting accounts of the origins of the present tree that grows at Bodh-Gayā. Some say it grew from a shoot taken from the Anurādhapura tree, while others say it grew from the roots of its uprooted predecessor. However that may be, the present tree is a grandchild, or more probably a great- or great-great-grandchild, of the original *assattha* tree under which, in a night of the year 528 BC, the ascetic Siddhattha Gotama became the Buddha.

528 BC

2

The foundation of the Order and the beginning of the mission

FIRST SERMONS

According to tradition, the young Buddha spent the first seven days after his enlightenment at the foot of the *bodhi* tree, 'enjoying the delight of liberation' (Mv 1.1.1). We can accept this statement as true, because the framework of the teaching still needed to be filled out with detailed recognitions, and a partly joyous, partly sentimental mood may have kept the Enlightened One at the spot which meant so much to him. We can give less credence to the statement that, after the seven days under the *bodhi* tree, he spent seven days under each of a number of other trees at Uruvelā. Under the Goatherd's Banyan (*Ficus indica*) he explained to a Brahmin who had questioned him the true nature of Brahminism, consisting of a pure and virtuous life and a good knowledge of the Veda (Mv 1.2). Still more fabulous is the event which is supposed to have occurred in the third week after his enlightenment under a mucalinda tree (*Barringtonia acutangula*). According to Mv 1.3, when a pre-monsoon storm broke out, the cobra living in the root of the tree wrapped its body round him and protected him from the rain with its outspread hood. The root of the legend could be that the reptile, being driven out of its hole by the rain, inflated itself before the Samaṇa, but did him no harm.

From the mucalinda tree the Buddha moved to a rājāyatana tree (*Buchanania latifolia*), under which he also stayed for a week. It was here that the merchants Tapussa and Bhallika, who were travelling from Ukkalā (in Orissa?), presumably to Rājagaha, gave him barley gruel and honey as alms, 'so that it might bring them happiness and good fortune'. He ate the proffered food, and the two merchants 'took refuge in the Enlightened One and his teaching' – which he had not yet promulgated – thus becoming his first lay followers (Mv 1.4).

The fifth week after his enlightenment he spent once more in the shade of the Goatherd's Banyan. Possibly inspired by a request from Tapussa and Bhallika for instruction, he considered whether his doctrine, which was 'profound, hard to see, hard to grasp, factual, excellent, inaccessible to (mere) logic, subtle, to be apprehended by the wise (only)', should be kept to himself or revealed to other people. The Pāli texts (Mv 1.5 and MN 26) record these doubts in the form of a conversation with the God Brahmā Sahampati ('Lord over himself'). Apparently the Buddha, in order to make his inner conflict understandable, made use of this well known god-figure to present the counter-arguments when he hesitated to teach. That he, like the majority of his contemporaries, believed in the existence of gods (who, too, were mortal and subject to the law of rebirth), is undoubted. But that he really saw Brahmā so vividly with his own eyes, as the texts declare, is probably the interpretation of later monks.

In the following 'dialogue', which has been cut down to essentials, personal and quietist arguments are opposed to altruistic ones. The latter win the day.

The Buddha 'This world delights in the pleasures of the senses, but my teaching (*Dhamma*) aims at the renunciation of all attachments and the destruction of craving. If I were to teach this doctrine, which goes against the stream, and people did not understand me, that would be a weariness and a trouble to me.'

Brahmā 'The world will perish if the Fully Enlightened One does not decide to teach his doctrine. May the Exalted One therefore teach it! There are some beings with little dust on their eyes. If they do not hear the Dhamma they will be lost. But if they hear the Dhamma they will attain [to liberation]!'

Brahmā's arguments aroused Gotama's compassion for the beings, and with the cry: 'Let the doors to Deathlessness be opened to all who are able to hear!' he agreed to teach. Satisfied, Brahmā bowed to the Buddha, circled round him to the right according to Indian etiquette, and vanished. The gods, too, know how to behave towards an enlightened one.

When he came to consider to whom he should first declare his teaching, the Buddha thought first of his one-time teachers Āḷāra

Kālāma and Uddaka Rāmaputta. Learning that they were both dead, he next thought of the five companions of his ascetic period, who, he knew, were staying in the deer-park at Isipatana ('Seer's Rest') near Benares (Vārāṇasī). They, he knew, would quickly grasp the teaching. In the triumphant consciousness of having the means to save mankind in his hands, and determined to devote himself to his mission, he set out for Benares. If we take into consideration the fact that he had to beg for alms-food every morning, and that the hot midday hours were unsuitable for walking, we must assume that he took at least fourteen days over the journey (210 km as the crow flies).

Between Uruvelā and Gayā, soon after the commencement of his journey, he met a certain Upaka, a naked ascetic of the Ājīvika school, an exponent of extreme determinism. Upaka was struck by the inner exaltation and the radiance of the Buddha, and he asked him who was his teacher and what was his teaching. Proudly the Buddha declared that he was emancipated through the destruction of craving, he was the victor and had, therefore, no teacher, but was a teacher himself. Unimpressed, Upaka heard him and said: 'It may be so, brother', and shaking his head, took another path to one side (Mv 1.6; MN 26; MN 85). It would have been easy for the compilers of the Pāli Canon to have cut out this episode, which is somewhat detrimental to the Buddha's image. That they did not do so speaks for their respect for historical truth.

Koṇḍañña, Bhaddiya, Vappa, Mahānāma and Assaji were not at all pleased when Gotama, their one-time companion who had deserted them, approached them in the deer-park at Isipatana. In fact they agreed neither to greet him nor to rise in his presence. But as he approached, they were so overwhelmed by his dignity as one liberated that they treated him with all courtesy. They took his alms-bowl and his upper robe, prepared a seat for him, washed his feet and addressed him, out of habit, as 'Brother' (*āvuso*). But the Buddha rejected this form of address:

> 'Monks, do not address the "Thus-Come" (*tathāgata*) as "Brother" (as if he were one of yourselves). Monks, the Thus-Come is a Holy One (*arahant*), a Fully-Enlightened One.'
>
> (Mv 1.6.12 = MN 26; i, 171)

A Buddha represents a unique category of being, who shares indeed the outward appearance of mankind, and like human beings is subject to physical decay (as a result of unexpired *kamma*), but who is no longer bound to the cycle of birth and death. Until his final extinction he lives as one emancipated in the world, but inwardly detached from it. All bonds, including family and social ones, have been broken for him.

The claim of their former companion to have discovered the way to deathlessness (= liberation), to have found and realized the truth and the teaching (*dhamma*), was met by the five ascetics with scepticism. How could it be, they asked, that one who had abandoned asceticism in favour of a life of plenty could have won through to the truth? The Buddha explained to them that he had by no means succumbed to a life of abundance, and to make things clear he preached a sermon (*sutta*) to them, the famous Sermon on the Turning of the Wheel, with which his mission begins. The *sutta* presents the Dhamma as the middle way, and sets forth the system of the Four Truths: the logical framework within which all detailed teachings are contained.

> 'There are these two extremes, monks, which one who has left the world should not pursue. Which two? (On the one hand) giving oneself up to indulgence in sensual pleasure; this is base, common, vulgar, unholy, unprofitable. (On the other hand) giving oneself up to self-torment; this is painful, unholy (and also) unprofitable. Both these extremes, monks, the Perfected One has avoided, having found that it is the Middle Way which causes one to see and to know, and which leads to peace, to (higher) knowledge, to enlightenment and Nibbāna.
>
> (1) This, monks, is the Noble Truth of Suffering (*dukkha*): Birth is suffering, old age is suffering, sickness is suffering, death is suffering; sorrow, lamentation, pain, grief and distress are suffering; being joined to what one does not like is suffering, being separated from what one likes is suffering; not to get what one wants is suffering: in short, the five aggregates of clinging (which make up the empirical personality) are suffering.
>
> (2) This, monks, is the Noble Truth of the Origin of Suffering: It is

that craving (*taṇhā*) which gives rise to rebirth and, bound up with pleasure and passion, now here now there, finds ever fresh delight: it is Sensual Craving (*kāmataṇhā*), Craving for Existence (*bhavataṇhā*), Craving for Non-Existence (*vibhavataṇhā*).
(3) This, monks, is the Noble Truth of the Extinction of Suffering: it is the complete removal and extinction of this craving, its forsaking and giving up, abandonment and detachment from it.
(4) This, monks, is the Noble Truth of the Path Leading to the Extinction of Suffering. It is this Noble Eightfold Path, namely:

Right View (*sammā-diṭṭhi*)
Right Resolve (*sammā-sankappa*)
Right Speech (*sammā-vācā*)
Right Action (*sammā-kammanta*)
Right Livelihood (*sammā-ājīva*)
Right Effort (*sammā-vāyāma*)
Right Mindfulness (*sammā-sati*)
Right Concentration (*sammā-samādhi*).'

(Mv 1.6.17+19–22=SN 56.11.5–8)

The five listened to his words with breathless attention, and even as he spoke, Koṇḍañña gained full understanding of the teaching: 'Whatever is subject to the law of origination, is also subject to the law of decay' (Mv 1.6.29). Soon afterwards, he asked the Buddha to accept him as a disciple, and the Buddha, with the formula: 'Come, monk, the doctrine has been well explained: lead a life of purity in order to attain to the end of suffering!', accepted him as a monk (*bhikkhu*) (Mv 1.6.32). Koṇḍañña was thus the first monk in the history of Buddhism, and his ordination marks the beginning of the order of monks (*saṅgha*) which exists to this day. In Buddhist Asia the 'turning of the Wheel of Dhamma' is celebrated annually at the full moon of the month of Āsāḷhā (June–July). Thus a period of two lunar months (fifty-six days) is assumed to have occurred between Gotama's enlightenment in Vesākha and the sermon at Isipatana.

Soon the Buddha's instruction led to Vappa's and Bhaddiya's understanding of the Truth (the Dhamma), and they too were accepted as monks. While the bhikkhus (literally 'mendicants') Koṇḍañña,

Vappa and Bhaddiya went on the alms-round to provide food for the group, the Teacher gave private instruction to Mahānāma and Assaji. In a little while they too gained the requisite insight, and sought ordination (Mv 1.6.33–7). There were now six bhikkhus in the world – the Master and his five disciples.

A few days after the ordination of the five, the Buddha gave them a discourse on non-self (Mv 1.6.38–46 = SN 22.59). It is remarkable in that it introduces an idea that was not hinted at either at the time of the enlightenment or in the Isipatana sermon, and which is surprising in a non-materialistic system: the denial of the existence of a soul. This shows that the Buddha had already developed his doctrine philosophically since his enlightenment.

The 'Discourse on the Marks of Non-Self' starts from the assumption that the empirical personality consists of five – and only five – 'groups' (*khandha*) of constituents, namely body, feelings, perceptions, the mental reactions to these (*saṅkhāra*), and consciousness. Since in India an ego, self or soul (*atta*, Skt *ātman*) always implies something that survives death and is eternal, and since none of the 'five groups' is permanent, the conclusion is drawn that none of them constitutes a soul. In the five groups which exhaustively form the personality there is mental or psychic life, but no soul in the sense of a permanent entity: the personality is 'non-self' (*anatta*), without a soul.

A second argument supports the first. The mutability and perishable nature of the five groups render each of them 'painful' (*dukkha*), and something that is painful (and unsatisfactory) cannot be a soul.

When the five bhikkhus heard this explanation from the Buddha, their minds were freed from all influences (*āsava*) leading to rebirth, and thus they became 'saints' (*arahant*) (Mv 1.6.47). Their understanding of the saving doctrine was now as vast and profound as that of the Buddha, and they differed from him only in the source of their understanding. A Buddha is dogmatically defined as one who has found his liberation for himself, whereas an Arahant has gained it under instruction (SN 22.58).

The relative ease with which the first five, as well as many later monks and lay people, attained enlightenment, has led some readers of the texts to assume that people in the Buddha's time were more predisposed to spiritual insight than we are today. This is possible, because in world history periods of greater and lesser spirituality can be found. A further reason for the frequent declarations of Arahantship is that in ancient India the conviction prevailed that understanding and realization were the same thing. Whoever fully comprehends the Four Noble Truths and, in accordance with the second one, recognizes craving (*taṇhā*) as the cause of rebirth and suffering, has by this very insight destroyed craving and has thus become an Arahant. Today we are less optimistic about the effectiveness of recognition.

SĀRNĀTH – THE ARCHAEOLOGICAL SITE

After the noise of car-horns and rickshaw-bells in Benares, Sārnāth seems like an oasis of peace. The busy Hindu city is only 8 kilometres from the quiet of the deer-park of Isipatana, the modern Sārnāth (Skt *Sāranganātha*, 'Lord of the Deer'), but how different the world seems here – ordered and solemn. The last part of the asphalt road is fringed by mighty mango and tamarind trees. The site, which is enclosed by a stone wall, is carefully tended by the Indian Archaeological Service. Between the complexes of ruins are grassy lawns, dotted here and there with the red and violet blossoms of bougainvillaea.

The most striking monument at Sārnāth is the 44 m-high Dhamekh Stūpa, a round tower, 27 m in diameter, standing on a stone base, built of brick with, in places, ornamental stonework, narrowing halfway up to two-thirds of its base diameter. This all grew through numerous claddings and vertical extensions out of a small brick and clay stūpa from Asoka's time (third century BC).

The origin of the name Dhamekh was disputed until the discovery of a burnt-clay votive tablet settled the matter. Its inscription denotes the stūpa as *Dhamāka* (Skt *dharmacakra*). This means that it marks the spot where the Buddha, in addressing the five ascetics, 'set the Wheel of Dhamma' (Pāli: *dhammacakka*) in motion. Pilgrims venerate the stūpa, which like all stūpas is solid and so cannot be entered, by right-handed circumambulation, an ancient Indian way of paying respect to highly placed persons.

Passing the remains of old monasteries and numerous votive stūpas, the pilgrim proceeds from the Dhamekh Stūpa to the former main temple of Sārnāth, whose 2 m-thick brick walls remain standing to a height of about 5 m. Judging by the strength of the masonry and the statements of Hsüan-tsang, the original temple tower must have been about 60 m high. The remains of the walls enclose an area of 13 by 13 m. This is the floor of the former inner hall of the temple which, as Hsüan-tsang describes it in the seventh century AD, contained a metal statue of the Buddha. The temple probably dates from the second or third century AD, and stands on the site where the five monks erected a hut of leaves for the Master, in which he spent the rainy season of 528 BC. The spot is a favourite meditation-place for pilgrims from Śrī Laṅkā, Burma and Thailand. Often, too, Tibetan monks in their purple robes can be seen here holding a Pūja (religious ceremony), or venerating the memory of the Teacher by 108-fold prostration and the setting-up of oil lamps.

To the west of the main temple the visitor finds a monolithic edict-column of the Emperor Asoka (third century BC). Seventy cm thick at the base and 55 cm above, originally 16 m high, the column is now broken into several pieces as the result of the destruction of Benares and Sārnāth by General Qutb-ud-Din in 1194. The capital of the column, now in the local museum, is rightly famous. It represents four finely sculptured lions, sitting back-to-back, for, just as the lion has the loudest voice among beasts, and roars in all directions, so too the Buddha was the teacher most clearly heard in his time, and he spread his Dhamma in all directions. The lion capital is today the state crest of the Republic of India, and the twenty-four-spoked wheel which appears four times in the base of the capital – which is a symbol both of the Buddha's teaching and of just government – now appears on the Indian national flag.

The imperial edict engraved in Brāhmī script on the still-standing portion of the pillar does not really fit in with the dignity of the place. It warns monks and nuns against schism, and commands that schismatics must put on white clothing (instead of the yellow robe of the Order) and must leave the community of the Order. Lay followers are urged to observe special rules on the *Uposatha* days (new moon, full moon, and the days at the mid-point between the two). Since the edict makes no reference to the events of Isipatana, it has been

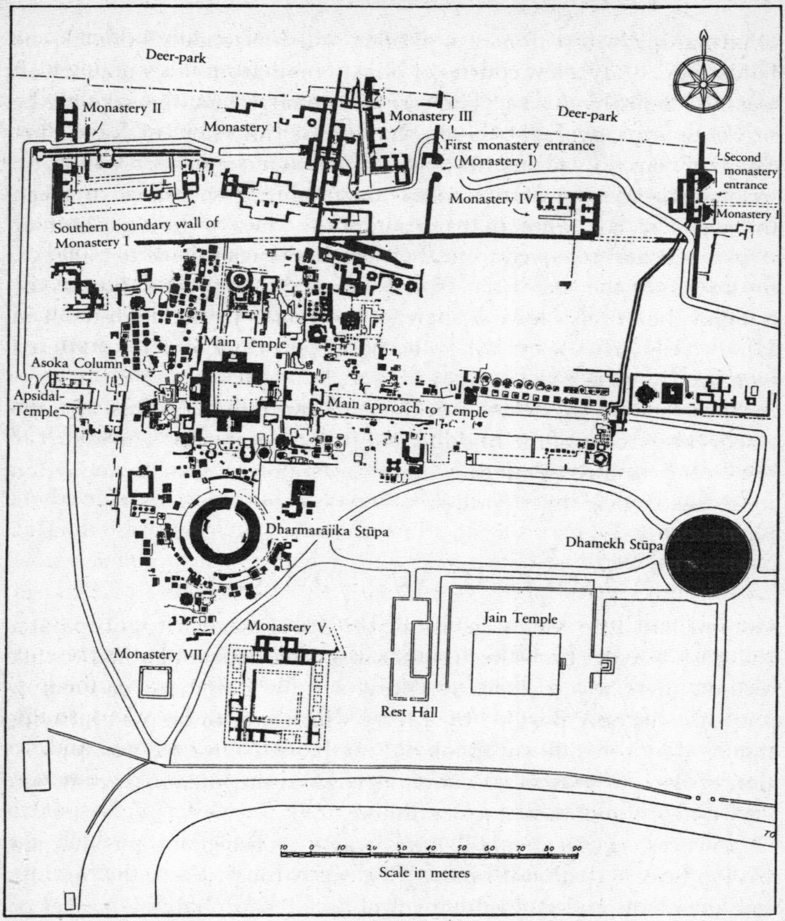

Sārnāth (Isipatana), the site of the Buddha's first discourse and of the foundation of the order of monks (present-day archaeological state).

concluded that the pillar was brought to Sārnāth from somewhere else. The content of the edict is consistent with its having come originally from Kosambī.

A few metres south of the main shrine and the Asoka pillar the visitor observes a circular platform. This is the basis of the former

Dharmarājika Stūpa, once 30 m high, which originally bore a stone balustrade. Only a few courses of brick remain from this stūpa, which was also built by Asoka. The rest was removed for the sake of the bricks in 1794 by Jagat Singh, the Diwan (minister) of Rāja Chet Singh of Benares. During the demolition a round stone urn was found 9 m below the top of the stūpa, containing a reliquary of green marble. This contained that portion of the ashes of the Buddha that Asoka had had removed from their original burial place to Sārnāth, in order that the site of the First Sermon and the foundation of the Saṅgha should also have a share of the relics. Jagat Singh dealt in Hindu fashion with the ashes: he had them ceremonially scattered over the Ganges.

Nevertheless, the demolition of the Dharmarājika Stūpa and the discovery of relics of the Buddha had its fortunate side. The report of the local British Resident drew public attention to Sārnāth and led to its archaeological investigation.

GROWTH OF THE COMMUNITY

Gotama had little interest in visiting the city of Benares from Isipatana (Sārnāth). Apart from the fact that it was an hour and a half's walk distant, there was a river, the Varuṇā (now Barṇā) to be crossed, and this was only possible by a ferry which had to be paid for with money that a mendicant monk did not have. Above all, the population of Benares was so resistant to religious mendicants that it was very difficult to obtain alms-food there.

However, contact with Benares was established for the Buddha without any action on his part. This was through Yasa, the son of a rich merchant and guild president of Benares, probably a banker or wholesale cloth merchant. Yasa was a spoilt young man who had had his fill of the pleasures of life, which had left him inwardly empty. The Pāli Canon (Mv 1.7.1f.) mentions the three houses he lived in, according to the season, the female musicians who surrounded him, but towards whom he was indifferent, and the golden shoes – presumably embroidered with gold thread – that he wore.

So Yasa, bored by marriage and luxury and spiritually unsatisfied, visited the deer-park at Isipatana early one morning, greeted the

Buddha, and sat down at a respectful distance. Gotama, who recognized the young man's world-weariness, gave him a 'graduated discourse'. The method, which shows his didactic skill, and which he first used with Yasa, consisted of mentioning first such readily comprehensible matters as the giving of alms, ethical rules, heaven, and the worthlessness of sense-pleasures. If the listener was capable of taking in more, he went on to teach the Four Noble Truths, i.e. about suffering and its origin, its cessation and the way to achieve this. This pedagogical method proved an immediate success with Yasa. He gained the 'dust-free and spotless insight into Dhamma, namely, that whatever is subject to the law of origination, is also subject to the law of decay' (Mv 1.7.6).

In the meantime Yasa's mother was getting worried about her son, and begged her husband to go in search of him. And so Yasa's father came to Isipatana, and he asked the Buddha where his son was. Instead of replying directly, the Buddha asked him to sit down, and then delivered to him the same 'graduated discourse' which had proved so successful with Yasa. But as Yasa's father was too worried to take in more, he only gave him the first and easier part of the teaching. Thereupon Yasa senior took his refuge in 'Buddha, Dhamma and Saṅgha', and declared himself a lay follower (*upāsaka*). And so he was, after Tapussa and Bhallika, the third lay member of the Buddhist community, though the first to be converted with the threefold formula of Buddha, Dhamma and Saṅgha which is still in use today.

Finally, Yasa's father discovered his son among those surrounding the Buddha and begged him to return home for the sake of his grieving mother. But Yasa looked so pleadingly at the Buddha that the latter declared that it was impossible for one who scorned worldly life as much as Yasa to resume his former existence. Yasa senior could only accept the Buddha's argument, but he invited the Buddha to a meal for the following day, accompanied by Yasa. The Buddha accepted by silence, the usual Buddhist form of agreement – probably accompanied by the still-current indication of acceptance, describing a horizontal figure-of-eight with the chin. As soon as his father had gone, Yasa junior begged for ordination as a monk. Gotama acceded to his request, and before long the bhikkhu Yasa attained to sainthood. 'Now there were seven Arahants in the world' (Mv 1.7.7–15).

Despite its edifying character this story is a moving document of the times. It not only characterizes the religious yearning which had seized India in the sixth century BC, and which drove numberless people to leave their houses and huts to venture on a wandering mendicant life, it also shows us the mental distress which parents, or in other cases wives and children, suffered at the departure of a son, a husband or a father.

The meal to which Yasa senior had invited his son's Teacher and the son himself took place next morning. 'Accompanied by the Venerable (bhikkhu) Yasa', the master made his way to the house of Yasa's parents, where Yasa's mother and his 'former wife' welcomed the guests. After they had received the graduated discourse (in full) from the Buddha, both ladies took the threefold refuge, thus becoming Gotama's first female lay followers (*upāsikā*). Thereupon, assisted by Yasa senior, they served the monks with the meal (Mv 1.8).

Yasa's conversion had consequences. The fact that a spiritual doctrine had induced the satiated youth to abandon his life of ease and become a *samaṇa* was proof enough to his friends that this teaching must be something extraordinary, and inspired four of them to imitate him. Vimala, Subāhu, Puṇṇaji and Gavampati, all, like Yasa, merchants' sons and of the Vessa caste, were accepted as monks on Yasa's recommendation, and all became Arahants (Mv 1.9). Not long afterwards, a further fifty of Yasa's friends from the surroundings of Benares entered the Order, and also became Arahants. The number of Arahants had thus risen to 61 (Mv 1.10).

BENARES ORTHODOXY VERSUS THE *SAMAṆA* MOVEMENT

Even in the lifetime of the Buddha Benares had the reputation of a place that was especially auspicious for those seeking salvation, though not to the same degree as later, in Hindu times. The belief of many that ritual bathing in the Gaṅgā (Ganges) at Benares was specially salvific, and that the dead whose remains were cremated at the Ghāṭs (special bank-sites) of the city went straight to heaven, gave the place an aura of sanctity.

The name of Vārāṇasī or Bānārasī, from which the modern forms Banāras or Benares are derived, comes from the names of the two rivers between whose mouths the city lies on the left (or western) bank of the Gaṅgā, the Var(u)ṇā (Barṇā) and the Asi, the latter of which is in the dry season a mere trickle. The right (eastern) bank of the Gaṅgā, which at Benares flows first from south to north and then turns north-east, is uncultivated, a broad expanse of grey sand, which is covered by deep water every monsoon. Anyone dying on the east bank opposite the city is believed by the inhabitants to be reborn as a donkey.

The tradition that Benares was a royal foundation carries little conviction. The city rather seems to have developed out of a trans-shipment port that grew up in the angle of the Varuṇā and Gangā, north-east of the present Malavīya bridge, where goods were unloaded from the punts and barges coming down the Varuṇā to larger sailing-ships on the Gaṅgā. Here, and at the nearby Rāj-Ghāṭ, archaeologists have discovered the remains of the oldest stone buildings of the city, dating back to the sixth century BC, just about the Buddha's time. The commercial centre of the city lay 2 km to the south-west on a hill, corresponding to the present-day Chauk (Chowk). This hill is about 40 m above the water-level and protects its inhabitants from the risk of flooding to which the parts of the city along the banks are annually exposed.

Already in antiquity, Benares was known for its fine textiles. Benares cotton, delicate muslin and the heavy brocades, often threaded with gold, were famous, and found customers throughout the sub-continent. Any man with the requisite commercial initiative and some capital to invest, who advanced the money for thread to the weavers and provided the fashionable patterns for them, and who then took care of the export and sales of their product, could make a fortune. This may well have been how Yasa's father became a rich man.

Some other branches of industry and trade were directly related to the religious role of the city: the manufacture of clay and copper vessels for the water-cult, the sale of incense and fuel for the Vedic fire-ceremonies and cremations, the trade in sacrificial animals and in garlands. A considerable proportion of the Benares inhabitants (who perhaps numbered 120,000 at this period) also lived by providing services connected with the pilgrimages, whether as sacrificial or cremation celebrants, as guides, servants in the inns, or as tricksters preying on the pilgrims. And round about the city in a wide arc were to be found 'publicity agents' of various kinds who eloquently proclaimed the virtues of the holy city and its value for the salvation of one's soul.

Though Benares, with its busy riverside life, was a bustling city in the Buddha's time, we must picture it as architecturally comparatively modest. Those visual elements we think of today at the mention of Benares did not yet exist. There were neither images nor temples, because the Vedic sacrificial cult was carried out in the open air. There were no stone stairs down to the river, but just banks of clay, and there was no imposing city skyline: there were merely secular buildings of brick and clay, and they did not even have the appearance that we regard today as typically Indian.

The spiritual landscape, too, was poorer: we have to picture an India still without a *Rāmāyana*, a *Mahābhārata*, a *Bhagavadgītā*; the classical mythology was still in its infancy, and Śiva, whose citadel Benares was to become, was an unimportant minor deity, nor had the worship of the sacred cow developed. Also – as now – there was no regulating authority in religious matters: all cult acts were performed, not by groups or communities, but by individuals. Every man performed, or had performed for him, whatever observances and rites he considered effective.

What then was Benares like in the Buddha's time? True, it was a place of Upanishadic wisdom, where the still fresh ideas of reincarnation and the natural law of retribution were discussed and passed on: but far more than this it was a centre of the Vedic sacrificial cults, which were in the hands of a professional guild of Brahmins, as well as of the cremation business – a city in which a heavenly after-life was offered for sale. Clearly, all those who were making a good profit out of this business were no friends of the emancipated *samaṇa* movement with its scorn for the sacrificial practices.

The majority of the Benares citizens, therefore, were cold and unfriendly towards the wandering mendicants who camped outside the city in such alarming numbers, and preached heretical ideas. If one of them ventured into the centre of the city, his alms-bowl might remain empty and he himself might be abused. Accordingly, most of the *samaṇas* kept to the outskirts and avoided contact with the towns-people.

The Buddha did the same. Out of the forty-five years of his mission, he spent only one rains retreat near Benares, namely in 528 BC, the year of his enlightenment and the foundation of the Saṅgha, and that was in the deer-park at Isipatana (Sārnāth). Later he stayed at Isipatana two or three times again, presumably on his way to or from Kosambī, but he confined his visits to the centre of Benares to a minimum. If he was not provided for by the Yasa family, he went for alms not into the city, but to the cattle-market on the outskirts (AN 3.129). He had too little in common with the orthodox citizens and their ritualism.

In point of fact, Gotama supported all the views that were anathema to the Vedic-Brahmanists of Benares: he considered (1) ritual washing and (2) fire-sacrifices as useless, (3) he spoke out against animal sacrifices, and (4) to the Vedic cult he opposed his view that all cults could be dispensed with.

1 The belief that water could wash one free, not only from dirt, but also from the consequences of errors and omissions of ritual, or of breaches of the caste code of behaviour, was general in Benares, but elsewhere as well. There were other sacred rivers besides the Gaṅgā. Flowing water was supposed to have a greater purifying power than that in ponds and reservoirs. The water of the ocean was considered not only ineffective for purification but positively dangerous, because it harmed the aura.

The more enlightened Brahmins did not have quite such a naïve faith in the purifying quality of the water. For them, it only annulled a person's sins when he not only totally immersed himself, but did so clearly conscious of the ritual character of his washing, combining it with the right attitude of mind. It was the inner attitude alone that distinguished the ritual bath from a mere cleansing bath. However, since this requirement was usually overlooked, the washings were, for most people, empty acts, mere external forms.

A typical adherent of the water-cult was the Brahmin Sundarika-Bhāradvāja: when the Buddha visited Sāvatthi this Brahmin asked him in surprise if he did not bathe in the nearby river Bāhukā, because this river brought liberation, was a source of merit and purified one from evil deeds (MN 7, p. 39). The Buddha rejected this idea as false: no amount of bathing could wash the perpetrator free of the after-effects of wicked acts. One should bathe only in pure deeds, in order to bring inner peace to all beings.

He gave similar instruction to the Brahmin Sangārava, who bathed morning and evening with the express intention of washing away his sins committed in the night and the day respectively (SN 7.21). Gotama explained to him that the teaching was the pond and moral discipline the bathing-place, and that whoever should bathe here would reach the other shore i.e. liberation. He made a similar utterance at the time of the Aṣṭaka festival at Gayā when he saw a group of matted-hair ascetics (*jaṭila*) ritually bathing: 'They will not become pure through water, all those who bathe here. He in whom truth and justice are at home *is* pure – he is a Brahmin!' (Ud 1.9).

Lay people and monks, too, sometimes gave expression to the Buddhist contempt for ritual washings. When someone reminded the Licchavī minister Nandaka from Vesāli, during a discourse by the Buddha, to take his evening bath, he replied: 'Enough of that, my good man! Never mind the outer washing – the inner washing is good enough for me, namely my discipleship to the Enlightened One!' (SN 55.11.3.10).

The theme is varied in verses by Puṇṇā, the daughter of a domestic slave-girl of the Buddha's rich supporter Anāthapiṇḍika, who had set her free because she had won the Brahmin Sotthiya for the Buddha's teaching. Having become a nun, Puṇṇā put into verse-form the arguments with which she had brought about Sotthiya's conversion:

> 'Only an ignorant person can have declared to you, the ignorant, that bathing frees one from (the consequences of) evil deeds. If that were so, then fish, turtles, frogs, water-snakes and crocodiles – whatever lives in the water – would go straight to heaven. All those who perform evil deeds (or follow an impure trade) such as sheep- and pig-butchers, huntsmen, fishermen, thieves and murderers would be freed from bad Kamma by sprinkling themselves with

water! Besides, if these rivers were to wash away the evil you have done, they would also wash away your religious merits, leaving you behind, hollow and empty!' (Thīg 240–3)

The argument is easy to follow, but only applies to those who believe in the mechanical purification by water.

2 The Buddha's attitude to the fire-cult is not so widely attested. To the Brahmin Sundarika-Bhāradvāja previously mentioned, who believed in purification by fire as well as by water, he declared:

'Think not, Brahmin, that by laying wood
Can purity be gained. That's external.
He who seeks it by such outward means
Will not be purified, so say the wise.

'I reject the heaping of logs on the altar,
The fire I kindle is within myself.
My fire burns always, ever clear and bright:
An Arahant, I lead the holy life.'

(SN 7.1.9)

The versification is of a later date, but doubtless correctly reflects the meaning of the saying.

Fire rituals existed in various forms in ancient India. The most important was the Vedic-Brahmin fire-sacrifice, which was carried out to order by professional Brahmins while observing elaborate cultic prescriptions, in order that the fire-god Agni would carry the sacrifice up to the gods. Other fire-ritualists tried to purify their own souls by burning their impurities in the sacred flame. Among these were the matted-hair ascetics (*jaṭila*), several groups of whom went over to the Buddha. One former leader of the Jaṭilas, Nadī-Kassapa (Kassapa of the River), reproached himself, having become a bhikkhu, for his former belief in the effectiveness of the fire-cult.

'Many an offering I've made,
Poured upon the sacred flame.
"Thus I'm purified!", I thought –
Foolish worldling that I was.'

(Thag 341)

3 Although the washing rituals and fire-sacrifices had no religious value in the eyes of the Buddha, at least they harmed no one. Blood-sacrifices were different. In ancient India these cost the lives every year of some human beings and of several thousands of animals. It must be credited as a cultural achievement to Buddhism that the ritual killing of living beings no longer belongs to the standard customs, and that animal sacrifices are today found only in Bengal, where the Hindu goddess Kālī ('the Black') is supposed to demand them.

Animals were for the Buddha fellow-beings with a perfect right to life, and his love (*mettā*) and compassion (*karuṇā*) were extended to them no less than to mankind. He disliked their slaughter for human food, though he was sufficient of a realist to see that universal vegetarianism could not be enforced. But he regarded their ritual killing as an aberration, especially since many people believed that the slow killing of the sacrificial animal increased the efficacy of the sacrifice. Often the animals – cattle, horses or goats – were strangled. There is to this day a place on the banks of the Gaṅgā at Benares which is called, in memory of a royal sacrificial ceremony, Daśāśvamedhaghāṭ, 'Ghāṭ of the Ten-Horse Sacrifice'.

That innocent animals had to give their lives for the religious aims of men offended not only Gotama's compassion but also his sense of justice. He was convinced that everyone has to pay for his own deeds, and that neither bribing the gods nor the transference of the results of evil deeds (*kamma*) to another – the vicarious atonement by means of a sacrificial animal – was possible. Whenever opportunity offered, he opposed such ideas, of course not as a prophet threatening condign punishment, but as an emotionally detached sage who taught and inspired, but did not attempt to force acceptance of his teaching on people. As he said himself, he avoided striving with the world (SN 22.94). All that he threw into the scale was the reasonableness of his thoughts and the magic of his personality.

He countered the great Vedic blood-sacrifices with pointing out their uselessness. When King Pasenadi of Kosala prepared a great sacrifice of 500 bulls, 500 oxen, 500 cows, 500 goats and 500 rams, and compelled his servants and slaves to collect the animals from their owners, presumably without payment, Gotama commented that neither human nor animal sacrifices bore any fruit. The wise kept away from vast sacrifices at which goats, cattle and other animals were killed. On the other hand, sacrifices without bloodshed and without great expense helped the sacrificer and pleased the gods (SN 3.1.9).

The rich Brahmin Kūṭadanta of Khānumata planned an even greater sacrifice of 700 of each kind of animal, but the Buddha talked him out of it. By telling him a tale in the style of the *Jātakas* ('stories of the Buddha's previous lives'), he convinced Kūṭadanta that regular gifts to *samaṇas*, building monasteries, taking refuge in the Buddha's teaching and keeping the precepts (refraining from killing and stealing, sexual misconduct, lying and drunkenness), and meditation were sacrifices not only easier to make but more effective, in fact the most beneficial of all sacrifices (DN 5.22–7).

He used additional arguments against blood-sacrifices when he was asked by some professional Brahmins from Kosala whether there were still today (i.e. in the sixth century BC) Brahmins who lived according to the old rules. He denied this, and described the Brahmins of earlier times as celibate men without possessions, living entirely on alms, who would not let cows be killed, regarding them as their best friends who provided them with ointment, food, strength, beauty and happiness (SNip 295ff.). Later on the Brahmins, led astray by the example of the rulers' splendid life, had urged these to perform horse and human sacrifices, for which they could demand a fee. Then the king had had 'many hundred thousand' head of cattle killed with the sword, which even the gods regarded as sinful. Through this slaughter of innocent living beings the sacrificial priests had fallen away from the right path, and the wise and the general population for good reason reproached the offerers of such costly sacrifices (SNip 299–313).

4 Another thing the orthodox held against the Buddha was his opposition to ritual. It was not that he objected to all rules and customs – there were rules and customs within the Buddhist community as well. What he objected to was the idea that rites and rituals were important for salvation – that one could even compel salvation through them. He expressly included 'attachment to rites and ritual' as one of the ten fetters (*saṁyojana*) to be broken, and one of the four attachments (*upādāna*) in his system. It is easy to imagine

the feelings of the professional Brahmins, who made their living as ritual technicians and ceremonial experts, when they heard of these articles in the Buddhist code which ran so contrary to their interests.

THE RAINS RETREAT IN ISIPATANA

Unloved by the citizens of Benares, in so far as they noticed him at all, and without the expectation of finding much acceptance of his teaching in Benares outside the ranks of the Yasa family, the Buddha and his little band of monks spent the rainy season 528 in the deer-park at Isipatana (Sārnāth). There was not yet a proper monastery. The only accommodation consisted of a few leaf-huts or at best huts of bamboo and reed-mats, which the bhikkhus had constructed for the Master and themselves.

The monsoon is more than a period of rainfall. It is an event that one longs for from April or May onwards as a climatic relief, and which then comes step by step and far too slowly. A natural phenomenon that precedes the monsoon is the blossoming of beautiful flowering trees, although many of those which grace the Indian scene today were brought by European seafarers. India in the Buddha's time was poorer botanically speaking. But the orange-coloured blossoms of the kadamba (*Nauclea cordifolia*), the campaka (*Michelia champaka*) with its scented golden yellow blossoms, the brilliant red flame of the forest (*Butea frondosa*), the queen's tree (*Lagerstroemia flos-reginae*), covered with pale blue candles, the golden shower (*Cassia fistula*) with its magnificent cascades of yellow, the shining red coral tree (*Erythrina indica*), and the Asoka tree (*Saraca indica*) with its balls of blossoms which turn from orange to red – all these must have already existed to delight the Indians of the sixth century BC.

The glorious spectacle of flowering trees in April-May is followed by a short period of leaflessness, during which the branches reach skywards thirsty and skeleton-like. The dew that had hitherto supplied trees and bushes with a little moisture in the early mornings no longer falls. The fields are grey beneath a merciless sun. The earth is like dry clay, and shows a pattern of deep cracks. In places the hot air rises up in spirals which, like funnels, draw up dust from the fields into the air.

Some days later, heralded by falcons and crows fleeing before it, a storm breaks out. Huts lose their roofs, trees are bent over, but just as quickly as it came, the storm passes. And then at last, about the middle of June, the longed-for monsoon rain begins. From mighty clouds thick individual drops fall and quickly become more frequent, and suddenly, with lightning and the roar of thunder, a downpour breaks out, which soon turns into continuous rain. Naked children run delightedly through the sheets of rain, and even the adults are glad to expose their faces briefly to the refreshing wetness.

After a period of continuous rain the clouds reach a compromise with the sun, each dominating the scene in turn for a few hours. In the intervals between rain showers the landscape is steaming, and an oppressive closeness takes the place of the previous heat.

The change in the landscape is enormous. The previously sluggish rivers are now broad streams, brown and gurgling, which threaten the riverside dwellings by their rapid rise; roads and paths sink in the mud and become impassable. Many clay huts dissolve and cause the (anyway not very watertight) rush roofs to sink down on the inhabitants. The animal kingdom, too, presents a new aspect: snakes, scorpions and millipedes that have been driven out of their holes by the water are frequently to be seen, jolly little frogs hop across the road, and the mooing of the ox-toad is heard. In the houses the geckos that run about the walls and ceilings in search of mosquitoes and moths develop fat tummies.

The atmosphere of the approach and arrival of the monsoon and the transformation it brings about was later to inspire more than one Buddhist poet, and assuredly the Master and his pupils too will have observed this natural spectacle in the deer-park at Isipatana. But this first rains retreat of 528 was mainly devoted to the training of the monks. Besides the Sermon on the 'Turning of the Wheel of Dhamma', and that on the 'Not-Self' (both Mv 1.6), three further discourses from those weeks are preserved in the Canon. In one (Mv 1.13 = SN 4.1.4) he recommends to his monks – although they were supposed to be Arahants already – systematic thought (*yoniso manasikāra*), which he declares had brought him to enlightenment; in the second (Mv 1.11 = SN 4.1.5) he declares that he and his monks are freed from heavenly and earthly snares; and in the third (AN 3.15) he gives them the parable of a carriage-maker who had to make two wheels for a chariot for a (legendary) King Pacetana. One wheel, which was made with utter care, and had taken six months to produce, remained standing after the running test when the impulse was exhausted; the other, finished in six days, tottered and fell over because there were flaws in felloe, spokes and hub. In the same way the monks must get rid of the faults and flaws in their deeds, words and thoughts.

The Pāli Canon contains four more discourses of the Buddha delivered at Isipatana, all of which date from his two or three later visits to the place. This can be seen from the fact that his audience consists of persons who only joined his community after 528.

Towards the end of the rainy season the Buddha gave two instructions which were to be of great importance for the future development of the monastic order. He decided not to confine the promulgation of the Dhamma to himself, but to include the monks in this task. Accordingly, he called his disciples together, and gave them instructions to disperse as missionaries:

> 'Go forth, monks, on your (own) way for the profit and happiness of the many, out of compassion for the world, for the profit, gain and happiness of gods and men. Let no two go together. Teach, monks, the Teaching (*Dhamma*) that is lovely in its beginning, lovely in its middle, lovely in its ending, in the spirit and in the letter, and propagate the perfectly pure holy life. There are beings whose eyes have little dust on them, who will perish if they do not hear the teaching. But if they hear the teaching, they will gain liberation. I myself, monks, will go to the garrison-city of Uruvelā, there to preach the Dhamma.' (Mv 1.11.1)

The monks went forth as instructed, and before long their mission produced successes. They brought men from all directions to Isipatana for ordination. However, they complained that the Buddha had reserved the right to ordain for himself, and requested this right for themselves. The Master did not easily grant their wish. First he considered in private, and then he discussed it with the monks. Finally he decided:

> 'I allow you, monks, yourselves in the various countries and districts

to grant the going-forth into homelessness (*pabbajā*) and the ordination (*upasampadā*). It is to be done in this way: Let him (the candidate) first have his hair and beard shaved off, let him put on yellow robes and cover one shoulder (the left) with his upper robe, and when he has saluted the feet of the (ordaining) monk (as a sign of discipleship), let him squat down and honour the ordaining monk with joined palms. Then he should be bidden to repeat: "I take my refuge in the Buddha, I take my refuge in the Dhamma, I take my refuge in the Saṅgha" – this he must repeat a second and a third time. I allow you, monks, to grant the going-forth and the ordination (of a new bhikkhu) by means of this threefold refuge.' (Mv 1.12.3–4)

By the granting of permission to the monks to ordain, the Buddha cut the umbilical cord binding the Saṅgha to its founder, and enabled it to live a life of its own. The ordination procedure was later further formalized (Mv 1.28.3–5), and supplemented by specific provisions in regard to the ordinand and the ordaining chapter.

The year 528 BC had been a successful one for Gotama, and he had become the head of a school within the *samaṇa* movement. Now the rainy season, and with it the annual period of immobility, was over. Forests and fields were green, and the rice that had been planted in mid-June now stood a hand's breadth above the surface of the water in the fields. Wells and ponds were full, the roads were again passable, and the oppressive closeness of the monsoon had given way to moderately warm days and mild nights. As he had announced, the young Buddha left the deer-park of Isipatana and set out for Uruvelā.

BACK IN URUVELĀ

Gotama's reason for visiting the scene of his enlightenment once more was to teach the Dhamma to the householders who had once supported him with alms while he was an ascetic. The Pāli Canon (Mv 1.14) reports a charming episode of his walk back there, which is said to have occurred in a grove called Kappāsiya. As the Buddha rested at the foot of a tree, some excited young men, obviously of better class, ran to him and asked him if he had seen a woman hurrying past. They explained that there were thirty of them who had come to the grove with their wives for amusement. One of them, being unmarried, had brought a prostitute along. They were in pursuit of her, because she had stolen their property and disappeared.

The Buddha 'What do you think, young men? Is it better to look for this woman, or for yourselves?'
Young Men 'Lord, it would be better for us to look for ourselves.'
The Buddha 'Well then, young men, sit down, and I will teach you Dhamma.'

Then he gave them the graduated instruction and explained the Four Noble Truths to them. Won over to the Buddha's teaching, the thirty young men requested ordination as monks, which the Buddha immediately granted.

The episode is probably historical; only the end seems to have been 'improved' by the redactors of the Pāli Canon. That all thirty young men, full of the joy of life, became not lay followers but monks, so that twenty-nine young wives had to return to their village as 'monks' widows', is hard to believe.

Apart from the historicity of the episode, the ordination formula that the Master used should be noted. It was not the triple refuge the Buddha had prescribed, but the words: 'Come, monk . . .', the same as he had used when he accepted Koṇḍañña as the first bhikkhu (Mv 1.6.32). It seems that this was the ordination formula that only the head of the school was allowed to use.

The Mahāvagga relates the incidents that occurred on the Buddha's return to Uruvelā with pedantic stiffness and a determination to turn everything into a miracle. We will confine ourselves to those episodes from which a crumb of historical information can be extracted.

Near Uruvelā were three brothers called Kassapa who led the life of matted-hair ascetics (*jaṭila*) and practised the fire- and water-cult. Each of them was the head of a school. Uruvela-Kassapa had five hundred *jaṭilas* as his pupils, Nadī-Kassapa ('Kassapa of the River') had three hundred, and Gayā-Kassapa ('Kassapa of Gayā') two hundred, though these figures are not to be taken literally.

As the Indian winter had already started and night temperatures were not much above zero, the Buddha went to the hermitage of Uruvela-Kassapa and asked if he could spend the night in the cult hut in which the fire maintained by the *jaṭilas* was burning. Taken by the stranger's self-confidence and personality Uruvela-Kassapa did not dare refuse, but declared that the hut contained a large and venomous serpent. But the Buddha did not allow himself to be frightened off, and spent the night in the hut safely 'owing to his magic powers' (Mv 1.15).

He passed further nights in the forest near Uruvela-Kassapa's hermitage, and three times the forest around him was illuminated. Kassapa, who invited the Buddha to a morning meal in his hermitage, was deeply impressed to learn that Gotama had been visited by radiant deities: in the first night by the 'Four Great Kings', in the second by Sakka (Indra), and in the third by Brahmā Sahampati (Mv 1.16–18). The historical kernel of this legend could be that the Buddha lit a fire at night as a protection against the cold and against wild beasts.

Meanwhile, the great annual sacrifice was due at Uruvela-Kassapa's hermitage, and visitors were expected from the whole of Magadha and the land of Aṅga which lay to the east. Fearing that the Buddha might attract some supporters of the *jaṭilas* to himself, Kassapa secretly wished that Gotama might not be present at the sacrifice. Sensing what Kassapa was thinking, the Buddha tactfully stayed away from the hermitage on the day of the sacrifice. Kassapa was astonished that Gotama could read his thoughts (Mv 1.19).

After the Buddha had observed Uruvela-Kassapa and his pupils for some time, he took the occasion of a boastful utterance on the part of the aged ascetic to bring him down to earth. Speaking directly to his conscience, he said: 'Kassapa, you are not an Arahant or even on the road to Arahantship. Your way of life is not such that you can become an Arahant by it, or even enter on the road to Arahantship!' Kassapa, to whom nobody had ever spoken like that before, was completely shattered. Falling at the Buddha's feet, he begged to be accepted into his Order (Mv 1.20.17).

It says much for Gotama's sense of justice that he did not at once accept Kassapa's submission, but warned him to consider the consequences of such a step for his followers: 'Kassapa, you are the head of a school of five hundred *jaṭilas*. Discuss the matter with them, so that they can do what they think right!' Kassapa took his advice, with the result that all (?) his disciples were converted with him to the Buddha's school. They cut off their matted locks, and threw their shoulder-poles and the implements used for the fire-cult into the river Nerañjarā. Then the Buddha gave them ordination as monks of his Order (Mv 1.20.17).

When the locks of matted hair and the wooden cult utensils floated down the Nerañjarā past the hermitage of Nadī-Kassapa, he was frightened that some misfortune had befallen his brother. He went to the latter's hermitage, and Uruvela-Kassapa explained to him the benefits of joining the Buddha's community, and he too joined the Saṅgha with all (?) his three hundred followers (Mv 1.20.20f.).

The same thing occurred in the case of Gayā-Kassapa, who had also gone to see if his brother was all right on seeing the cult objects floating by. He too joined the Order with all (?) his two hundred followers (Mv 1.20.22f.).

With his numerous new followers (even if they probably did not number a thousand), the former *jaṭilas* whom he had ordained as bhikkhus in Uruvelā, the Buddha proceeded to Gayā, which was not far distant, where the group camped on a hill 1 kilometre south-west of the city called Gayā Head (Gayāsīsa, now Brahmayoni). Here the Master delivered a sermon which alluded thematically to the practices of the *jaṭila* cult. It is the Fire Sermon (Mv 1.21 = SN 35.28), which begins with the famous words: 'Everything is ablaze!' The *sutta* is based on the Buddhist theory of perception, according to which there are not five senses but six: besides eye, ear, nose, tongue and body as tactile organ there is also the mind (*manas*) or, better, the organ of thought. Corresponding to these six senses are the sense-fields which are external to the person: forms, sounds, smells, tastes, tactile sensations and concepts (*dhamma*) or objects of thought. As soon as an organ of perception (e.g. the eye) and the corresponding sense-field (e.g. forms) come into contact, a consciousness of perception (e.g. sight-consciousness) arises. In this way the object is taken into consciousness, and perceived by man. All reality is brought to us by the six senses: the senses create our individual world.

It follows that the way in which we see the world depends on the nature of our senses, and on whether they convey the image of the object to consciousness without distortion and in its true colours. If anyone's senses are ruled by greed, hatred and delusion, all his perceptions will kindle, because they arouse further desires and aversions in him: for him the world is on fire. But whoever exerts control over the six senses is free from lusts and passions, and will gain freedom from rebirth.

It must have made a deep impression on the bhikkhus who were former followers of the fire-cult, to hear fire spoken of in this profound philosophical sense.

528–508 BC

3
The first twenty years

THE CONVERSION OF KING BIMBISĀRA

The Buddha was very well aware that the attitude of the kings towards him would be of decisive importance for the spread of his teaching. He therefore made Rājagaha, the capital and residence of King Bimbisāra of Magadha, in whose kingdom he was, his next goal.

There were some points of contact. He could not only refer to his first, somewhat cool meeting with the king at the beginning of his quest (534 BC); he could also count on the fact that Bimbisāra would regard the leader of an order as a former of opinions, and therefore a potential political influence whom it would pay him to get to know.

Rājagaha, 70 km south-west of Patna near the modern small town of Rājgir, was the most powerful royal city of northern India after Sāvatthi, the capital of the kingdom of Kosala. Its importance was of recent date, as only Bimbisāra had extended the older city of Giribbaja ('many mountains') and raised it to the status of a royal capital as Rājagaha ('Kingsbury').

Two things had been decisive in the choice of this place, despite its unfavourable situation as regards communications, as the capital of Magadha. South of Rājagaha there was iron ore which was obtained as iron oxide by open-cast mining, and which was largely turned into weapons and tools in the city. And to the south-east there was also copper ore. The wealth and power of Magadha depended on these mineral resources and the small industries involved with their processing.

The second factor was strategic. The city lay between long chains of mountains which formed a Z-shaped valley with good defensive possibilities. The defensive value of the situation was increased by a Cyclopean wall running along the ridges, which at the time was under construction, and which eventually reached a length of 40 km. The centre of Rājagaha, the old Giribbaja, was in addition protected by an older wall. The surrounding mountains kept every breeze away from the city, so that in summer the atmosphere in the valley was extremely oppressive. There were four pass-roads leading out of the city, each originally guarded by a defensive gate, which was shut at night.

The centre of Rājagaha did not fill the entire valley, but only the cross-bar of the Z; this was the area of Giribbaja, inside the inner wall. Here was Bimbisāra's palace, and here too were the houses of the nobility and the wealthy citizens, as well as the bazaar and the royal smithies. The royal palace was built on foundations of undressed stone (which have been exposed by archaeologists and can be seen today), but the building itself was of wood. The extensive areas of valley between the inner and outer walls contained scattered dwellings of clay, but consisted mainly of fields, mango-groves and pastures.

As soon as the Buddha and his retinue of monks, among them the three Kassapa brothers and the other former matted-hair ascetics, had reached Rājagaha and rested themselves in the Laṭṭhivana ('truncheon-forest') to the south-west of the town, Bimbisāra heard of the arrival of the '*samaṇa* Gotama, son of the Sakiyas', and at once set out with a company of Brahmins, householders, courtiers, orderlies and guards for the forest, in order to greet his visitor. In ancient India it was the custom for kings, just like private citizens, to go to see the religious and not to invite them to visit them. In this way they showed their respect for those who had renounced the world, and refrained from infringing the liberty of those who sought it.

Since the royal party did not know for certain who was the teacher of the other, Gotama or Uruvela-Kassapa, the Buddha subjected Kassapa to a kind of interrogation. The dialogue between the two may have been planned in advance; in any case, especially as it is given in the Pāli Canon in verse, it creates the impression of an act put on for the king's benefit:

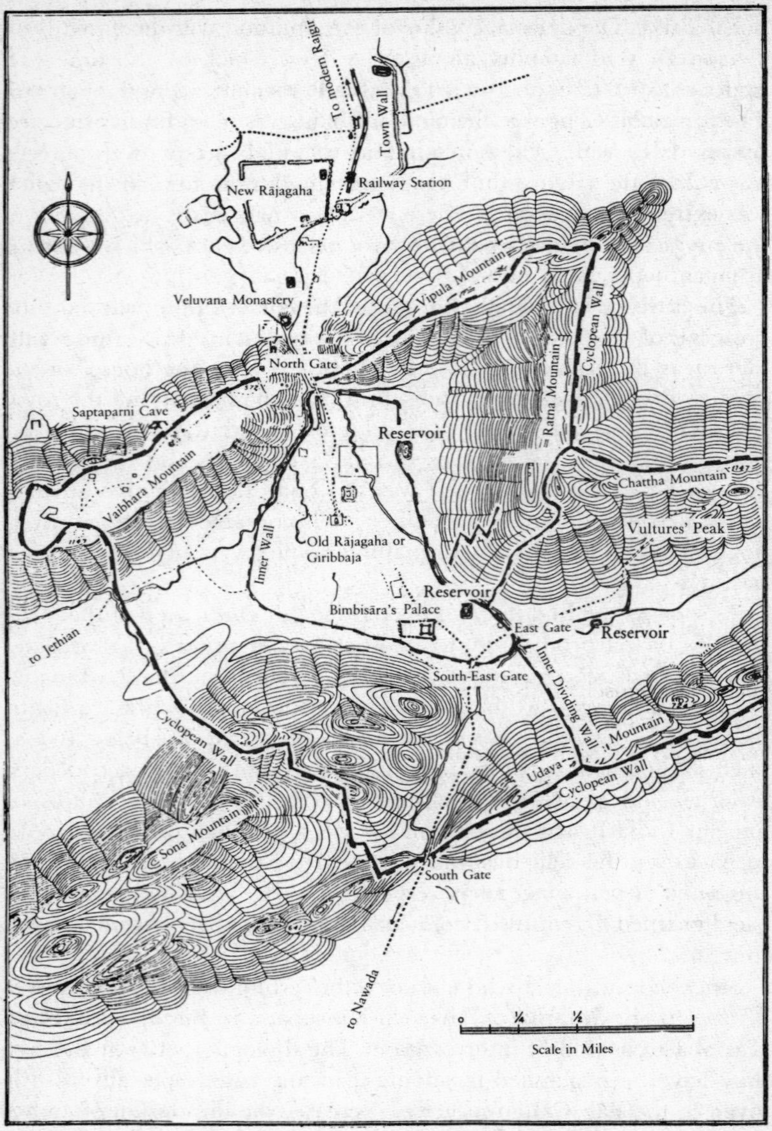

Rājagaha, the capital of the Kingdom of Magadha.

The Buddha 'Kassapa, until recently you practised the fire-cult in Uruvelā. Why did you give it up?'
Kassapa 'The reward that these sacrifices hold out is of a sensual nature, pleasures and women. Realizing that worldly things are impure, I lost interest in making sacrifices.'
The Buddha 'If your mind no longer finds pleasure in that, what does it rejoice in now?'
Kassapa 'I have come to know the state of peace (i.e. Nibbāna), which depends on nothing and which each man must realize for himself. It is for that that I have abandoned the practice of fire sacrifices.' (Mv 1.22.4–5, paraphrased)

After these words, Uruvela-Kassapa prostrated himself before the Buddha and declared: 'The Blessed One is my teacher, I am his pupil – the Blessed One is my teacher, I am his pupil!' (Mv 1.22.6). The ceremonial submission of the aged Kassapa to the spiritual guidance of the still scarcely known *samaṇa* Gotama must have impressed the king. The effect was increased by the fact that Kassapa uttered the words twice, thus giving them the force of an oath.

The Buddha at once took pedagogical advantage of the undivided attention which was now his. He delivered a graduated discourse to the assembly, after which all (?) those present, including the king, declared themselves his lay followers (Mv 1.22.8).

The narrative gives another, separate version of the king's conversion. When Seniya Bimbisāra, King of Magadha, it says, had grasped the teaching, penetrated it and gained confidence in it, he said to Gotama:

'As a prince I had five wishes, which have now been fulfilled. I wanted to be a king, and to be visited in my kingdom by a Fully-enlightened One. I also wished that I might be able to receive that Fully-enlightened One with honour, that he might teach me his doctrine and that I might understand it. Now all these wishes of mine have been fulfilled. It is as if someone were to set up what had been knocked down, or to point out the way to a man who had got lost, or to bring an oil-lamp into a dark place, so that those with eyes could see what was there. Just so the Blessed One has expounded the Dhamma in various ways. I, Lord, go to the Blessed

> One, to the Dhamma and to the Saṅgha of monks for refuge. May the Blessed One accept me from this day forth as a lay follower as long as life shall last!' (Mv 1.22.9–11, abridged)

He then invited the Buddha and his monks to a meal the following day, and the Master indicated his acceptance by silence.

Next morning, Bimbisāra served the Buddha and his monks with his own hands – a high honour seldom accorded to anybody. But the king had a still greater surprise in store: he presented, in the words of the declaration of gift, 'to the Order of monks with the Buddha at their head', his recreation park Veḷuvana ('Bamboo Wood'), which lay before the north gate of Rājagaha, so that the Master might settle there, near the city but in a quiet place, accessible to visitors but suitably withdrawn. The donation was given legal force with the usual ceremony: the donor poured water over the hands of the recipient into a bowl (in this case, naturally, a golden one). The Buddha did not utter any formal thanks, because this would have counterbalanced, and therefore cancelled, the religious merit which the donor had acquired for himself. Instead, he expressed his pleasure by delivering a discourse to Bimbisāra (Mv 1.22.15–18).

The conversion of the King of Magadha can be dated to the last month of 528 or the first two months of 527 BC. The second date is the more probable. Bimbisāra was five years younger than the Buddha and at thirty-one had already been king for sixteen years.

There was no question of the king's conversion to the teachings of Gotama arousing the envy of other religious teachers. It was and is in the spirit of Indian tolerance for one to be a follower of one school of thought, without rejecting the others. No Indian religious doctrine has ever laid claim to exclusivity. There were disputes between the schools, but no fights, and the Buddha's religion, too, is based on peaceful co-existence. We hear several times of how Gotama instructed new followers to continue to give alms to the monks of the school they had left (e.g. Mv 6.31.10f.).

There are many signs, not least his loyalty to the Buddha over the decades till his murder, that show that King Bimbisāra was deeply stirred by the Sakiya's teaching. The charisma of the Buddha, the conviction carried by his very presence, his nobility and eloquence, as well as the balanced nature of his views, which were expressed in the 'Middle Way', his high ethical standards and, not least, the mystical fascination of his goal of deliverance – all these things fascinated the king: he experienced an encounter with the numinous such as fills a man with bliss and kindles in him an inner light for life. At thirty-one, Bimbisāra was young enough to be inspired by religion, and yet old enough not to lose rational control over his enthusiasm.

The importance of Bimbisāra's conversion for the success of the Buddha's mission can scarcely be exaggerated. Thousands of citizens of Magadha followed their king's example and adopted the Dhamma as their guide. Many will probably have done this to gain favour with Bimbisāra, but most did so from conviction. In fact, the new doctrine had something to offer everyone, and every caste. It appealed to the warrior-nobles by its lofty tone and its compatibility with the duties of state service, and to the Brahmins by its rationality and philosophical precision. It impressed the merchants by its rejection of costly sacrifices, supposed to ensure commercial success, and by its understanding of mercantile thinking; for the artisans and the casteless, its attraction was its devaluation of hereditary privilege. Despite its negative judgement of the world, it was felt to be a religion of hope, which showed everyone how he could make use of the law of Kamma to work his way up within the social hierarchy, and finally gain liberation. With King Bimbisāra's conversion the Buddha's teaching had become socially acceptable and a subject of discussion on everyone's lips. The way was open for it to spread over the whole of India.

SĀRIPUTTA AND MOGGALLĀNA BECOME DISCIPLES

Gotama was not, of course, the only heterodox teacher in Rājagaha. Another prominent head of a school in Bimbisāra's capital was Sañjaya. Among his followers, who are said to have numbered two hundred and fifty (Mv 1.23.1) were two especially talented senior pupils, the friends Sāriputta and Moggallāna.

Sāriputta's home was the village of Nālaka (now Sarichak?) near Rājagaha, and he belonged to the Brahmin family of Upatissa. He had three younger brothers (Cunda, Upasena and Revata) and three sisters. His father's name was Vaṅganta, and his mother was called Rūpasārī. He was called after her Sāriputta ('Son of Sārī'). Moggallāna, who was often called Kolita because he lived in Kolitagāma (now Kul?), the next village to Nālaka, was the same age as Sāriputta, and they had played together as children. His mother Moggallānī, after whom he was named, was from the Brahmin caste, while his father, the village chieftain of Kolitagāma, belonged to the warrior (khattiya) caste which at that time was still considered the highest. It is said that the two friends had decided at the annual 'mountain-peak meeting' – perhaps a kind of fair – to become wandering mendicant followers of Sañjaya, which they shortly did. They had promised that if either of them should attain to insight, he would teach the other.

It was while he was a disciple of Sañjaya's that Sāriputta, during an alms-round in Rājagaha, met the bhikkhu Assaji, who had once been Gotama's companion during his ascetic practices and had later been ordained in the deer-park at Isipatana as one of the first five bhikkhus. Sāriputta was so struck by the noble and restrained bearing of the strange monk that he waited until Assaji had finished his alms-round, and then asked him who was his master. The bhikkhu replied that he was a disciple of the *samaṇa* of the Sakiya clan, and Sāriputta asked him about this master's teaching. Although (according to Mv 1.6.47) he was an Arahant, Assaji was not able to give a full account of the teaching. He said he was new, having only recently accepted the Buddha's teaching, but that he could give its contents in brief form. Then he uttered the famous verse which has since been adopted as the creed of Buddhists of all schools:

> 'Of *dhammas** arising from a cause,
> The Perfect One has explained the cause.
> And how they come to cessation,
> That too the Great Sage has taught.'
>
> (Mv 1.23.5)

Sāriputta, whose analytical and philosophical intelligence is often praised in the sources, at once grasped the sense of this statement: 'Whatever is subject to the law of origination (e.g. the empirical

*Here 'factors of existence'.

person and its suffering) is also subject to the law of destruction.' This means that it can, if no cause for further rebirth is created, be transcended in the state of cessation, which is Nibbāna. Overwhelmed by this insight, Sāriputta hastened to his friend Moggallāna in order to acquaint him with this new truth (Mv 1.23.5–6).

Moggallāna, an especially gifted meditator, grasped the meaning no less quickly than Sāriputta, and he proposed that they should both at once go to the Buddha and become his pupils. Sāriputta, however, declined as they first had to consult their *samaṇa* companions and Sañjaya. They did so, and their fellow-*samaṇas* declared their readiness to go over to the Buddha; Sañjaya, on the other hand, promised that if they stayed with him they would share in the leadership of his school. When Sāriputta and Moggallāna refused his offer, and went with all two hundred and fifty (?) of his followers to the Veḷuvana Park to request acceptance into the Buddha's order, Sañjaya was so disappointed that hot blood issued from his mouth. Meanwhile, the two friends were ordained by the Buddha (Mv 1.24), and soon became Arahants: Moggallāna in a week, and Sāriputta shortly after. They soon became Gotama's two chief followers, and remained such for more than forty years.

Not long after Sāriputta and Moggallāna had become monks in his order, the Buddha received a visitor from his home-town of Kapilavatthu. This was Kāḷudāyin, 'dark Udāyin', as he was called on account of his dark complexion. He was a friend of the Buddha's youth whom Rāja Suddhodana had sent out to look for his son and try to persuade him to visit Kapilavatthu.

Kāḷudāyin carried out his mission with great skill. He joined the Saṅgha and thus had access to the Buddha at any time. Then through vivid descriptions he tried to make the Master homesick for the Sakiya land. With lyrical enthusiasm he described the beauty of trees in full blossom, as the wanderer sees them at the side of the road:

> Trees are there, Lord, which glow in crimson now,
> In quest of fruit they've cast aside their leaves.
> But still the blossoms hang there, red as blood.
> Now is the time, o Lord, to travel there.

For trees in blossom give us high delight,
They spread the sweetest fragrance all around.
The loss of leaves betokens coming fruit.
Now is the time, o Lord, for setting forth.

This is the season that is full of glee:
Not over hot is it, nor over cold.
Let Sakiyas and Koliyas behold
You when you westward cross the Rohinī.

(Thag 527–9)

Indeed Gotama allowed himself to be persuaded. He promised Kāḷudāyin that he would visit Kapilavatthu, not at once, but after the next rains, which he planned to keep in Rājagaha. Kāḷudāyin was delighted, and hurried back to Kapilavatthu to convey the news to Rāja Suddhodana. He probably did so in flowery language, for he was a master of the flattering compliment, as is shown by the verses (Thag 533–5) in which he sings the praise of Suddhodana as father of the exalted Buddha, and honours the memory of the Buddha's deceased mother.

THE RAINS IN RĀJAGAHA

According to plan the Buddha spent the rains of 527 BC in Rājagaha, where, in the meantime, huts for the monks had been erected in the Veḷuvana park – the beginnings of a monastery. This was the second rains period since the beginning of his mission, and it was not without its problems. The continued growth of the Saṅgha raised unexpected difficulties for the leader.

The concentration of so many wandering mendicants doing the rounds in Rājagaha every morning and standing silently before the doors with their alms-vessels – which were not mere bowls but pots – waiting for food, had the effect that many of Rājagaha's possibly 60,000 inhabitants were sick of the sight of alms-seekers and considered the 'bald beggars' and 'scroungers' a nuisance, whatever school they belonged to. In addition, there was the negative social effect of mendicancy. Men who had previously earned their living and led a normal family life with wives and children suddenly took a fancy to the life of a *samaṇa*, joined the Saṅgha, and left their families destitute. The complaint was heard: 'The *samaṇa* Gotama lives by making (us) childless, making (wives into) widows and splitting up families. He has converted a thousand matted-hair ascetics and the two hundred and fifty followers of Sañjaya, and even cultured young men from the best families in Magadha are following the path of purity under his leadership!'

Often the monks were teased, especially by children, with a verse they had picked up from their elders:

> He came to Giribbaja, the master on his way,
> Leading the (bhikkhus) which he took from Sañjaya away.
> Who will be next (converted and) fall under his sway?

The Buddha, who heard this invective stanza from his monks, was unperturbed. The noise would not last long, he said, but as a smart tactician, knowing human nature, he resorted to a counter-measure. He uttered a reply in verse, which the monks promptly spread about with success:

> The mighty heroes, truth disclosers,
> They guide by dhamma, true in sooth.
> Who could be jealous of wise (masters)
> Who lead men on by teaching Truth?

As the Master had foreseen, the criticism ceased after a few days (Mv 1.24.5–7). Perhaps, too, King Bimbisāra had taken steps to restrain popular discontent with the yellow-robed *samaṇas*.

Hand-in-hand with his efforts to gain respect for the Saṅgha among the general population went the Buddha's inward-directed efforts for the disciplining of his monks. It had become clear that through the mass conversion of matted-hair ascetics and followers of Sañjaya, a number of men had come into the Order who lacked the most elementary breeding, and who by their bad behaviour and aggressive demands for alms were causing offence. To teach them manners, the Master issued a series of instructions. He ordered the monks to dress in proper monastic style, to behave modestly in front of those who gave them alms, and to eat in silence (Mv 1.25.5). Cases of disrespect towards those who instructed the new monks led him to issue rules on this subject too. He ordered the bhikkhus to obey their preceptor (Mv 1.25.8ff.), to look after his robe (Mv 1.25.10+23), to wash his alms-bowl (Mv 1.25.11), and to clean his lodging (Mv 1.25.19).

As we learn from the introductory descriptions of many *suttas*, the Buddha also expected the same services for himself. Almost always he was accompanied by a duty monk (*upaṭṭhāka*), whose job it was, among other things, to fan the Master while he preached in the hot weather (MN 12.1, p. 83); if no young monk was present, prominent monks like Sāriputta were not ashamed to do this. The duty monks frequently changed, until, in the twentieth year of the Buddha's mission, his cousin Ānanda took on this post and devotedly served in it till the end of the Master's life.

THE BUDDHA VISITS HIS HOME TOWN

True to his promise to Kāludāyin, the Buddha set out for Kapilavatthu as soon as the monsoon was over. He did not go alone: Sāriputta and some other monks accompanied him. The distance was 60 'ox-stages' (*yojana*): one such stage being about the distance a yoked ox could go – roughly 10 km. For the 600 km between Rājagaha and Kapilavatthu, Gotama allowed sixty days. After the first quarter of the journey north-westwards, the Ganges had to be crossed.

We can obtain some idea of what such journeys were like if we think of the long marches undertaken, in our own day, by Mahātma Gāndhi and Vinobha Bhāve. The master generally goes on alone or occasionally in conversation with one of his supporters. Five steps in front are a few resolute disciples who clear the way for him and guard him against pestering watchers, and behind him come the rest, some in attitudes of devoted attentiveness or mental concentration, others tired and resigned. Only three outward signs distinguished the Buddha from the Mahātma and Vinobha: his garment was not white, but coloured yellow-brownish with *kāṣāya* clay, he walked barefoot, and did not carry a stick. In ancient India sticks were regarded as weapons, and Gotama refrained from using them.

The events following his arrival at Kapilavatthu are narrated in the Pāli Canon only in fragmented form, out of chronological order, and with various discrepancies, but still we can form a picture of what happened.

Since custom forbade the Buddha, as a wandering monk, to pay an unsolicited call on Rāja Suddhodana, he took up residence in the Nigrodha Grove, a place in front of the city frequented by ascetics and *samaṇas*, where old banyan trees (*nigrodha*, *Ficus bengalensis*), whose aerial roots had developed into a forest of supporting trunks, provided welcome shade. The rāja was not immediately told of the arrival of his son. It was only next morning, when Siddhattha had been seen going round the streets of Kapilavatthu with his alms-bowl, that Suddhodana heard of his presence.

The first conversation between father and son did not pass off harmoniously. Suddhodana reproached his son for degrading himself as a beggar in his home town in front of everybody. Siddhattha, on being thus scolded like a child, defended himself by saying it was the custom for *samaṇas* to live on alms, and that the Buddhas of the past had also lived this way.

The Buddha's former wife Bhaddakaccānā (Yasodharā), who had lived for eight years as a 'monk's widow' and was embittered about it, found a way to express her anger. When the Buddha paid a second visit to his father's house, about a week after the first, she sent their son Rāhula, now aged eight, to him, saying: 'Rāhula, that is your father. Go and ask him for your inheritance!' Little Rāhula did as he was told. He greeted the Buddha politely, and waited till he had left the house. Then he followed him with the words: '*Samaṇa*, give me my inheritance!' The Buddha's reaction was as dignified as it was effective. He instructed Sāriputta to accept the boy there and then as a novice. Sāriputta thus became Rāhula's preceptor.

Suddhodana was inconsolable when he heard that now his grandson, too, had been withdrawn from the family, and implored his son never to grant the novice ordination (*pabbajā*) to anyone without the permission of his parents. If he had hoped that the Buddha would cancel Rāhula's novitiate, he was disappointed. The Master simply promised to do as requested in future cases (Mv 1.54).

Despite the efforts of the texts to present the Buddha's first visit to Kapilavatthu as a successful mission, it is clear that its success was restricted. Only a few accepted the Dhamma. The citizens of

Kapilavatthu had too vivid memories of the rāja's son as a spoilt young man to believe in his role as a Buddha, an 'Enlightened One'. Political caution also played a part. It was still uncertain how King Pasenadi of Kosala, who resided in Sāvatthi and was overlord of the Sakiya republic, would view this new school.

One Sakiya who had been ordained as a monk, perhaps before Rāhula's novitiate, was Nanda Gotama, Siddhattha's half-brother, the son of Suddhodana and Siddhattha's aunt and stepmother, Mahāpajāpatī. According to the canon, Siddhattha talked Nanda into becoming a monk, and he consented unwillingly out of respect for his brother who was a few days older than himself.

There is evidence (Jāt 182) that Nanda, at least at first, was not wholly committed to the bhikkhu life. Perhaps in reply to doubts expressed by his fellow-monks about Nanda's fitness for the celibate life, the Master praised his qualities, but in such a diplomatic formulation that in the praise he outlined a path of practice for Nanda: guarding of the sense-doors, restraint in eating, watchfulness over mind and body and rejection of all mental and emotional excitement (AN 8.9). The admonition was necessary, for Nanda was good-looking and harboured thoughts of love and considerations of giving up the yellow robe and returning to worldly life. It was only when the Master indicated to him the relatively slight beauty of his ex-wife or ex-beloved Janapadakalyāṇī that he began seriously to practise monastic self-discipline. He even became an Arahant (Ud 3.2).

The Buddha ordained seven more Sakiyas, not in Kapilavatthu but in Anupiyā, a place in the Malla republic that he passed through on his return from Kapilavatthu. The seven had left the Sakiya capital in order to become wandering mendicants on their own. But when they met the Buddha in Anupiyā, they felt it was more sensible to accept his guidance than to experiment for themselves.

The first member of this group whom the Buddha accepted was the former barber Upāli (Cv 7.1.1–4), a modest man whom no one expected to develop as he did into a specialist in monastic law and etiquette. Anuruddha and Ānanda were cousins of the Buddha – sons of his father's brother Amitodana by different wives. Both distinguished themselves by particular devotion to the Buddha. Other members of the group were Bhagu, Kimbila and Devadatta. The latter was also a cousin of the Buddha's, the son of his mother's brother Suppabuddha, and so a brother of Siddhattha's ex-wife Bhaddakaccānā.

The most prominent of the seven was Bhaddiya, the son of Kāḷigodhā, 'dark Godhā', who as the eldest of the Sakiya ladies had the position of a dowager. She may have been the widow of a Rāja who had for a time ruled the Sakiya republic either before Suddhodana or as his representative. This would explain why Bhaddiya is described (Cv 7.1.3) as the rāja ruling over the Sakiyas, through confusion with his father.

From Anupiyā, we are told (Cv 7.2.1), the journey went to Kosambī, capital of the kingdom of Vaṁsā, where the Master and his companions lodged in the grove of the merchant and banker Ghosita. This grove was open to wanderers of all denominations. Some time later Ghosita presented it to the Master when, after visiting Sāvatthi on business and hearing the Buddha there, he became his disciple.

BACK IN RĀJAGAHA

The year 526 BC saw the Buddha once more in Rājagaha, where, as before, he spent the rains in the Veḷuvana 'monastery'. One of the places he visited most frequently was the Vultures' Peak (Gijjhakūṭa), a natural platform on the southern slope of Mount Chatha with a fine view of the southern part of the Rājagaha valley, where it was possible to enjoy the breeze which is so seldom felt in the valley below. The Vultures' Peak soon became a favourite spot for the Master, and he ascended it sometimes even in the rain and at night. Here he could conduct conversations undisturbed and devote himself to the instruction of the monks, and dozens of discourses were delivered here. There were two natural caves on the north side of the mountain, the larger of which was the so-called 'Boar's Cave', and these gave protection from storms and could be used in an emergency for a night's lodging.

In the second Rājagaha rains period the Buddha had two encounters which were to prove important and valuable for him and his Order. They were with Jīvaka and with Anāthapiṇḍika.

The contact with Jīvaka came about as follows: being tired from his long wanderings, Gotama had left the inner city of Rājagaha, making for the Vultures' Peak, and had sat down to rest outside the east gate of the inner city wall in the shade of a mango grove. The grove belonged to the king's physician, Jīvaka Komārabhacca, of whom it was said that he was the son of the town courtesan of Rājagaha, who had exposed him after birth. A prince, it was said, had found the boy and brought him up (Mv 8.1.3–4). In any case the fact was that Jīvaka had for seven years studied medicine at the famous university of Takkasīla (Skt Takṣaśīla = Taxila in Pakistan) (Mv 8.1.6), and had become famous through some spectacular cures. He had recently cured King Bimbisāra of a fistula, whereupon the king had appointed him his physician in ordinary and official physician for the royal ladies and the Buddha's Order (Mv 8.1.13–15). This physician, Jīvaka, seized the opportunity of Gotama's visit to his mango grove in order to have a few words with the great *samaṇa* for whose health, by royal command, he was responsible. Being committed through his profession to the preservation of life, he asked the Buddha about his attitude towards the slaughtering of animals and vegetarianism.

'I have heard it said that animals are killed on your account, and that you eat meat that has been specially provided for you. Is that right?'

'Jīvaka, whoever says that is not telling the truth. I say, rather, that meat is not to be accepted (as alms-food) in three cases: if one has seen, heard or suspects (that the animal was specially killed for the monk). But if that is not the case, a monk may accept meat.

'If a monk goes on the alms-round through a village or market-town with an inner attitude of loving-kindness (*mettā*) towards all beings, and a householder invites him for a meal the next day, he may accept the invitation. But, when he is eating next day in that house, he should not have the idea that he would like again to be invited to such a fine meal. He should rather eat the alms-food without being caught up in the pleasure of eating. Do you think, Jīvaka, that a monk who acts like this is harming himself or another being?'

'No, Lord.'

'(If you speak of deliberate destruction by me, Jīvaka, that is true in only one sense:) I have destroyed greed, hatred and delusion in myself so that they cannot arise again. Anyone who kills for my sake or for that of one of my disciples commits a fivefold evil: by leading up the animal, tormenting it, killing it, and thereby tormenting it again, and finally by treating me or one of my disciples in an improper manner.' (MN 55, paraphrased)

Won over by Gotama's words, Jīvaka declared his accession to the lay community. And when the Buddha on a later occasion again rested in his mango grove, he sought instruction in the duties of a lay follower (AN 8.26).

Jīvaka henceforth gladly undertook the task of medical attendant to the Saṅgha, though it gave him a great deal of work for no fee. The Buddha once consulted him about a 'disharmony of the body-fluids', which Jīvaka cured with oil-massage, laxatives, warm baths (in the hot springs near Rājagaha), and fruit-juice (Mv 8.1.30–33). To monks who looked pale he recommended physical exercise and a heatable bathing-hut (Cv 5.14.1) – no doubt a reasonable prescription.

Jīvaka's appointment as physician to the Saṅgha had one undesirable side-effect, when men with various disorders joined the Saṅgha as bhikkhus in order to get free treatment from the famous doctor. Jīvaka, therefore, begged the Buddha to exclude the sick from ordination. The Master accepted this suggestion and issued appropriate instructions (Mv 1.39.5–7).

Deducing from his frequent visits to his mango grove that Gotama was specially fond of this place, Jīvaka presented it to the Master (Jīvakāmbavana). Of the monastery which once existed there, the foundations can still be seen of four long halls with smaller side-buildings, all once spanned with vaulted roofing.

The second especially prominent lay follower who declared himself a supporter and friend of the Buddha in that same year 526 BC was Sudatta 'Anāthapiṇḍika', the 'Feeder of the Poor', as he was called because of his generosity. Anāthapiṇḍika lived in Sāvatthi and was married to the sister of a merchant from Rājagaha. A gold-dealer

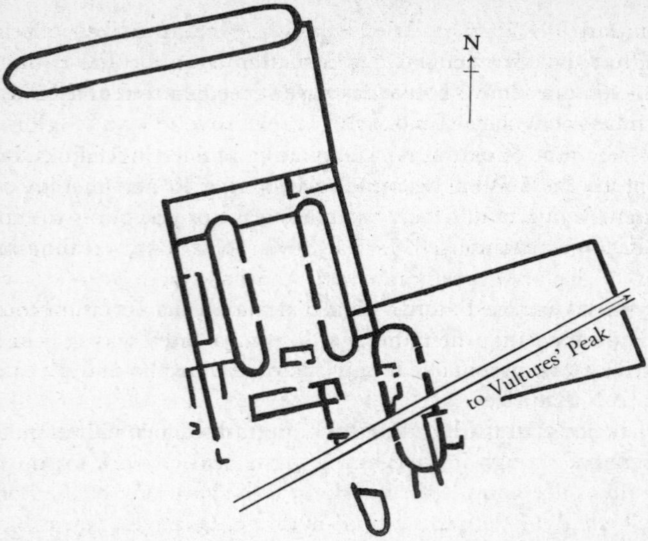

Jīvaka's mango grove (Jīvakāmbavana) near Rājagaha, the monastery donated to the Buddha by King Bimbisāra's personal physician. The narrowness of the four apsidal halls was due to the barrel-vaulting.

and banker by profession, and as the leading member of that branch in Sāvatthi its guild-president, he had come to Rājagaha to do some business with his brother-in-law.

With amazement Anāthapiṇḍika observed the extensive preparations being made in his brother-in-law's house for feeding the Buddha and his monks on the following day. Filled with curiosity about the man who bore the honoured title of a Buddha, an 'Enlightened One', he passed a sleepless night and then arose before dawn to seek out the Buddha. The Master had camped on the charnel-ground 'Cool Grove' (Sītavana), and had already risen. He was walking up and down to enjoy the coolness of the morning. A conversation soon developed, during which the Buddha gave Anāthapiṇḍika graduated instruction. By pronouncing the Three Refuges, Anāthapiṇḍika declared himself a lay follower of the Dhamma, and invited the Buddha for a morning meal the following day (Cv 6.4.1–5).

This meal, too, took place in the house of Anāthapiṇḍika's

brother-in-law in Rājagaha. It ended with Anāthapiṇḍika's offering the Buddha and the Saṅgha a place of retreat for the rains in Sāvatthi. Gotama's only stipulation was that such a retreat should be situated in a lonely place (Cv 6.4.7).

On his return to Sāvatthi, Anāthapiṇḍika at once looked out for a suitable plot of land. What he found was a park of Prince Jeta, a son of King Pasenadi of Kosala. Jeta, however, was unwilling to surrender possession. He would not sell the park even for a hundred thousand *kahāpaṇas*, he declared, a remark which Anāthapiṇḍika, who was well versed in the law, immediately reported to the royal arbitration court. The court decided that the naming of a sum, even by way of refusal, constituted a commitment to sell (since any one who did not want to sell would not name a price). And so the park passed into Anāthapiṇḍika's hands who, according to popular belief, had to cover practically the whole area of the park with coins as the purchase price (Cv 6.4.9–10).

KING PASENADI BECOMES A LAY FOLLOWER

Anāthapiṇḍika's promise to provide the Order with a home in Sāvatthi (110 km north-east of Lucknow) induced the Buddha, not long after his conversation with the banker, to set out for the capital of Kosala. His march followed the usual caravan route via Vesāli (Cv 6.5.1), capital of the Licchavī republic, and presumably also through Kapilavatthu, where however, realizing that a prophet is without honour in his own country, he did not stop this time. Arrived in Sāvatthi, he took up residence in the Jetavana ('Prince Jeta's Park'), which Anāthapiṇḍika had just acquired, and which was apparently open to representatives of all religions. Next morning there was a meal for the monks at Anāthapiṇḍika's house, at which the following conversation took place:

Anāthapiṇḍika 'Lord, how shall I arrange matters with the Jetavana?'
The Buddha 'Have it arranged for the Order of the four points of the compass, both present and future.'
Anāthapiṇḍika 'Very good, Lord.' (Cv 6.9)

There was no water-pouring ceremony for the formal transfer of ownership, simply the grant of the right of use to the Saṅgha – but

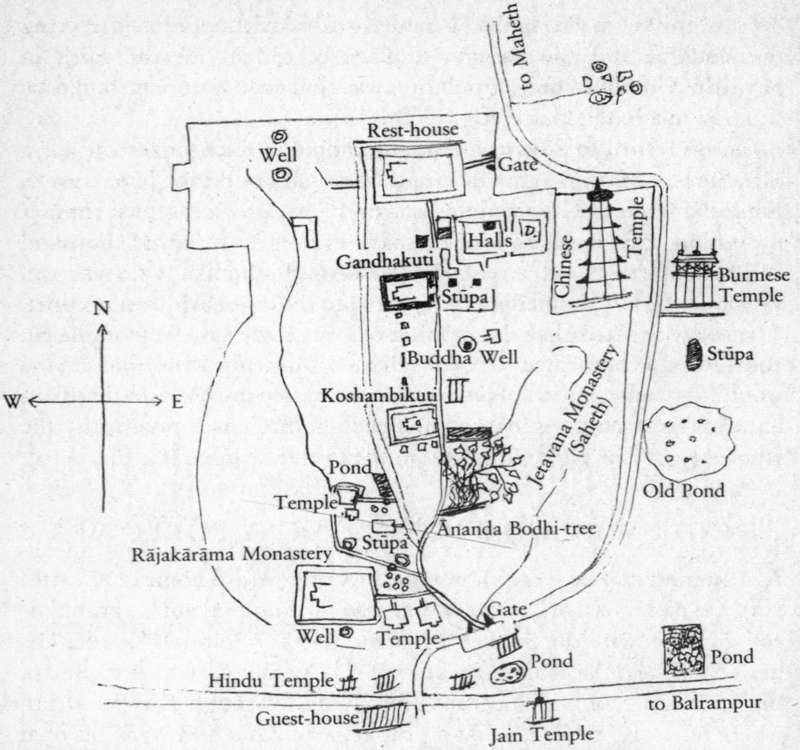

The Jetavana complex, south-west of Sāvatthi, with the Jetavana monastery founded by Anāthapiṇḍika and the Rājakārāma monastery of King Pasenadi. The Ānanda *bodhi* tree is supposed to have been planted by Ānanda, at the request of the citizens of Sāvatthi, by bringing a shoot of the *bodhi* tree from Bodh Gayā (improvised map of a local tourist guide).

this, thanks to the Buddha's clever answer, was to continue beyond his lifetime into the distant future. Anāthapiṇḍika remained the legal owner of the park, which he placed at the disposal of the Buddha's Order as a permanent loan.

Although we are told that Anāthapiṇḍika at once built a monastery in the park after purchase (Cv 6.4.10), and although we hear of such building work a second time after Anāthapiṇḍika had placed its right of use in the hands of the Saṅgha (Cv 6.9.1), it seems that rain-proof buildings were only very slowly erected over the years. It was not till eleven years later (515 BC) that Gotama – after various short stays in other seasons – passed the rains in Jetavana. From 508 onwards he made Sāvatthi his annual rains residence, and spent eighteen monsoon periods in succession at the Jetavana. A further six he spent in the 'East Grove Monastery' (*pubbārāma*) at Sāvatthi, a foundation of the generous female lay follower Visākhā Migāramātā.

The Jetavana lay about 500 m south-west of Sāvatthi (now Maheth), and is now known as Saheth. The old books describe it as being thickly planted with shady trees, partly mangoes. Children used to play near the park, and sometimes came to paddle in the pond which the Buddha used for bathing in. The pond, in a ruinous state, now lies outside (to the east) of the area that is shown to visitors to Saheth as the Jetavana. No trace remains of the buildings from the Buddha's time.

Among the inhabitants of Sāvatthi who did not shirk the walk to the Jetavana to hear the Buddha and rejoice in his sight (*darśana*), was King Pasenadi of Kosala, who was about the same age as Gotama. He approached the Buddha in a sceptical spirit:

> *Pasenadi* 'Do you also, Gotama, claim to have attained perfect enlightenment as a Supreme Buddha?'
> *The Buddha* 'I do indeed make such a claim.'
> *Pasenadi* 'The *samaṇas* and Brahmins known to me as heads of schools have all replied, in answer to my question, that they are perfectly enlightened. How can you be such a one, since you are so young in years and junior in ordination?'
> *The Buddha* 'There are four beings (and things), Your Majesty, that should not be despised because they are young: a warrior, a snake, a fire, and a monk.' (SN 3.1, paraphrased)

The king, who understood the reference to his own youthful age, was impressed by this quick reply, and declared himself a lay follower of Gotama's by pronouncing the Three Refuges.

Whether we believe that Pasenadi's conversion took place immediately following their first conversation, or not, it is a fact that a feeling of trust and friendship soon grew up between the king and the great *samaṇa*. The Saṃyutta Nikāya alone contains (in Saṃyutta 3) no fewer than twenty-five dialogues, spread over the years, between the two, in which Pasenadi reveals his thoughts, observations and experiences, and the Buddha states his opinion. Some of these conversations have a pastoral character, as when the Buddha calms the king's disappointment when his chief wife Mallikā bears him a daughter instead of the hoped-for son (SN 3.16), when he consoles him at the death of his grandmother (SN 3.22), and helps him overcome his grief at the passing of his beloved Mallikā with reflections on the inevitability of death (AN 5.49). On other occasions the Buddha gave him a friendly warning. Thus it is recorded that Pasenadi, who was a glutton and had developed a large corporation, once came to see the Buddha puffing and blowing so much that the Buddha warned him:

'A man who always lives with care,
And shows restraint while taking food,
His sensuality's reduced,
He grows old slowly, keeps his strength.'

At once the king ordered the young man who was fanning him to remind him of this verse before every meal (SN 3.13).

Just as the acceptance of the Dhamma by King Bimbisāra had initiated a missionary breakthrough for the Buddha in the kingdom of Magadha, so now Pasenadi's conversion assured equal success in the kingdom of Kosala. The news of the king's 'taking refuge' in the teaching of the *samaṇa* Gotama spread like wildfire, and soon reached the subject republics, including that of the Sakiyas.

PASENADI AND THE KINGDOM OF KOSALA

The portly King of Kosala comes to life in the descriptions of him in the Pāli Canon – a very human mixture of rich living, bonhomie, philosophical reflection and political cunning.

He was the son of King Mahākosala. His father had handed the rulership over to him soon after his return from his studies of Takkasīla, and after he had proved himself as governor of Kāsi (Benares). The University of Takkasīla, the capital of Gandhāra, was the finest educational establishment in south Asia, with an attractive syllabus. Besides philosophical and theological subjects (study of the Vedas, philosophy, ritual skills, magic, Vedic grammar) and the secular studies of law and politics, various practical skills were taught (medicine, elephant training, fencing and archery). The university was open to any member of the warrior or Brahmin caste with the necessary qualifications. The fees were high, but poorer students could have their fees remitted in return for services to their teachers (Jāt 252). All students lived on the university campus under strict discipline. The penalty for breaches of order was corporal punishment.

Both Pasenadi's addiction to the pleasures of the table, and his urge to make up for lost time in love-affairs, can perhaps be traced back to his spartan existence as a student in Takkasīla. His numerous wives are often mentioned. Casting aside all social and caste conventions, he had chosen for his chief wife the lovely Mallikā, the daughter of a garland-maker, who had successfully consoled him with her charms after the loss of a battle. The king had a high regard for her common sense, and consulted her often before taking political decisions. We know the names of four further wives of his: the sisters Somā and Sakulā, and Ubbīrī and Vāsabhakkhattiyā, who was of Sakiyan birth. When Pasenadi had wanted to have a wife also from the Sakiya clan, she had been sent at his request from Kapilavatthu. She became the mother of the crown prince Viḍūḍabha.

Pasenadi's studies in Takkasīla had sharpened his intellect, but had scarcely fitted him for government. Sometimes philosophical ideas inhibited his decision-making, and such thoughts occasionally arose in the midst of state business, which then bored him. He told the Buddha that he was so upset by the many lies he had to listen to as president of the law court that he handed over the conduct of the case to another judge (SN 3.7.2). He several times used the expression to Gotama: 'When I was quietly sunk in meditation, the thought occurred to me . . .' (SN 3.4.2, etc.) – a formulation that clearly reveals his contemplative nature.

If reasons of state had permitted, Pasenadi would probably have devoted more time to his philosophical-religious interests. However, political considerations compelled him to exercise restraint, and to distribute his favours evenly among those religious schools that were able to influence popular opinion. He balanced his gifts for the Buddha's Saṅgha – of which the most evident was the monastery hall in the Jetavana compound, and the King's Grove Monastery (*rājakārāma*) – by granting the tax-income of three villages to three professional Brahmins famous for their learning in the Vedas. In fact he never renounced the Vedic sacrificial religion, and once, without caring about the Buddha's abhorrence, he arranged a great blood-sacrifice (SN 3.9).

This furtherance of religion demanded a great deal of money. In one case, when the king wanted to dig deep into the state purse for the benefit of the Buddhist Order, his minister Kāla tried to stop him. His courage cost him dear. The Buddha showed by his behaviour disapproval of Kāla, whereupon Pasenadi dismissed his minister from office. This case shows Gotama's influence on the king, and demonstrates that he knew how to defend his interests.

Pasenadi's kingdom of Kosala was 350 km long from west to east, and 270 broad from north to south. Its most westerly point lay 70 km west of modern Lucknow. From here the frontier swung north and north-east, taking in the central Tarai, and then bent eastwards to the Gandak (= Sadānīra) river, which it followed for a while southwards, then continued southwards to the Ganges, running parallel with this upstream till it left the river north-east of Benares, continuing north-westwards to the starting-point. A third of the oval described by this boundary-line, the whole north-eastern and eastern part, was not the heartland of Kosala, but consisted of territories ruled over by locally elected rājas. These were the republics and tribal territories of which Pasenadi was overlord.

The administrative apparatus that Pasenadi had received from his father for ruling this extensive realm was not very effective, and did not make the task easy. Apart from the two dependable chief ministers, Ugga and Ārohanta, without whose advice the king seldom decided a political issue, there was generally disunity among his ministers, and their quarrelling was more than once the talk of the town. It was also because these ministers insinuated to the king that General Bandhula was aiming at the crown, that the king was led to have the general killed, with consequences which will be mentioned later.

The quarrels among his ministers, and Pasenadi's ever-watchful suspicion of their loyalty, make it understandable that he reserved to himself all dealings with the republics and tribes under his overlordship. In matters concerning the vassal states the ministers had no say. The king dealt direct and personally with the rājas, and compelled their obedience because he had placed 'their' generals under his personal command. The rājas reported at intervals at rāja conferences, which took place in Sāvatthi under Pasenadi's chairmanship. One *sutta* of the Saṃyutta Nikāya (3.12) tells of a conference of five rājas, but does not say who the four rājas assembled around the Mahārāja Pasenadi were. They were probably the rāja of the Sakiya republic from Kapilavatthu, the rāja of the Koliya tribe from Rāmagāma, the rāja of the Moriya tribe from Pipphalivana, and one of the two rājas of the Malla republic, either from Kusināra or from Pāvā. Instead of one of these, the rāja of the Kālāma tribe from Kesaputta could have been present.

The *sutta* does not tell us what the political purpose of the conference was, but merely lets us see that the kings occasionally also discussed philosophical matters – in this case the question of which sense-organ – eye, ear, nose, tongue or sense of touch – provides the greatest pleasure. At Pasenadi's suggestion the question was put to the Buddha, who replied that each sense-organ was the bearer of both pleasant and unpleasant sensations. No one sense-organ could be rated higher than another, but in the case of competing sense-pleasures that which gave the strongest pleasure must be considered chief, irrespective of which organ it was that provided it. We can assume that this consultation, at Pasenadi's proposal, increased the prestige of the Buddha in the rājas' countries of origin, and eased the way for the acceptance of the Dhamma.

We should not overestimate the size of the capital of Kosala. The city wall of Sāvatthi (Skt Śrāvasti, now Maheth) can still be made out. It forms an oblong which borders in the north on the river Acirāvatī (Rāptī), and which takes in about 3 square kilometres. A dip in the ground, south of the city, seems to suggest that Sāvatthi used to be surrounded by a moat.

The city owed its prosperity less to its function as seat of government than to its favourable communications. The Acirāvatī linked Pasenadi's capital with the Ganges river-traffic. The caravan road from Takkasīla in the west forked at Sāvatthi, the south-eastern branch leading to Rājagaha, and the southern one to Kosambī. Sāvatthi thus lay on one of ancient India's most important trade-routes.

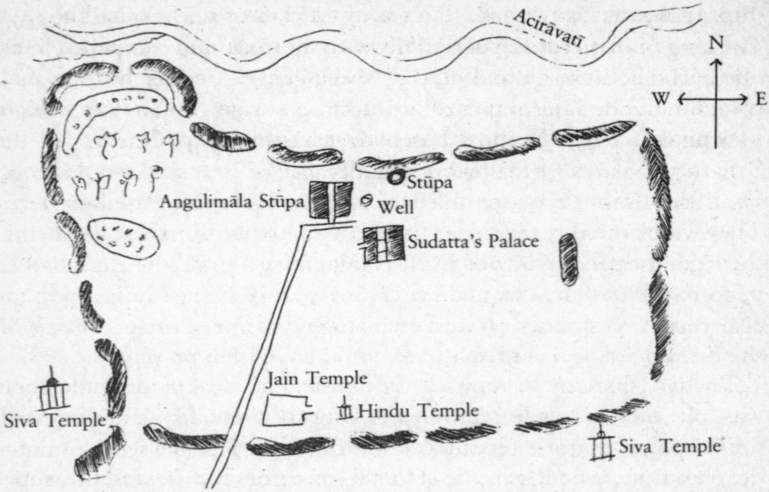

Sāvatthi (Skt Śrāvasti), capital of the Kingdom of Kosala (present-day archaeological state: improvised map of a local tourist guide).

This brought in money, but also increased the problem of security. Pasenadi had to wage an unending war against robbers and gangs in his kingdom, and sometimes had to order the arrest of 'large numbers of people' (SN 3.10). Especially dangerous was the 'Blind Man's Wood' (*andhavana*) which stretched southwards from Sāvatthi, and where robbers had once blinded a bhikkhu. Even the king was not safe here. Once, when Pasenadi was about to traverse the wood with a small entourage, his spies brought the news that robbers were on the watch for him. He at once had the wood surrounded by troops. The robbers were captured and impaled.

RAIN RETREATS IN RĀJAGAHA AND VESĀLI

The simplest thing would have been for Gotama to spend the rains of 525 BC in Sāvatthi, where Anāthapiṇḍika's Jetavana would have been at his disposal. But, either because the accommodation in the Jetavana seemed still too provisional for him, or because he had promised King Bimbisāra to spend the monsoon this year, too, in

Rājagaha, at any rate all sources agree that he again spent the rainy months of 525 at Rājagaha. This was the third monsoon from which he had sheltered in the capital of Magadha.

The Buddha also spent the monsoon of the following year in Rājagaha, although disturbed by unforeseen circumstances. In that year (524 BC) the great rains had already set in south of the Ganges, and the Buddha was preparing to spend three quiet months in the Veḷuvana in meditation and the systematic training of the monks, when a messenger arrived in Rājagaha from Vesāli, the capital of the Licchavī republic. It was Mahāli, a friend of King Bimbisāra's, and he reported that there was great distress in Vesāli (now Vaiśāli): there was no sign yet of the rains, and it was feared that they would pass by the Licchavī republic. A famine had broken out, and many people had died, and now in addition a stomach and intestinal disease was raging (cholera from the polluted wells), which had claimed further victims. Mahāli therefore begged Bimbisāra to persuade the Buddha to go to Vesāli to help the city and the republic.

If this account (reported in the commentaries) states Mahāli's arguments correctly, it points to a new way of viewing the Buddha. He is here no longer viewed as a teacher proclaiming a way to liberation from the round of rebirths, but as a man who can influence nature and cause rain to fall. Five years after his enlightenment, the Buddha had in the eyes of the people become a superman (*mahāpurisa*).

The text does not say whether Gotama tolerated or rejected this view of himself. He complied with Mahāli's request at the prompting of Bimbisāra, left with some followers for Vesāli, and crossed the Ganges five days later. Scarcely had he landed on the north bank, in the Licchavī republic, than the floodgates of the sky opened, and the longed-for rain came down over this country as well.

The Buddha left the task of combating the cholera to his disciple Ānanda, to whom, we are told, he gave the 'Jewel Sutta' (*Ratana Sutta*) for the purpose. Indologists may doubt whether this *sutta* (SNip 222–38) goes back to the Buddha himself; but it is significant that it was just to this *sutta* that a curative effect was ascribed. It is one of those Buddhist texts which are based on the previously mentioned, pre-Buddhist idea that every truth, irrespective of the importance of its contents, possesses magic power, and that through the pronouncement of this truth, through its 'activation' (*saccakiriyā*), any desired effect can be achieved – even if the 'truth' involved is an article of faith:

> 'Whatever wealth there is, here or beyond,
> Whatever jewels there may be in heaven:
> There is none equal to the Perfect One.
>
> The greatest of all jewels is the Buddha:
> *Through this truth* may there happiness prevail.
> (Ratana Sutta, SNip 224)

Within a short time, Ānanda succeeded in mastering the cholera with this truth-spell. Modern interpreters, of course, will rather ascribe this success to the plentiful supplies of fresh water which again became available with the coming of the monsoon.

The Licchavī republic (with Vesāli as its capital), which had joined together with the Videha republic (with its capital at Mithilā) and some tribes as the so-called Vajji Federation, is sympathetically described in the Pāli Canon. The 14,000 or so members of the Licchavī warrior-noble caste who managed the affairs of the estimated 250,000 inhabitants of the republic, and provided the rājas, are several times praised for their sense of political responsibility. The public council sessions in Vesāli which were called by the sound of drums and at which one or other of the three Licchavī rājas presided, were well attended, and the measures agreed on by consensus were energetically translated into actions. Justice was dispensed swiftly and objectively.

In spite of their relative prosperity, the Licchavī nobles lived modestly. Many of the young warriors slept on straw mattresses and practised their military skills (SN 20.8). They also trained fierce dogs for war and were especially feared as archers. However, occasionally their high spirits came to the fore, and they tussled and snatched things like sugar-cane, candy, cakes and sweets from the goods entering the city. Sometimes – perhaps as a test of courage? – they slapped women and girls on the bottom (AN 5.58).

Although the people of Vesāli took trouble to make the Buddha's stay in their city a pleasant one, and though he was comfortably accommodated in the Gabled Hall in the Great Forest (Mahāvana), Gotama did not feel entirely at home on this visit to Vesāli. We do not know the reason, but we are told that, although he had been invited and was hailed as a saviour from disaster, he left the city after seven days (or, in another version, a fortnight) and returned to Rājagaha, where he spent the rest of the rains retreat.

FOUNDATION OF THE ORDER OF NUNS

Allegedly, while the Buddha was still in Vesāli he heard the news that his father Suddhodana was dying in Kapilavatthu. In order to reach his father before he died, the Master flew through the air to Kapilavatthu, and was just in time to deliver a discourse to Suddhodana by which he became enlightened, so that the old rāja was able to enter Nibbāna on his deathbed. Such is the legendary story according to one commentator.

The historical truth is that Suddhodana died in the second half of 524 BC, and that Siddhattha visited his home town again in 523, by which time Suddhodana had long been cremated, and a new rāja elected. We do not read anywhere in the Canon that this new rāja was a member of the Gotama family.

It was probably on this second visit to Kapilavatthu that the Buddha acted as mediator in a conflict over the use of the water of the river Rohinī. The Rohinī (now Rowaī) formed the frontier between the Sakiya republic and the tribal territory of the Koliyas, and was blocked by a dam built jointly by Sakiyas and Koliyas, from above which they drew off water for their fields. When in May-June 523 the water-level was so low that it only sufficed for the irrigation of one side or the other, a quarrel broke out between the Sakiya and Koliya field labourers. Insults were hurled back and forth and a struggle – the text calls it a 'war' – seemed inevitable. Then the Buddha stepped between the fronts as mediator. His fame as an 'enlightened one', his position as an intimate of King Pasenadi, to whom both Sakiyas and Koliyas were subject, and his eloquence brought about the scarcely-to-be-expected miracle. Using the argument that water was of less value than human lives, he succeeded in preventing bloodshed and calming the angry contestants (Jāt 536).

On the occasion of this visit of the Buddha's to Kapilavatthu, his stepmother Mahāpajāpatī approached him with a proposal which he found extremely unwelcome and irksome. Through the renunciation of Siddhattha, Rāhula and her son Nanda, she had no one to care for but her daughter Sundarīnandā; after the death of Suddhodana she had no more domestic duties, and so at an advanced age she turned to religion. One day she sought out the Buddha in the Nigrodha Grove outside the city and said: 'It would be good if women too could go forth into homelessness (i.e. as nuns) in the Dhamma proclaimed by you.' The Buddha was evasive and negative, and even kept to his refusal when Mahāpajāpatī twice repeated her request. In tears at this refusal, which she interpreted as base ingratitude, Mahāpajāpatī returned to Kapilavatthu (Cv 10.1.1).

A little later the Buddha left his home town and by easy stages reached the Licchavī capital of Vesāli, where he was put up, as in the previous year, in the Gabled Hall. Meantime, Mahāpajāpatī had plucked up fresh courage, had cut off her hair and put on yellow robes like a monk, and had followed the Buddha on his journey, accompanied by a few Sakiya women. With swollen feet and covered with dust, she arrived in Vesāli, where Ānanda found her at the approach to the Gabled Hall. With tears in her eyes she told Ānanda of her wish that the Master might permit the foundation of an order of nuns (Cv 10.1.2).

She could not have found a more skilled advocate. Touched, Ānanda passed on Mahāpajāpatī's dearest wish to the Buddha, who again refused. So Ānanda began to argue the case:

> 'Lord, would women who should go forth into homelessness in your Dhamma and discipline be able to attain perfection (i.e. enlightenment)?'
>
> 'Yes, Ānanda.'
>
> 'Lord, since they are capable of this, and since Mahāpajāpatī Gotamī has been of great service to you, both as the Blessed One's aunt and also, after the death of your real mother as stepmother, guardian and wet-nurse, for that very reason it would be good if (you would permit) women to go forth into homelessness in your Dhamma and discipline.'
>
> 'Ānanda, if Mahāpajāpatī promises to observe eight additional rules, let this count as her ordination.' (Cv 10.1.3–4, abridged)

And he named the eight points to Ānanda, all of which are aimed at subordinating the nuns (*bhikkhunī*) to the monks. Even a nun of high seniority ranked below the most junior monk, and had to greet him respectfully. On learning the eight points from Ānanda, Mahāpajāpatī agreed to the conditions (Cv 10.1.2–5), and so was ordained as the first bhikkhunī of the Buddhist Saṅgha (Cv 10.2.2).

The Buddha had not willingly agreed to the foundation of the order of nuns; it was only the moral compulsion to fulfil the heart's desire of his stepmother that induced him to abandon his original refusal. What he thought of the order of nuns came out in his words to Ānanda when the latter reported to him Mahāpajāpatī's acceptance of the eight points:

> 'Ānanda, if women had not obtained the (right to) go forth into homelessness in this Dhamma and discipline, the holy life would have lasted long, the true Dhamma would have lasted for a thousand years. But now that women have this right, the holy life will not last long, the true Dhamma will last for only five hundred years.
>
> Households with many women and few men fall an easy prey to robbers and thieves of the household treasures (and so too with an order to which women are admitted). Just as a rice-field with the blight and a cane-sugar field attacked with red rust perish (so too an order in which there are nuns). Just as a man who builds a dyke for the construction of a reservoir, so that the water does not overflow, so I have fixed these eight rules for the nuns, Ānanda.'
>
> (Cv 10.1.6, abridged)

But things turned out better than the Master had prophesied. The order of Buddhist nuns, indeed, died out in the twelfth century, but the doctrine and the order of monks outlived the prophesied five hundred years many times over, and is still today alive and vigorous.

PROBLEMS WITH KOSAMBĪ

The greatest Indian rulers of his time, the Kings of Magadha and Kosala, were Gotama's friends and the number of his followers ran into several thousand. He felt that the time was ripe to establish relations also with Rāja Udena who resided in Kosambī and ruled the kingdom of Vaṁsā, between the rivers Ganges and Yamunā.

The Buddha was well-informed about the king at second hand: he had spent the rains of 521 BC in Suṁsumāragiri ('Crocodile Mountain'), the home of the Bhagga tribe which belonged to Udena's kingdom, and he knew the Vaṁsā capital of Kosambī (55 km south-west of the modern Allāhabād) from repeated visits. Thanks to the generosity of some Kosambī merchants who had heard the Master preach in Sāvatthi and had placed parks at his disposal in their home town, the Order possessed established refuges and a considerable following in Kosambī. In particular, the monastery-grove of the banker Ghosita, who as the richest man in Kosambī was president of the guild as well as royal treasurer, had developed into a lively monastic centre. The ground therefore appeared ready for an extended mission, and so the Buddha went once again to Kosambī in 520, to instruct the monks during the rains and perhaps also to gain King Udena's adherence to the Dhamma.

The attempt was a failure. The Vaṁsā king was worldly-minded and did not bother about questions going beyond the here and now, and he avoided a meeting with the great Teacher. He had had enough of the religious arguments between his wives, Sāmāvatī and Māgandiyā, whom he had married recently. Sāmāvatī was a follower of the Buddha, whereas Māgandiyā was opposed to him. She stopped at nothing to blacken her Buddhist rival's name to the king. Saying that Sāmāvatī used to watch the Buddha from her window as he went on his alms-round, she aroused jealousy in Udena's mind so that he had Sāmāvatī's window bricked up. Later on, she tried by means of intrigues to represent Sāmāvatī as a secret foe who was plotting against the king's life. Though he did not believe her, but was still suspicious, the king seems to have subjected Sāmāvatī to an ordeal. He shot an arrow at her, which however missed. Some time later she perished in a fire in the women's quarters of the palace. The king found out that Māgandiyā had caused the fire and subjected first her scheming relatives, and then Māgandiyā herself to a painful death.

The king's dislike of religious questions did not restrain the ladies of the court from taking an interest in religion. Once, when Udena went to sleep during an excursion in the Udaka forest near Kosambī, his wives seized the opportunity to listen to a discourse by the bhikkhu Piṇḍola. When the king woke up, he was furious and threatened to have Piṇḍola thrown into a nest of red ants (Jāt 497), a threat which he might have carried out, but for the fact that Piṇḍola was the son of the court Brahmin Bhāradvāja, whose loyalty he did not want to lose.

With increasing age, Udena became more tolerant towards Buddhism, perhaps for political reasons, since the Dhamma had by this time turned into a political factor even in the Vaṁsā kingdom, and perhaps also because his own son Bodhi (rāja) had become a supporter of the Buddha. The question of what motives could induce a vigorous man to subject himself to self-discipline once even induced him to seek out the bhikkhu Piṇḍola, and Piṇḍola explained to the king the impurity of desires, of the body and of sense-perceptions, and the advantages of self-control (S 35.127). Much later, after the Buddha's death, Udena gave his concubines permission to receive instruction in the Udaka park from the aged Ānanda. But when they told him how many cloths for robes they had given Ānanda, he was annoyed. He wondered whether Ānanda wanted to set up in business with the material, and in spite of his advanced years he did not scorn the exertion of going out to confront the bhikkhu (Cv 11.1.12–14).

When Gotama arrived in Kosambī in 520 BC, all such things still lay in the future. The king's indifference to the Saṅgha, however, was obvious and was reflected in the low morale of the local monks. How embarrassing for the Buddha to find the bhikkhu Sāgata lying before the city gate of Kosambī, dead drunk! On his alms-round, he had drunk a cup of palm-wine at every door. It was not exactly a triumphal procession in which the monks carried their intoxicated confrère back to the monastery, doubtless to the accompaniment of witty comments from the citizenry. This event provided the occasion for the Buddha to issue an order prohibiting alcohol for the monks (Sv 51.1). Later he decreed that novices who were found to be drinkers should be refused the full ordination (Mv 1.60).

If we are to believe the commentary, it was a lavatory water-jar – water being used in Asia for the same purpose as we now use paper – that nearly led to a schism in the Order. A monk of the Ghosita monastery in Kosambī had left it outside the latrine without throwing out the remaining water – an offence against cleanliness. The Vinaya

Piṭaka (Mv 10) tells the rest of the story. The forgetful bhikkhu, on being reproached by a fellow-monk, declared that he did not regard his carelessness as a disciplinary offence. The assembled chapter that dealt with the affair, however, found him guilty of negligence and suspended him. But the monk so disciplined had friends and pupils among the local brethren, who supported him. And so there were two groups of monks who held different views about the legality of the suspension. At this state of affairs, the matter was referred to the Buddha.

In the meantime, the two groups of monks had come into open conflict, and even struck each other in front of lay followers. The Buddha made an emphatic appeal to the monks:

> 'Monks, if an Order is divided (in its opinions), if it is not behaving according to rules, if there is unfriendliness, then you should sit down and consider: "At least we will not behave improperly towards one another in deeds and words – we will not come to blows!"' (Mv 10.2.1)

The warning was only effective in so far as physical violence ceased; the arguments continued unabated.

Some time later Gotama was asked by one of the moderate monks to calm a group of bhikkhus who were once again violently disputing the same question of discipline. In view of the impossibility of bringing them to reason, the Buddha cut them short: 'Enough now, monks, no strife, no quarrels, no contention, no disputing!' But the monks were so angry that even the Buddha's command was powerless. Insolently, one of the monks cried out to the Teacher: 'Let the Master of Dhamma be patient and let him sit down here unconcerned and at ease. This strife, quarrel, contention, dispute is our affair!' (Mv 10.2.2). Ignoring this impertinence, the Buddha told the bhikkhus a long cautionary tale, but this too had no effect. Disgusted and sad, he left the assembly (Mv 10.2.20).

Towards the end of the rains (520 BC) the Buddha again took to wandering, and beyond Bālakaloṇakāra village, in the Eastern Bamboo Grove, he met the bhikkhus Anuruddha, Kimbila and Nandiya, who presented a picture of perfect friendship. 'I have given up my own will and live according to the will of the other two. We have different bodies but only one mind,' Anuruddha declared to the Master, and the others agreed (Mv 10.4=MN 128).

The Buddha passed the monsoon of the tenth year of his mission (519) in the Pārileyya forest near Kosambī, where there were wild elephants. Accompanied by a few close companions, he devoted himself chiefly to meditation. He needed to be alone for once (Mv 10.4.6) in order to seek in peace and quiet for a solution to the conflict in Kosambī, which threatened the unity of the Order.

The solution came about as a result of new circumstances, while Gotama was staying, about the turn of the year 519/518, in the Jetavana grove at Sāvatthi. The monks of Kosambī had quarrelled so fiercely in the eighteen months since he had left the city that the lay followers on whom they depended for their food lost patience. They had decided to refrain from saluting and supporting the bhikkhus, so that the Saṅgha in Kosambī faced acute problems of supply. Therefore, both groups of monks hastily sent deputations to the Master in Sāvatthi, begging him to settle the dispute by his decision.

Gotama's procedure proves his understanding and skill. When the friends of the suspended bhikkhu had explained that he now recognized his fault, Gotama told them to reinstate him. When this had been done, he spoke to the other group of monks, who had originally brought about the suspension. He explained to them the reason for the reinstatement, and made it clear that the monk's recognition of his guilt retrospectively proved the legitimacy of the act of suspension. He then asked them to recognize the reinstatement. This too was done: by silence (i.e. by not raising any objection) the assembly confirmed the bhikkhu's re-ordination. Outward harmony was re-established (Mv 10.5.11–14). Each faction had won on the point they regarded as most important – neither side had lost face.

But the monks of Kosambī continued to be quarrelsome. In the thirty-five years left to him, the Buddha never again passed a monsoon in Kosambī, or anywhere else in King Udena's kingdom of Vaṁsā.

THE SECOND DECADE OF THE MISSION

After the first decade of the Buddha's mission the historical material of the Pāli Canon becomes sparser. Not that there is a lack of general information – the three dozen volumes of the Canon and the commentaries are full of material – but this consists mainly of edifying stories and discourses explaining points of doctrine, with scarcely any historical details. Also, the first decade had marked out the area of the Buddha's activity. From now on the same places recur again and again, so that the Master's traces are confused and indistinguishable.

One example of a historically unproductive episode, which nevertheless illustrates Gotama's life and his self-assuredness, is the following, which can be dated to the eleventh year of his mission (518 BC).

On his alms-round the Buddha had reached the edge of the village of Ekanāla, south of Rājagaha, just as the rich Brahmin Bhāradvāja was giving out milk-rice to his ploughmen for their breakfast. Silently, the Buddha joined their ranks and waited to see if he would be given food.

Bhāradvāja 'I plough and sow, and having finished work, I eat. You too, *samaṇa*, should plough and sow, and then you would have food.'

The Buddha 'I too, Brahmin, plough and sow, and when I have done that, I eat.'

Bhāradvāja 'We see do not see Master Gotama use yoke or plough, and yet he speaks thus?'

The Buddha 'I sow faith, my plough is wisdom, energy is my draught-ox, the fruit of my labour is Deathlessness. Whoever performs such work, is freed from all sorrow.'

But when Bhāradvāja then offered the Buddha a bowl of milk-rice, Gotama refused it. A gift won by rhetoric was no proper alms and brought the giver no merit. Bhāradvāja, however, would not take the rice back. It was beneath his dignity to eat what had been rejected or to offer it to his labourers, so he poured it into a nearby rivulet.

How very applicable the parable of the sower was to Bhāradvāja's own case became apparent before long. The word-seeds that Gotama had sowed in the Brahmin's heart ripened, Bhāradvāja was converted to the Dhamma and became a monk (SN 7.2.1).

The year 517 BC was a year of famine. At the invitation of a Brahmin lay follower, the Buddha and some of his companions spent the rainy season near Verañja, a place to the south of Sāvatthi (Sv Par 1.1.9). The village council had issued ration-tokens to the starving population, and alms were so hard to come by that the monks often returned with empty bowls. Fortunately some horse-traders from northern India were also staying at Verañja with their beasts, and they gave the monks some bran. Ānanda supplied the Buddha with this food, who calmly declared that one day there would be better times again (Sv Par 1.2.1).

In 515 BC Rāhula, the Master's son, attained the age of twenty (from conception), and having reached the minimum age he was ordained from novice to bhikkhu. After the Buddha had spent the rains in the Jetavana monastery near Sāvatthi, he one day asked Rāhula to accompany him on an excursion into Blind Man's Forest, and Rāhula readily agreed (MN 147).

As is often the case with the sons of great fathers, Rāhula was a nebulous personality. A certain tendency to romance and fantasize, which possibly pointed to a gift for story-telling, had been driven out of the youth when he was fifteen, as 'lying' (MN 61), and likewise the eighteen-year-old's feeling of self-confidence based on pleasure in his own handsome figure (MN 62). Rāhula had none of the urbanity, political skill and power of conviction of his father, let alone his charismatic radiance. But how, indeed, could he have developed such qualities, which only grow in confrontation with the world? Brought up from the age of nine exclusively in the male company of the Saṅgha, trained by Sāriputta and the Buddha to concentrate on liberation and conform to the monastic ideal of self-discipline, he could not enjoy his childhood in play. Prevented from developing his capabilities and brought up in a narrow line of development, he had become a man gifted with understanding, but receptive and trained to obedience: the only qualities he had been allowed to develop were diligence and strictness of monastic observance. He was, as all agreed, a clever and charming young man, but nothing more than that.

The relationship between the Buddha and Rāhula was trusting and friendly, but not cordial or intimate, since this would in the Buddha's view have meant creating an inner bond which could only be productive of suffering. Understandably, the Canon does not report really private conversations between father and son: the discourses to Rāhula are not distinguished in any way from those which the Master gave to other monks. Such, for instance, is the instruction he gave Rāhula as they sat together under a tree in Blind Man's Forest. It concerns the method for keeping oneself free from emotions based on sense-perceptions.

> 'What do you think, Rāhula? Is the eye, are visible forms, is eye-consciousness something permanent or impermanent?'
>
> 'Impermanent, Lord.'
>
> 'Are the ear, the nose, the tongue, the sense of touch and the mind (as organ of thought), the corresponding objects and consciousnesses something permanent or impermanent?'
>
> 'Impermanent, Lord.'
>
> 'But is something that is impermanent painful or pleasant?'
>
> 'Painful, Lord.'
>
> 'Would it be right to think concerning that which is impermanent, painful and subject to the law of change: "This is mine, I am this, this is my self"?'
>
> 'No, Lord.'
>
> 'Rāhula, when an attentive disciple realizes that, he turns away from the (six) senses, their objects and the corresponding consciousnesses (i.e. no longer allows himself to be attracted by them). In this way he becomes passionless and free, and brings about the cessation of (re)birth.' (MN 147, abridged)

Even as his father spoke, Rāhula grasped the deeper meaning of this teaching, and the 'influences' (*āsava*) leading to rebirth and suffering fell away from his mind. Thus he too had become an Arahant.

Perhaps it was in the same year 515, as the Buddha was spending the rains in the Jetavana near Sāvatthi, or perhaps at some other of his numerous visits to the capital of Kosala, that the Buddha entered into a confidential relationship with the rich laywoman Visākhā. They had first met more than a decade earlier, when Visākhā, then aged seven, was still living with her parents in Bhaddiya (in the Anga country). In the meantime much had happened in her life. Her father Dhanañjaya had moved with his family to Sāketa, and here his pretty daughter had caught the eye of the marriage-brokers of the merchant Migāra, who was looking for a bride for his son Puṇṇavaddhana. The marriage took place, and from then on Visākhā lived in Sāvatthi with her husband, to whom she bore numerous children.

Among all the female benefactors of the Saṅgha, Visākhā held chief place. She gave the monks rain-clothes, provided food for monks who were departing or arriving, and cared for those who were sick, sending them food and medicines (Mv 8.15.7). The chief monument of her generosity was the establishment of the later famous 'East Grove Monastery' (*pubbārāma*), outside the east gate of Sāvatthi.

When the Buddha stayed in her monastery, Visākhā came to him more than once for consolation after disappointments. Once she had lost a law suit: King Pasenadi of Kosala, as chief judge, had decided against her. In the heat of the day, at a time that was not customarily used for interviews, she sought out the Master and related her problem to him. The Buddha, wise enough not to take sides, gave her this philosophical consolation:

> Painful is all subjection, bliss to be in control,
> Being bound is vexatious, hard to escape are bonds.
>
> (Ud 2.9)

Another time, years later, she came again at an unfitting time to see Gotama, her sāṛī and hair all wet. A beloved granddaughter of hers, she said, had just died, and that was why she was all wet (from the ritual purification bath after the funeral). The Master replied:

'Visākhā, would you wish for as many sons and grandchildren as there are people in Sāvatthi?'

'Yes, Lord.'

'How many people die every day in Sāvatthi?'

'Lord, perhaps ten people die, or nine or eight – at least one person dies every day. There is no lack of deaths in Sāvatthi.'

'What do you think, Visākhā, would there ever be any time when you would be without wet garments and hair?'

'Certainly not, Lord! I have sorrows enough with so many sons and grandchildren!'

'Visākhā, I tell you, whoever holds a hundred things dear has a hundred (causes of) suffering, whoever has ninety, eighty, fifty, twenty, ten, five, two dear things, has just so many causes of suffering. But whoever holds nothing dear has no suffering. I tell you, they are free from sorrow, free from dust, free from despair:

'All sorrows, griefs and sufferings which appear
In great variety here in this world:
They all originate from what is dear
And, if there's nothing dear, do not arise.

'Hence, those are happy and are free from grief
Who in the world hold nothing dear at all.
If you aspire to be sorrowless
Do not hold anything dear in this world.'

(Ud 8.8, abridged)

In the immediately following period, in which the Buddha spent the rains in Kapilavatthu (514 BC), in Āḷavī north of Benares (513), in Rājagaha (512 and 509) and at the (yet unlocalized) Cālika Mountain (511, 510), nothing of any historical importance is reported. Only in the year 508, from which time on the Buddha chose the monasteries of Sāvatthi for his regular rains retreats, is anything noteworthy again recorded.

A notable event of that year was the conversion of the dreaded robber Aṅgulimāla ('Finger-Necklace'), allegedly so called because he had made himself a necklace from the knuckles of those he had murdered. He was the son of the Brahmin Gagga, who held a post at the court of the King of Kosala, and had received an academic education at the university of Takkasīla. With his trained intelligence he avoided arrest, and all the police patrols that Pasenadi sent out after him returned without success. Aṅgulimāla had an ally in his mother, who warned him of the police activities.

As a highway robber and footpad, probably the leader of a gang who lay in wait for travellers and caravans, Aṅgulimāla was a member of the largest group of criminals in ancient India. In the villages, in which people lived in the sixth century BC proverbially 'with open doors', crime was rare. It was commoner in the cities. Burglaries did not happen frequently, because the well-to-do whose homes it would have paid to burgle were surrounded by servants day and night. It was more usual for a servant to disappear with his master's valuables, but this too had its limits, since most servants lived with their families in or near the master's house, which made flight scarcely possible. Armed robbery was the most promising way of getting rich quickly, and therefore it was the commonest, although this crime, which threatened both trade and the state's income, was threatened with such punishments as mutilation, blinding, impaling, strangling or beheading.

The Buddha ignored all warnings when he set out from Sāvatthi into the district made unsafe by Aṅgulimāla. Before long he met the robber, who was astonished at the courage of this solitary wandering mendicant. The conversation between them, as preserved in the Canon (MN 86) is probably a later invention, the more so as it is in verse. But the fact remains that Aṅgulimāla finally begged the Buddha to admit him to his Order, and that the Buddha at once agreed. They returned to Sāvatthi as master and pupil, and put up in Anāthapiṇḍika's Jetavana monastery.

With all respect for the Buddha's powers of persuasion, Aṅgulimāla's change of heart does seem rather too sudden to be credible as a purely religious conversion. His hasty swing to the path of virtue becomes more logical if we assume that Aṅgulimāla, by joining the Saṅgha wanted to avoid punishment, since the religious orders were not subject to worldly jurisdiction. King Pasenadi was curious to see the ex-criminal he had sought so long and so unsuccessfully. On a visit to the Jetavana monastery, he had a conversation with the now shaven-headed, yellow-robed Aṅgulimāla.

If Pasenadi could forgive the converted robber, the citizens of Sāvatthi, who wanted vengeance, thought differently. As the monk Aṅgulimāla went on the alms-round in the city, they stoned him, causing serious injury. Bleeding, with torn robes and a broken bowl, he appeared before the Buddha in Jetavana, and was told: 'Endure it, Brahmin! You are experiencing here and now the ripening of your (evil) deeds, for which otherwise you would have to endure hellish pains for a long time!' (MN 86, ii.104). Aṅgulimāla did not live for long in the Order. He died soon, perhaps as the result of a second attack.

Aṅgulimāla's conversion was noised abroad and further enhanced the Buddha's prestige. This aroused the jealousy of other groups of *samaṇas*, whose supply of alms was reduced, and they considered ways and means of discrediting Gotama. They found a tool in the female mendicant Sundarī, whom they persuaded to visit the

Jetavana as often as possible and to be seen by as many people as possible. She did as they asked, and after some time she was murdered by her sponsors and dumped in the Jetavana. Shortly after this, these evil *samaṇas* announced that Sundarī was missing, and was probably to be found in the Jetavana.

The corpse was soon found in a well-ditch at the Jetavana, and was brought to Sāvatthi, where the murderers made a great outcry: 'Look, everybody, at the deed of the Sakiya son's followers! They are shameless, unprincipled, wicked, liars and unchaste! How can a man, after intercourse, kill the woman!' This false denunciation was not without its effect; it was repeated, and the monks had a lean time on their alms-round.

The Buddha reacted as he had done in Rājagaha, when he had been called a 'widow-maker' and 'snatcher of sons'. He gave his monks a verse to counter the attacks of their abusers:

> Hell is the lot of him who tells untruths,
> And of him, too, who won't admit his deed.
> For both when having died, will be in store,
> A vile existence in another world.
>
> (Ud 4.8 = Dhp 306)

There was no proof of innocence and public rehabilitation of the Saṅgha, but the conviction rapidly spread that the Buddha's Order had had nothing to do with the murder.

The twenty-first year of his mission (508 BC) brought the Buddha some relief in that his cousin Ānanda took on the office of his permanent adjutant and personal servant (*upaṭṭhāka*). The Master, now in his fifty-sixth year, was tired of the frequent changes of persons among his surroundings, especially as, of the various monks and novices who had served him in a personal capacity – Nāgasamāla, Nāgita, Upavāna, Sunakkhatta, Cunda, Sāgata, Rādha and Meghiya – not all had performed their duties equally conscientiously. When he asked the senior monks if one of them would take on this task, it was the kindly Ānanda who offered himself. In order to avoid any suspicion that he had taken on the job for the sake of personal advantage, Ānanda begged the Master never to pass on to him food or clothing that was given to the head of the school, and not to take him when invited, but to tell him the contents of all discourses that he gave in Ānanda's own absence. The Buddha agreed to all these points. For twenty-five years, Ānanda remained the Master's faithful and devoted shadow (Thag 1039–45). He prepared his night's resting-place, brought him water, washed his alms-bowl, protected him against curious intruders, presented worthy visitors to him, and informed him of the events of the day, until the Master's death (483 BC) made such services unnecessary.

4
The doctrine, the Order, the laity

THE DOCTRINE

Suppose we could go back two and a half thousand years in time and converse with the Buddha, and we were to call him a 'philosopher'. He would only accept such a label with reservations. He would approve of it in so far as a philosopher is literally a 'friend of wisdom', but would qualify this by saying that as a pragmatist he valued only such wisdom as pertained to liberation from suffering. He would also approve of the title of philosopher in the sense of a seeker after the nature of the world and the principles that govern it. But if by philosopher we meant the creator of a speculative system, he would reject the title for himself as unsuitable.

He did not regard himself as the inventor of an ideological structure, but as the revealer of discovered natural laws. He firmly rejected the reproach put about by the Licchavī nobleman Sunakkhatta, who had left the Saṅgha (MN 12; i.68), that he had invented a theory or proclaimed a dogma of his own devising. He was convinced that in the law of Kamma (i.e. of rebirth according to the quality of one's deeds) he had described an objective truth, and that with the Eightfold Path he had drawn the proper conclusion in terms of liberation from this law. According to the Buddha, everyone is subject to the natural law of rebirth according to his deeds, even if he denies the teaching.

The fact that partial aspects of the truth revealed by him had already been recognized by others did not worry Gotama in the slightest: whatever knowledge which served the cause of liberation was passed on, was welcomed by him. Nevertheless, his contemporaries found his doctrine novel. No one had previously combined the denial of a self with the apparently incompatible idea of rebirth, no one had so clearly formulated the painfulness of all existence and preached it with such eloquence. In Gotama's Dhamma old and new insights were combined to form a harmonious system, which was readily intelligible, and yet, since it pointed beyond the world of the senses, profound and mysterious.

Its principles can be set out in a few propositions:

> Existence in all its forms is suffering (*dukkha*), for whatever has life is subject to the phenomena of suffering: pain, impermanence, loss, separation and unattainability.
>
> All unliberated beings are subject to rebirth: their suffering does not end with death, but continues as and in the next form of existence.
>
> Rebirth is regulated by the natural law of ethical conditionalism, according to which good deeds (*kamma*) or, more precisely, intentions (*saṅkhāra*), condition rebirth in better circumstance, and bad deeds in worse. Good deeds are wholesome, bad deeds are unwholesome.
>
> Since there is no 'soul' that survives the body, rebirth takes place not in the form of metempsychosis, but through a series of conditionings.
>
> The forces that keep the cycle of rebirths in operation are craving (*taṇhā*) and ignorance (*avijjā*), the destruction of which each can bring about in himself through self-control.
>
> Emancipation consists in the stopping of the cycle of rebirths and in the cessation (*nibbāna*) of the empirical personality.

His conviction that he had found, with these recognitions, the key to deliverance from suffering, is the reason for the Buddha's self-confidence; the optimism of his followers stems from the conviction that everyone who strives for emancipation will gain it. Despite regarding existence as suffering, Buddhism is not pessimistic; in its followers it establishes confidence and relaxed mood. A follower of the Dhamma is like someone to whom the doctor has explained his disease, but with the assurance that a cure is possible without any external operation, solely through the patient's own efforts.

1 Suffering (*dukkha*)

That Siddhattha, who was born to a high position and favourable circumstances, should have developed a particular sensitivity to suffering as a consequence of his socially secure position, is psychologically understandable. But we may ask: How was it that all the good fortune that he enjoyed did not make him happy? It would be foolish to assume that the son of Rāja Suddhodana of Kapilavatthu was not aware of his happy circumstances. The only thing was that he saw more deeply and demanded more. He had a philosophical idea of happiness (*sukha*) which he did not find realized in his life, which in fact was realized nowhere. True, he was lucky in the world, but was this continually threatened condition really happiness? And what was the worth of small 'happinesses'? The few minutes of pleasure at a rhetorical success, flights of the imagination in conversation with friends, passion in a woman's arms, the pleasures of the table – what were they all worth, these joys that lasted such a short time, only to yield immediately once again to the normal condition of boredom, dissatisfaction and dread of the future – in other words to suffering (*dukkha*)? They were mere episodes, blissful escapes, not the happiness of being. Any happiness that is worthy of the name must be a stable happiness beyond all that threatens it, must be permanent freedom from suffering – that was Siddhattha's conviction when, at the age of twenty-nine, he gave up family, home and possessions in order to devote himself to the quest for this happiness.

First, he had to become clear in his mind about the nature of the suffering which he sought to escape from. And so, of the *Four Noble Truths* with which he outlined his teaching in 528 BC, in the Deer Park at Isipatana, to the five ascetics who had once been his companions, the first gives the definition of suffering (*dukkha*):

'This, monks, is the *Noble Truth of Suffering*:

(a) Birth, old age, disease and death are suffering;
(b) Sorrow, lamentation, pain, dejection and despair are suffering;
(c) Being joined to what one dislikes, and being separated from what one likes, is suffering;
(d) Not getting what one wants is suffering;
(e) In short, the Five Groups of Grasping are suffering.'

(Mv 1.6.19)

The message of this definition of suffering is not just presented but has to be deduced by analysing the various sentences and drawing the necessary conclusions.

(a) Birth, old age, disease and death are aspects of life and are inseparable from the existence of the individual. In establishing their nature as suffering, Gotama makes it clear that no form of existence *can* be free of suffering.

(b) Sorrow, lamentation, pain, dejection and despair are reactions to the loss of loved things. In the end everything to which our heart has become attached must lead to the bitter pain of parting: every inner attachment is productive of suffering.

(c) In addition to the forms of suffering that belong to the category of *Time* (= Impermanence) there are those that belong to the category of *Space* (= Nearness or Separation), i.e. being joined to what one dislikes or being separated from what one likes.

(d) Our suffering is further increased by our wishes, which generally can only be partly fulfilled. What is longed for and not obtained leads to pain: unfulfilled wishes, whether to be, to do or to have something, turn to suffering.

(e) By the 'Five Groups of Grasping' (*pañcupādānakkhandhā*), the constituents of the empirical personality are meant. The individual, who consists of the Five Groups and only of these, is the focal point of all experiences of suffering, and must therefore itself be rated as suffering. The Five Groups are:

The Body (*rūpa*) with its six sense-organs: eye, ear, nose, tongue, sense of touch and organ of thought (*manas*). By the contact of the senses with the objects of the outside world there arise:

Feelings (vedanā), i.e. sensations or impressions, which become

Perceptions (*saññā*), whereby the object is mirrored in the mind of the observer. Such perceptions give rise to

Mental Reactions (*saṅkhārā*), i.e. conceptions, longings, volitions, acts of will or intentions.

Consciousness (*viññāna*), finally, arises out of the perceptions in the form of becoming aware of the external object or the object of thought (*dhamma*).

As we can see, the Five Groups are not only the constituents of the empirical person; they also explain, in their functional succession, the process of perception. They are called 'Groups of *Grasping*' because in the process of rebirth they are grasped at as a new personality, as determined by *kamma*.

To sum up: What is the central message of Gotama's 'Noble Truth of Suffering'?

Starting from the point that every individual existence *brings suffering with it*, because (a) certain forms of suffering are inseparably connected with physical existence, (b) others arise through our emotional attachment to what is impermanent, or (c) distant, or (d) through our wishes, it leads to the conclusion that (e) individual existence *is* suffering. 'Suffering', *dukkha*, is in the Buddha's teaching a philosophical expression for the basic nature of existence – for the condition of being unemancipated, in the world.

In order to see that this is so requires spiritual maturity. The average human being allows himself to be fobbed off by occasional happy states and momentary pleasures and so is prevented from seeing that everything is suffering. 'If the body (and the other Groups forming the person) were exclusively painful, connected solely with suffering and not also with pleasure, then beings would not crave so much for the body (i.e. physical existence),' the Buddha declared to Mahāli, while on a visit to Vesāli (SN 22.60.6). In modern terms: Our moments of happiness are the pennies the gambling-machine returns to us. They lead the gambler to carry on with the game, though he should know that in the long run he will be the loser.

2 *Saṃsāra*, rebirth and its laws

The impermanence of all beings and things, which is the cause of so much pain and sorrow in the world, would in the last analysis be a blessing if suffering were to end with death. But – death as liberation from the evils of existence: for the Buddha the solution of the problem of suffering is not as simple as that! He saw it differently: All beings are bound to the cycle of rebirth (*saṃsāra*), and they all re-arise after death according to their deeds.

Rebirth, the necessity to endure suffering over and over again, to be exposed to the plagues of birth, sickness, pain, loss, separation, disappointment and death, again and again, is something which Indians feel as extremely frightening. It is true that rebirth offers the chance of working one's way up to a better form of existence, but even the highest form, that of a god, is not free from suffering and impermanence, and thus is no real liberation. Gotama distinguished (MN 12; i.73; AN 9.68) five levels of existence (*gati*, 'destinations') in which one can be reborn:

> The heavenly world, whose inhabitants, the gods (*devā*) enjoy a long and happy but not eternal life, and are, like all beings, subject to the transformations of *saṃsāra*.
>
> The human world, which offers the best chances of emancipation, since in it one can most readily learn of the teachings of a Buddha, and become a bhikkhu.
>
> The animal kingdom.
>
> The world of 'ghosts' (*peta*); and finally
>
> Hell, in which those beings must endure torments until they have worked off the evil *kamma* for deeds which could not be atoned for in other worlds.

In none of these worlds is existence eternal. When the deeds for which someone was born as a god in heaven or a being in hell have exhausted their effects, he has to leave heaven or hell for some other form of existence. The gods may lament this, but for those in hell such time limitation is the silver lining.

A glance into the past opens up frightening perspectives. Everyone has gone through innumerable existences in all sorts of forms of life, has proceeded for aeons from life to life, unaware that joy is ephemeral and suffering constant, and therefore ever desirous of a new existence. Only those who have developed higher mental faculties are able to remember their past lives in detail.

Since every existence is conditioned by the preceding one, the question arises as to the origin of this cycle of rebirths. In a discussion with the monks in Sāvatthi, the Buddha dismisses this question as unanswerable:

> 'Monks, this wandering (of beings in the cycle of rebirths) comes from beginningless time. No beginning can be found from which beings, trapped in ignorance, fettered by craving, have wandered and rushed around (in *saṃsāra*). What do you think, monks, is the greater – the water in the four great oceans or the tears that you have shed as you fared on and wandered round on this far path, weeping and wailing as you hated what was allotted to you and as you did not get what you loved?' (SN 15.1.7)

Then, from the past, one's look turns to the future: Can further existences be avoided? Is there a chance to untie oneself from the implacable wheel of rebirths that perpetuates our misery?

There is, the Buddha replies – and this is where his doctrine of emancipation takes its start – for the process of rebirth follows a law that one can get to know and utilize so that, if one is compelled to undergo rebirth, it can at least be into better (though not sorrow-free) conditions. The natural law of ethical conditionalism, the *Law of Kamma*, is the reason why good deeds (*kamma*) lead to rebirth in a better state, and bad deeds to rebirth in a worse state. Good deeds are wholesome (*puñña*, *kusala*) bad deeds are unwholesome (*apuñña*, *akusala*). For what anyone is now, he can only blame himself. Whatever he does now in the way of good or bad deeds, he will reap in the future in the form of a corresponding higher or lower rebirth. 'Deed divides beings into lower and higher' (M 135; iii, 203). As an oft-quoted verse puts it:

> Safely returned from distant lands a man
> With joy is welcomed by his friends and kin.

So too, a good man who has left this world,
By his good deeds is welcomed in the next.
(Dhp 219–20)

Rebirth in good or bad circumstances is not a reward or punishment for good or bad deeds, but their natural consequence. There is no need of a judge to see that justice is done and to apportion rewards and punishments – the law of *kamma* works automatically and inescapably. We cannot escape the results of our deeds (AN 10.206). Like all the laws of nature, this one can be made serviceable to man if man adapts himself to it.

The recognition of rebirth and of the steering function of deeds in the cycle of *Saṃsāra*, Gotama had found worded in the Brāhmaṇas, and the Upaniṣads, most clearly in the Bṛhadāraṇyaka (4.4.5) and the Chāndogya Upaniṣad (5.10.7). But the deepening and developing of the law of *kamma* is his own work, and shows him as an original thinker and fine psychologist.

If *every* deed, he reflected, were to contribute to an existence in another birth, which was always painful, then there would be no possibility of escaping from existence and its suffering. For nobody can refrain from all actions: every word one utters, every move of the hand is an action. Therefore the factor that determines the individual's future existence and its quality cannot be sought in the act itself, but must lie in its motivation. Kammic effects are created by good or bad volitions (*cetanā*), acts of will (*chanda*), the intentions behind the act (*saṅkhāra*). If anyone has an evil intent, and is only prevented from carrying it out by external circumstances, then the *intention* alone, the *will* to act, suffices to bring about the corresponding kammic results. So, for each individual the decisive factor for his future is his mental attitude.

This was a recognition of considerable significance. First of all, it shifted the kammic effect from the outward deed into the mind of the doer, and thus made it possible to comprehend the process of rebirth psychologically; and secondly, it showed the way in which one could act without kammic involvement. As the Buddha declared, all deeds that are motivated by greed (*lobha*), hate (*dosa*) and delusion (*moha*) are kammically binding for the doer. But whatever one does without the spur of these unwholesome states, and free from inner attachment, is without kammic consequences.

> 'Whatever deed, monks, is done without greed, hatred or delusion, when one has destroyed (these three affects), that deed is annulled, cut off at the root, made like an uprooted palm-tree, prevented from becoming (i.e. the kammic maturing), and not subject in future to the law of becoming.' (AN 3.33.2)

With this, the Buddhist path to liberation is outlined in principle: to act without desire for success, with goodwill towards all, and clearly aware. In so disciplining his mind everyone possesses an instrument to gain a better rebirth existence and finally to liberate himself from the compulsion of rebirth.

In Europe the law of *kamma* has sometimes been interpreted deterministically, as if a being whose existence was determined by his past *kamma* were also equally determined in his thinking, so that there was no room for freedom of will and action. Many utterances of the Buddha indicate that this interpretation is wrong. Actions, or more precisely, intentions to act, determine the sphere of rebirth, the circumstances of life, the physical appearance and the mental qualities of the being to be reborn, but not that being's thinking and action. Within the framework of his character, everyone has the liberty to choose the kammic intentions that will fix his kammic future. Everyone has control over his future, although the degree of such control depends on the sphere of existence in which one is. Of all beings, mankind has the best chances of turning consciously towards the positive, and in the direction leading to liberation, and for this reason rebirth in human form is considered favourable. For the Buddha, the gods were considered as too intoxicated with happiness to be able to see the need for liberation.

3 *Anatta* (non-self)

Inevitably, the doctrine of rebirth raised the question of the subject of rebirth: Who or what is it, that is reborn? Which part of the person remains constant in the cycle of rebirths, so that we can really speak of a *re*birth? The soul-seekers of the Upanishadic tradition presented themselves at this point, and wanted to know from Gotama what the soul or self (Skt *ātman*) consisted of, which put on the different rebirth existences as a person puts on new clothes.

His answer astounded them. The (Upanishadic) doctrine of a Self, he declared, was a foolish doctrine. The Self must by definition be something eternal. But none of the five groups (*khandha*) that go to make up the empirical person, is eternal. Not one of them survives death, and therefore none of them can be regarded as the entity that passes over into the next form of existence, as Self or 'soul'. There is rebirth, but in the absence of a soul, no transmigration. And so he taught his monks:

> 'What do you think, monks, is the body (the first of the five Groups) permanent or impermanent?'
>
> 'Impermanent, Lord.'
>
> 'Are (the other four Groups:) feelings, perception, mental formations and consciousness permanent or impermanent?'
>
> 'Impermanent, Lord.'
>
> 'But what is impermanent, is that painful or pleasant?'
>
> 'Painful, Lord.'
>
> 'But what is impermanent, painful and subject to the law of change, is it right to think, concerning that: "This is mine, I am this, this is my self?"'
>
> 'No, indeed, Lord.' (MN 22; i.138)

Rebirth without transmigration looked like a contradiction, but Gotama explained that there is only a contradiction as long as one thinks in the usual terms of substance. To anyone who assumes that there must be an enduring bearer, or sufferer, of rebirth, to anyone who supposes that rebirth must mean *complete* identity of the reborn person throughout the various forms of rebirth, the doctrines of *kamma* and Non-Self (*anatta*) must seem incompatible. However, if we replace thinking in terms of substance with thinking in terms of function, rebirth without transmigration becomes comprehensible. The successive existences in a series of rebirths are not like the pearls in a pearl necklace, held together by a string, the 'soul', which passes through all the pearls; rather, they are like dice piled one on top of the other. Each die is separate, but it supports the one above it with which it is functionally connected. Between the dice there is no identity, but conditionality.

If the question of self-identity in rebirth puzzled the Buddha's own disciples, it was even more mysterious to the followers of other schools. On an alms-round in Rājagaha, the naked ascetic Kassapa tackled the Buddha about this problem: 'Sir Gotama, is suffering caused by oneself or is it caused by another?' (i.e. are the doer of the deed and the one who later suffers the effects of the *kamma* so created identical, or are they different?). The Buddha denied both alternatives, and explained:

> 'If one says: "*He* acts, *he* (himself) enjoys (the fruit of his deed)", one comes to regard (man) as eternal (because then an immortal soul must be assumed as the link). If one says: "*One person* acts, *another* enjoys (the fruit of a deed)", one comes to regard (man) as destructible (because then the individual is assumed to cease at death). Not falling into either of these extremes, the Tathāgata has proclaimed the teaching by a Middle (i.e. Dependent Origination).' (SN 12.17.14)

Between complete identity of the persons involved in rebirth on the one hand, and complete separation of the two on the other, the truth lies in the middle: everyone *conditions*, by his deeds or intended deeds, 'his' rebirth, but is not fully identical with the being that thus comes to be. We should not think: '*I* will be reborn,' but rather: 'This chain of rebirths *takes place* according to *kamma*. All the empirical individuals in the chain will have the experience of egohood, but this empirical ego is not a permanent something, a soul, is not identical with previous and subsequent existences.' The ego or self is a phenomenon of experience, nothing substantial, not an entity.

Just how, in detail, rebirth takes place without a soul, is very precisely explained by the Buddha. It is not, as we have seen, the actual deeds (*kamma*) so much as the intentions that condition the next existence:

> 'If, monks, an ignorant man (in the sense of the teaching) produces a good intention (*saṅkhāra*), then his consciousness (*viññāṇa*) will incline to the good. If he produces a bad or a neutral intention,

then his consciousness will incline to the bad or the neutral.'

(SN 12.51.12)

The intentions to act pass on their ethical quality to consciousness.

The consciousness that is thus qualitatively coloured is now the factor that establishes the conditional contact to the next form of existence: it brings about in a woman's womb the development of an embryo, i.e. a new being, without, however, transmigrating into this embryo. The technical term for the new being is *nāma-rūpa*, 'name and form', in which 'name' denotes the incorporeal, 'form' the physical components:

'I have said: "Consciousness conditions name-and-form" (i.e. the new empirical person). That should be understood thus: If the consciousness (of one who has died) were not to descend into the mother's womb, would name-and-form (the new person) develop there?'

'No indeed, Lord,' (replied Ānanda). (DN 15.21)

Of course, consciousness is not the only factor conditioning the development of a new being. For a child to come into being there must be, besides the consciousness in search of a womb – in the Canon sometimes called a 'genie' (*gandhabba*) – there must be a woman in her season, and a man as begetter. Only when these three come together: mother, begetter and 'genie' (= consciousness), does new life come into existence (MN 38.28 Ip.265). The consciousness of the person who died works in the womb of the future mother as the spark that kindles life. It kindles the factors of mother and begetter into a flame (the child), but the spark is present in the flame that it conditions, not as something substantial, but merely as a condition *sine qua non*. In the course of development the child evolves its own consciousness, which is not identical with the consciousness that originated it. When the monk Sāti expressed the opinion that consciousness persisted through the chain of rebirths (i.e. as a kind of soul), the Buddha rebuked him sharply (MN 38.6; i, 258).

The process of 'rebirth without a soul' can be graphically displayed thus:

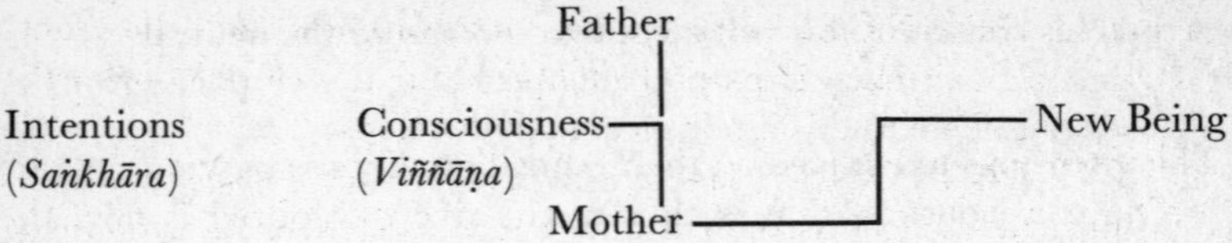

This scheme explains not only the mechanics of rebirth, but also how *kamma* exercises its influence on the newly-born being. The consciousness that seeks a womb does not choose any womb, but one that corresponds to its own kammic quality. A kammically 'good' consciousness will set in motion the development of an embryo in a mother who guarantees to the child good hereditary qualities and good social circumstances. *Kamma* takes effect not *in* but *as* the new being. The body is 'action of the past, brought about by intentions' (SN 12.37).

Practical requirements made it necessary to present this 'rebirth without a soul' in a readily grasped and memorized form. Accordingly, the *principle* of dependent origination (*paṭicca-samuppāda*) discovered by the Buddha was converted into the *formula* of dependent origination. It is not probable that Gotama himself actually formulated this *conditional nexus* of twelve links: it is more probably the work of early monks. As material they used three separate short chains of conditionality which the Master had used in sermons, and joined them up, irrespective of the fact that the twelve-linked chain thus created comprises three separate existences in a series of rebirths, but uses different terms to describe each of these existences. Nevertheless, the early monks considered this formula as such an important recognition that in compiling the Pāli Canon they attributed it to the Buddha.

In order to understand the conditional nexus we need to be clear about its inner relations. It is not a causal chain, as in philosophy a 'cause' is defined as something that produces an effect without the aid of any other contributory factors. Rather, each link in the chain functions as a *condition*: it is a necessary factor (*nidāna*) among other, unnamed factors for the arising of the next link in the chain.

This conditional nexus (according to MN 38.19; i, 26 and elsewhere) begins with

1 IGNORANCE (*avijjā*), i.e. unawareness of the fact that all existence is painful (*dukkha*) and therefore not worth seeking. Due to this ignorance, man develops

2 INTENTIONS (*saṅkhāra*): he creates *kamma* which must take effect as rebirth and a new existence. As explained above, the quality of these intentions colours the

3 CONSCIOUSNESS (*viññāṇa*), which after the death of a being leads to the development in a qualitatively appropriate womb of

4 NAME-AND-FORM (*nāma-rūpa*), that is, a new empirical person (but without passing over into this). With this, the second being in the conditional nexus comes into existence.

Since the new being thus reborn, like every other being, is equipped with six senses – sight, hearing, smell, taste, tactile sense and thinking – it perceives the world about it as a six-sense correlation, as

5 THE SIX SENSE-SPHERES (*saḷāyatana*). With these, through the sense-organs, there is established

6 CONTACT (*phassa*) with objects in the world. On this basis there arise in man

7 FEELINGS (*vedanā*). Owing to his tendency (due to continuing ignorance), to repress unpleasant feelings and to be seduced by pleasant ones, he develops

8 CRAVING (*taṇhā*), i.e. wanting to have, to enjoy, to be. This is the reason why he does not gain liberation, but continues his saṃsāric existence through

9 GRASPING (*upādāna*) at a new empirical person. He thus enters into a third rebirth existence within the framework of the conditional nexus.

This third existence is only summarily indicated in the nexus. It begins with

10 BECOMING (*bhava*), i.e. the development of the new being in the womb, soon to be followed by

11 BIRTH (*jāti*). The end, as always, is

12 DECAY-AND-DEATH (*jarā-maraṇa*). And so the rebirth-process continues: a cycle that repeats itself because of

the ignorance of beings concerning the true nature of existence and their craving for continued becoming.

So much for the conditional nexus. Not very lucid, it nevertheless gives expression to the principle of conditionality discovered by the Buddha.

4 Excursus: the Buddha's world-picture

Gotama saw the principle of conditionality, according to which everything that exists depends on *several* conditioning factors, as a universal principle which left no room for the assumption of an unchanging absolute. Consistently with this, he arrived at a pluralistic view of the world, which was thus diametrically opposed to the philosophy of the Upaniṣads.

The Upanishadic teachers postulated an immortal soul (*ātman*) in every being, and were convinced that all these souls were identical with one another as well as with the world-soul (*brahman*). They taught a monism, i.e. that there was an all-unity according to which the ground of the world was undifferentiated 'non-duality'. Whoever recognizes that you and I are essentially one, and that we are all in essence identical with the Absolute, whoever realizes that all the ostensible differences between beings are but deception (*māyā*), has gained liberation.

The Buddha contradicted these assertions in all points. There is, he declared, neither an immortal soul that survives the body, nor an Absolute in and behind all things. We can therefore not derive the multiplicity of the world from an Absolute, nor can we find liberation in being absorbed in that Absolute. It is wrong to assume a dichotomy between the phenomena composing our world and an Absolute. There is no Essence or noumenon behind beings, no 'Ding an sich' behind things. Phenomena alone compose beings and things, and these are far from being unreal. They are real, as we experience every day, and we should treat them as realities. The painful process of rebirth takes place in the only existing world, that is, the world of ever-changing phenomena. Just this process of change *is* life, for life is not *being*, but a continual *becoming* something different.

Owing to the absence of an Absolute behind the phenomena, there is no uniting link that runs through everything. Innumerable 'soulless' phenomena simultaneously arise, modify one another when they collide, combine with others and thus condition new phenomena which take the place of the old. The world is pluralistic; the only constant factor in the flux of phenomena is the law determining the way the fluctuation operates: conditionality (*paṭicca-samuppāda*).

Gotama does not seem to have made any statements describing the nature of the elements that lie behind appearances and form their components. He called them '*dhammas*', which we can here best translate by 'factors of existence', but as a pragmatic teacher of liberation he refrained from giving a detailed theory of *dhammas*. However, after his death, some monks eagerly took the subject up, counted the *dhammas* in scholastic manner, drew up lists and worked out a *dhamma* theory. In this way they created a Buddhism in which man appeared, scarcely as a feeling and suffering being, but simply as a conglomerate of *dhammas*. They spoke, if we may use a modern example, not of a pond, but of a collection of so and so many cubic metres of H_2O. The famous scholastic Buddhaghosa (fifth century AD) explains this depersonalized viewpoint in verse:

> For there is suffering, but none who suffers;
> Doing exists although there is no doer;
> Extinction is but no extinguished person;
> Although there is a path, there is no goer.
>
> (VM 16.90, transl. Ñāṇamoli)

> There is no doer of a deed
> Or one who reaps the deed's result;
> Phenomena alone flow on –
> No other view than this is right.
>
> (VM 19.20, transl. Ñāṇamoli)

5 What keeps *Saṃsāra* going?

Before the above excursus we spoke of rebirth without a transmigrating soul, and of the way in which *kamma* determines the next existence. This leads to the question of what the forces are that keep the cycle of *Saṃsāra* in motion. They must obviously be very vital powers.

In the second of the Four Noble Truths the Buddha gives the answer:

> 'This, monks, is the *Noble Truth of the Origin of Suffering*: it is this craving, leading to rebirth, pleasing, bound up with lust, finding pleasure now here, now there, that is to say craving for sense-pleasures, craving for becoming, craving for non-existence.'
> (Mv 1.6.20)

Thus it is Craving (*taṇhā*) – also more literally translated 'thirst' – that seduces us into remaining in *Saṃsāra*. Craving is the reason why beings, in the face of all reason, accept this long suffering in return for short-lived joys.

It shows the Buddha's profound knowledge of human nature that beside the craving for sense-pleasures (enjoyment, possessions, sexual satisfaction) and the craving for becoming (i.e. for a fresh rebirth), he set the craving for non-existence (i.e. for self-destruction). Even the wish not to go on existing is a form of craving which binds one to the cycle of rebirths. An unemancipated man who kills himself remains attached to the cycle of rebirths, and effects nothing but a change of state.

But craving can only fulfil its role of seducing us to stay in *Saṃsāra*, so long as a man is unaware of the painful nature of *all* existence, i.e. about the essentially painful nature even of pleasures. Knowledge, understanding and insight are the greatest foes of craving. Accordingly, the Buddha in addition to craving (*taṇhā*) also points out ignorance (*avijjā*), i.e. non-understanding of the true nature of things, as one of the forces propelling *Saṃsāra*. Many of his discourses refer to craving and ignorance as joint causes of suffering. Later, he systematized the factors of suffering in a group of three: Greed (*lobha*), Hatred (*dosa*) and Delusion (*moha*). He often used for them the collective names of 'influences' (*āsava*) and 'defilements' (*kilesa*).

The third of the Four Noble Truths simply states that for liberation the destruction of craving is necessary:

> 'This, monks, is the *Noble Truth of the Cessation of Suffering*: the utter stopping, destruction, giving up, rejection, abandonment and putting away of this craving.' (Mv 1.6.21)

Since this statement belongs to the very earliest core of the Pāli Canon, it does not yet speak of the equally necessary destruction of the factors of ignorance and hatred.

6 The path to liberation

After the philosophical mountain tour in the first three Noble Truths, in the fourth we enter the open plain of ethics. This truth describes the modes of behaviour which lead to the end of the 'defilements' and thus of the suffering they cause, for each individual. It draws the practical consequences from the understanding of the true nature of the world.

> This, monks, is the *Noble Truth of the Path leading to the Cessation of Suffering*. It is this *Noble Eightfold Path*, namely:
> 1 Right View, 5 Right Livelihood,
> 2 Right Resolve, 6 Right Effort,
> 3 Right Speech, 7 Right Mindfulness,
> 4 Right Action, 8 Right Concentration. (Mv 1.6.22)

The rules (*sīla*) are not 'commandments' but rather recommendations for a wholesome way of life. As a man develops ethical self-control by practising them, he improves his lot with every rebirth. At the same time he reduces craving and ignorance in himself, until he succeeds in bringing them to a complete halt, and thus to bring about his emancipation from *Saṃsāra*. Whether, and how far, he keeps to the rules, is his own business. The natural law of *kamma* operates mechanically and incorruptibly to ensure that each one receives the appropriate fruits of keeping or breaking the rules.

Just as these rules work inwardly on the individual, so too outwardly, because when all practise self-control, society also benefits. The relationship of mutual support is like that between two acrobats, one of whom balances a bamboo rod on his shoulder while the other performs tricks at its end. As long as each one looks after himself, he protects the other, and when he looks after the other, he protects himself (SN 48.19).

It is noteworthy that none of the rules makes demands of a ritualist character. The Buddha rejected ritual and cult observances; he considered that they only tended to attach us more firmly to *Saṃsāra*. And to whom in (early) Buddhism should a cult have been directed? The destruction of suffering is, according to the Dhamma, not a numinous affair. All the eight steps of the Path are related in a clearly visible way to their intended effect, liberation from suffering.

In the four and a half decades of his ministry the Buddha provided numerous explanations of the Noble Eightfold Path, which made clear what was to be considered 'right' in each rule. In addressing the laity he often started from the questioner's occupation, explaining the rules in relation to his means of livelihood and social status. Addressing the monks in Kammāsadhamma, the provincial capital of the Kuru tribe (DN 22.21), he defined the Eightfold Path as follows:

1 *Right View* (*sammā-diṭṭhi*) is the knowledge of suffering, of its origin, of its cessation, and of the Path Leading to its Cessation, i.e. familiarity with the Noble Eightfold Path.
2 *Right Resolve* (*sammā-saṅkappa*) is the decision for renunciation (i.e. turning away from excessive self-indulgence), for goodwill towards all beings, and for harmlessness.
3 *Right Speech* (*sammā-vācā*) is refraining from lying, slander, insult and frivolous chatter.
4 *Right Action* (*sammā-kammanta*) is refraining from taking life, from taking what is not given (i.e. theft) and from sexual misconduct (or excessive sensuality).
5 *Right Livelihood* (*sammā-ājīva*). The disciple of the Buddha must give up wrong ways of making a living, that is, through activities which harm or torment other beings.
6 *Right Effort* (*sammā-vāyāma*) is directed within. A monk – and here Gotama speaks expressly of a bhikkhu – strives to prevent the arising in himself of unwholesome mental states, and to overcome those that have arisen. He likewise strives to produce wholesome mental states, and to maintain those that have arisen.
7 *Right Mindfulness* (*sammā-sati*) is principally but not exclusively intended for monks. Here a monk, having put aside hankering and fretting for the world, abides contemplating body, feelings, mind and mind-objects. The purpose of this exercise is to bring under conscious control all his processes and functions.
8 *Right Concentration* (*sammā-samādhi*). This rule derives from the time of Gotama's ascetic practices and consists of the four Absorptions (*jhāna*) which had once (MN 36.34ff.; i, 247) made the mind of the young ascetic capable of attaining

enlightenment. The object of these absorptions is to cause the meditator to turn away from the world, to convey to him the experience of inner stillness and to prepare his mind for higher insights.

This, then, is the Noble Eightfold Path leading to liberation from suffering. The Buddha's early followers considered it to be the most important, as the practical part of the Dhamma, more important than the philosophical part. Without any mention of Gotama's wider-ranging recognitions, they defined his teaching:

> To refrain from all evil and develop the wholesome,
> To purify one's mind, is what the Buddhas teach.
>
> (Dhp 183)

Anyone who disciplines himself will sooner or later obtain release, even though his theoretical knowledge of the Buddha's teaching may be slight.

The needs of the early community made it necessary to supplement the Eightfold Path with a catalogue of things to be avoided. The resulting list of actions which lead to kammic decline consists of ten prohibitions, the first five for lay followers, and all ten being binding on novices and monks:

1 To refrain from taking life.
2 To refrain from taking what is not given (theft).
3 To refrain from unchastity (by this rule, lay people are bound to observe the sexual conventions, and monks to absolute celibacy).
4 To refrain from telling lies.
5 To refrain from intoxicating drinks.

The remaining rules for novices and monks are of a disciplinary nature, and are meant to ensure that the monks keep aloof from the vanities of the world and maintain modesty and mindfulness.

6 To refrain from eating after midday.
7 To refrain from attending performances of dancing, music and theatricals.
8 To refrain from using garlands, perfume, cosmetics and jewellery.

9 To refrain from using high and wide beds.
10 To refrain from accepting gold and silver (money).

7 Nibbāna

The goal of liberation which the Buddha promised his followers as a result of the destruction of greed, hatred and delusion, is closely connected with the doctrine of non-self (*anatta*). Every religion that teaches the existence of an immortal soul must assume that this soul continues to exist after salvation, and must therefore provide for its lodging in a realm of liberation, a sphere of salvation. The soul (Skt *ātman*), can be absorbed into the All-Soul (*brahman*) as in the Upanishadic philosophy, it can become united with God as in theistic Hinduism, or it can enter paradise, as in Christianity and Islam. Owing to his denial of an immortal soul, Gotama did not have to acknowledge any of these rationally difficult solutions. He did not have to bother about the fate of a soul; for him, liberation consisted in the final dissolution of the suffering individual and the breaking of the chain of rebirths: in fact in the extinction (*nibbāna*) of the empirical person. He rejected the accusation of certain Brahmins that he was a nihilist (*venayika*). He destroyed only one thing: suffering, he replied (MN 22; i,140). Since the so-called person is only a bundle of phenomena with no 'self', and since its existence is necessarily bound up with suffering, its ending is no loss. On the contrary – its dissolution, when not followed by any further rebirth, is to be welcomed as the liberation from suffering.

In view of the fact that Nibbāna is a liberation, we should not be surprised to find that many passages in the Pāli Canon define it by negatives. Nibbāna is the destruction of the craving that leads to rebirth (DN 14.3.1), the liberation from greed, hatred and delusion (DN 16.4.43), and the final pacification of the intentions (*saṅkhāra*) (DN 14.3.1), which always create *kamma* and so lay the foundations of further rebirths. Whereas all saṃsāric forms of existence are conditioned by intentions (*saṅkhatā*), Nibbāna is unconditioned or non-intended (*asankhata*) (AN 3.47). It cannot be gained by wholesome deeds alone, it is not the final station of a kammic path, but lies beyond all conditionality. It is outside of Saṃsāra, nevertheless it is not an Absolute.

The fact that Nibbāna can only be attained by the destruction of all desire has as a consequence that the very desire for Nibbāna hinders its realization. Eagerness for liberation stands in its own way. When the Buddha was asked how he had managed to cross the flood of suffering, he replied: 'Without tarrying (*appatiṭṭham*) and without hurrying (*anāyūham*), I crossed the flood . . . When I tarried, I sank, when I hurried (after liberation) I was whirled round. Only when I neither tarried nor hurried, did I cross the flood' (SN 1.1). For the gaining of liberation one requires a calmness that never loses sight of the goal but approaches it without haste or fanaticism. The proper attitude is one of unintentionality.

Beside negative definitions, the Canon does contain positive descriptions of Nibbāna. It is the highest happiness, peace, the quiet place, security, blessing, the deathless, purity, truth, the highest, the eternal, the uncreated, the unending, etc. Some of these expressions have an emotional character and must be understood in terms of the enthusiasm of the early Buddhist community which in the idea of Nibbāna made contact with the numinous and waxed lyrical on the wings of faith in liberation. It is reported of the bhikkhu Udāyin that he was surprised at the feeling-toned expression 'happiness' (*sukha*) that the bhikkhu Sāriputta had used in regard to Nibbāna, and asked how it could be that Nibbāna, in which there were no sensations, could be termed 'happiness'. Sāriputta replied: 'That is just what happiness is, where there are no more sensations' (AN 9.34).

Those passages in the Pāli Canon that refer to Nibbāna speak of it in two different ways. In one group of passages, Nibbāna is regarded as the *state* which *arises* in the liberated person when the factors causing suffering have been destroyed. According to this, Nibbāna is a condition of the mind that arises in that person, but then is irreversible, and can therefore be termed safe (*dhuva*), permanent (*nicca*) and enduring (*accuta*). The term *Nibbāna* itself, which literally denotes the process of the extinction of a flame and the resultant state of being extinct, supports this view.

The second way of referring to Nibbāna regards it as something unborn (*ajāta*) and unbecome (*abhūta*), and so as something given, that existed long before the liberation of that person, who by his liberation has *gained access* to it. In this way, Nibbāna necessarily took on the character of a place: 'There is, monks, a realm (*āyatana*) where there is neither earth nor water, fire nor air . . . Just this is the end of suffering' (Ud 8.1). The entry *of* Nibbāna is here interpreted as the entry *into* Nibbāna.

Further information about the state of liberation can be taken from the passages that deal with him who is liberated. Since Nibbāna does not necessarily coincide with the death of the liberated person, who may indeed, like Gotama, continue to live for years and even decades, it is necessary to distinguish between Nibbāna before death and that after death (Itiv 44). In the Nibbāna before death the liberated person is still in possession of the five Groups (*khandha*) which constitute 'his' empirical person – in other words, he continues to exist as a being perceptible to all. He has not transcended the sufferings of physical existence, ageing, sickness, accidents and pains: these are interpreted as surviving remnants of *kamma* which he still has to work out. However, he is, thanks to his freedom from the *kamma*-producing defilements, not capable of creating fresh *kamma*. Full of compassion (*karuṇā*, *anukampā*) and loving-kindness (*mettā*) for all that lives, but indifferent to whatever affects himself, he simply awaits the Nibbāna that will set in after his death.

This post-mortem Nibbāna, in which the five Groups have fallen away from the liberated one, so that he is no longer 'graspable' as a person, is generally called *Parinibbāna*, 'all-round extinction'. Several times in the Canon the question is raised as to whether a liberated being exists after death or not. The answer is 'neither yes nor no': such a one has entered a state beyond *Saṃsāra* which is inaccessible to our categories of thought or powers of description. In a discussion with a wandering mendicant of the Vaccha clan (Vacchagotta), the Buddha said that it is with a fully liberated person the same as with a fire. As long as it is burning, we know what fuel it consumes, but when it has gone out, no one can say in which direction it has disappeared to. In the same way, with one who has attained to 'all-round extinction', the fuel (i.e. the five Groups) has been consumed, and he is as deep, immeasurable and unplumbable as the great ocean (MN 72.18; i, 486f.).

The Udāna ascribes this stanza to the Buddha:

'He who's freed above, below and round about,
Will no more see himself as "this am I".
Though he failed earlier, now he crosses the flood
In order never to become again.'

(Ud 7.1)

And in the Sutta Nipāta the Master instructs Upasīva:

'As a flame when blown out by the power of wind
Goes to rest and eludes definition,
So a sage who is freed of Body-and-Name
Goes to rest and is lost to cognizance.

'There's no measure for him who has gone beyond
And no word that is apt to describe him,
When the Dhammas completely have fallen away
All paths of the language have ended.'

(SNip 1074 + 76)

THE ORDER

1 Legal basis

As the son of a rāja, Siddhattha had grown up in a household where political and legal questions were daily topics. He had attended dozens of sessions in the assembly and had been present at numerous trials. Thus he had gained a considerable knowledge of legal matters. Although politics and jurisprudence were not central to his thinking, which was essentially concerned with philosophical matters, nevertheless he was more proficient in law than the other leading teachers of his time, and this knowledge was of great assistance to him for the consolidation of his Order. There were two legal areas in which it was necessary to establish regulations: the relation of the Saṅgha to the state and society, and the internal law of the Order, which sets up a code of behaviour for monks and nuns and stipulates the penalties for misconduct.

The kings respected the Orders (*gaṇa, saṅgha*) as autonomous corporations with their own legal code outside secular jurisdiction. Bimbisāra of Magadha issued express instructions to his officials to take no action against mendicants of the Buddha's Order who might commit offences (Mv 1.42.1). Two cases recorded in the Pāli Canon make clear this exemption from secular justice.

A woman of the Licchavī tribe had committed adultery. Since her husband, when he found out, received permission from the tribal council to kill her, she fled to Sāvatthi, taking with her some articles of value, and succeeded by bribery in being accepted into the Buddhist order of nuns. Thereupon her husband appealed to King Pasenadi, but the king decided that since the woman had become a nun, no further steps could be taken against her (Sv Vin IV, p. 225).

The second case is that of the monk Dhaniya who, wishing to build himself a hut, took some planks away from King Bimbisāra's royal timber-store, telling the overseer that he had special permission from the king. The case was brought before Bimbisāra's court in Rājagaha. The king declared that the permission he had once given to the monks referred unmistakably to uncut timber lying in the woods. Dhaniya was well aware of this, and for his deception deserved flogging, prison or banishment. However, in view of his clerical status he, Bimbisāra, would refrain from imposing any punishment and merely give the defendant a solemn warning.

Not long afterwards, the case was tried anew by the Buddha, who sentenced Dhaniya to the penalty set for theft – expulsion from the Saṅgha (Sv Vin III, pp. 42–5).

The exemption of the Saṅgha from secular law reached its limit where it clashed with the security of the state. The kings did not allow the Orders to become refuges for those who had bound themselves to the service of the state. Thus king Bimbisāra requested the Buddha to ban the ordination of soldiers, because members of his army had fled into the arms of the Saṅgha when he wanted to send them into action over a frontier dispute. He made his request, to which the Buddha at once consented, in a friendly way, but not without emphasis. His legal advisers had advised him that a single monk or a chapter of monks who ordained men liable to military service so as to withdraw them from active service should be punished by beheading, having their tongues torn out or their ribs broken (Mv 1.40). Weakening the armed forces was considered such a severe crime that its organizer could not be saved from punishment even by his monastic status.

The Orders were also closely watched to ensure their political conformity. Any form of polemics, let alone action, against the state was something the kings and rājas would not put up with. They maintained extensive networks of spies and informers who also penetrated the Orders, and quickly reported anything that might harm the state. King Pasenadi once even gave the Buddha a description of how this spy-network functioned (SN 3.2.1). Nothing is known of any differences between the Buddhist Order and the state.

On the contrary, the Buddha, not least because of his own caste and upbringing, fulfilled all the expectations of the Kings of Magadha and Kosala. He ordered the monks to obey the kings (Mv 3.4.3) and to avoid politics. Even if they were of khattiya descent, they were not allowed to speak in the assembly. He bade the laity perform their duties towards the state and the community and to live in peace together, but beyond this he saw no necessity to act as a social reformer. The raising of living standards was a matter for the king and the local authorities; a monk's duty was to strive for his own emancipation. Social activity, being involvement in secular affairs, was a hindrance to his proper task.

Thanks to Gotama's clear delimitation of the spheres of activity, a triangular relationship was soon established between the king, the Saṅgha and the laity: the people supported the Saṅgha by giving alms and the king by paying taxes; the Buddha and the Saṅgha reminded the king to rule justly and the people to live in peace and discipline; the king provided for the safety of the country, for impartial justice, and for material conditions for the population sufficient to enable them all to give alms. He had the exceptional opportunity to gain more than average religious merit by establishing parks, dams, tanks, wells and homes (SN 1.47). Though abuse of power by the ruler and his officials occurred, and some bhikkhus were too demanding on their alms-round, the majority of the population were sufficiently content with what the king and the Saṅgha did, not to rebel against church or state. As far as we can tell, people felt neither exploited nor the victims of an unjust system. True, voices were occasionally heard raised against the 'lazy scroungers' and 'idle priests', but these were more the result of momentary annoyance than of any general dislike towards monasticism.

The model adopted by the Buddha for the organizational structure of the Saṅgha was that of the republics north of the Ganges. Having been brought up in the centre of power in one such republic, he had been familiar with the system of debates in the council chamber from an early age, and adopted this as a matter of course for the Saṅgha. He himself, as legislator and leader of the Order, resembled the rāja of a republic, however with the difference that he had not been elected but, as founder of the Order, had automatically grown into its leadership.

Next to the Master, leading functions in the Saṅgha were exercised by his chief disciples Sāriputta and Moggallāna. They owed their influence over the monks not to official appointment, but to their spiritual qualities. They had no authority to issue orders to the monks, but there is no recorded case of a monk's not following their suggestions. In due course a leadership group developed within the Saṅgha, composed of monks senior in ordination and those who were said to have attained to Arahantship. This stage of perfection had always to be recognized by others, because it was not permitted to speak of one's own attainments. Only in poetry was it permissible to sing of the joys of one's liberation.

Important decisions were originally taken by the full assembly, and later on, when the Saṅgha was too large for this, by local chapters. Whereas in the council chambers of the republics only members of the warrior nobility were allowed to speak, in the chapter meetings of the Saṅgha any monk or novice was entitled to express his opinions. There was no vote: the matter was discussed until a consensus was reached. Whenever, either through a change of mind on the opponent's part, or through sheer exhaustion, no further objections were raised, the matter was considered as settled. Silence all around was taken as agreement. However, the principle of consensus did not always work, as we see from the case of the dispute in the Order at Kosambī, in which the chapter repeatedly broke up without reaching an agreement.

We can see how important for the continuation of the Order these meetings of the monks, and the leadership of the senior monks, were in the Buddha's eyes, from his words to the chapter at Rājagaha. When Ānanda, on his instruction, had called the monks together, the Buddha addressed them as follows:

'Monks, I will teach you seven conditions of the welfare (of the Saṅgha). Listen, and pay careful attention.

As long as the monks hold frequent and well-attended assemblies (the Saṅgha) will prosper, and not decline.

As long as they meet in harmony, take decisions in harmony (i.e. by consensus), and carry out their functions in harmony;

As long as they do not authorize innovations and do not abolish what has been authorized, but proceed according to the rules of discipline;

As long as they honour, respect and listen to the elders of great experience who are long ordained, fathers and instructors of the order;

As long as they do not fall prey to craving which leads to rebirth;

As long as they are devoted to forest lodgings;

As long as they appreciate that like-minded companions will come to them, and those who have already come will feel at ease with them:

As long as the monks hold to these seven conditions, (the Saṅgha) will prosper and not decline.' (DN 16.1.6, abridged)

The code which set out the rules of the Order, and the penalties for infringement, is the Vinaya Piṭaka, the 'Basket of Discipline'. Its present form in five books is the product of a later period, but there is little doubt that its material is very old and that the majority of its rules and decisions go back to the Buddha himself. Each rule represents Gotama's conclusion in regard to a particular case. Thus, the Basket of Discipline is not a systematically constructed legal code, but the result of accumulated case-law. The Buddha's disciple Upāli was the one who specialized in memorizing the Master's legal decisions, although in doing so he perpetuated some things which were only meant for the moment.

Its unsystematic origin is readily observable in the Vinaya. The Pātimokkha, which is extracted from the Suttavibhaṅga section, represents the code of behaviour and of offences for the Order, and embraces four areas: offences of the monk or nun against persons, things, the Order and the religion. However, the offences are arranged not in accordance with this system, but according to the severity of the punishment or reprimand to be imposed for disregard of the rule. Thus seven very mixed categories of rules came about, while an eighth category gives methods of settling disputes.

1 *Pārājika* rules are those, a breach of which is punishable by expulsion from the Saṅgha. For monks there are four *pārājika* offences (sexual intercourse, theft, murder, and laying claim to higher attainments, e.g. magic powers). For nuns there are eight such rules. '*Pārājika*' means 'failure', as the commitment of a *pārājika* offence proves, that the bhikkhu or bhikkhunī failed in his or her vocation.

2 *Saṅghādisesa* ('involving a meeting of the Saṅgha') offences are those which the guilty person has to confess to before the assembly, and the penalty for which, when it has been carried out, must be confirmed by the assembly. The normal penalty is temporary suspension of the rights of the guilty party. For the monk there are thirteen, for the nun seventeen such offences.

3 *Aniyatā* ('to be decided') offences are such that the circumstances have to be inquired into in order to determine whether they belong to categories 1,2 or 5, the penalty being different accordingly. For monks there are two such cases.

4 *Nissaggiya-Pācittiya* ('entailing expiation by forfeiture'). Non-observance of these rules is an offence which must be confessed to the whole assembly, to the local chapter or to a single monk. This constitutes the expiation. All the rules of this class concern objects of possession of a monk or a nun (robes, bowl, etc.), which the guilty person must forfeit. There are thirty of these rules for both monks and nuns.

5 *Pācittiya* ('requiring expiation'). These are rules of the Saṅgha, non-observance of which is defiling. They are expiated by confession to the chapter or to a single monk. There are ninety-two such rules for monks, and one hundred and sixty-six for nuns.

6 *Pāṭidesanīya* ('to be confessed'). These are rules the breach of

which is to be contritely confessed to the chapter. There are four such rules for monks and eight for nuns.

7 *Sekhiyā* ('rules of conduct'): rules of etiquette and decent behaviour in regard to clothes, behaviour on the alms-round, eating, and personal hygiene. There is no formal sanction prescribed for breach of these. For both monks and nuns there are seventy-five such rules.

8 *Adhikaraṇa* ('settlement of litigation') rules deal with the procedures for settling disputes and eliminating differences of interpretation. Seven different forms of settlement are laid down.

An examination of the rules in detail shows that many are common to both Brahmanism and the *samaṇa* movement and were simply taken over by the Buddhist Saṅgha. The ascetic tradition of ancient India and the objects of the Order make the rules about sexual behaviour understandable. Nevertheless the number and minuteness of the rules on sexual discipline are noteworthy, as well as the severity of the penalties for contravention. We are also struck by the extensive rules of etiquette and behaviour. They prove not only that the Buddha was concerned to make his Order acceptable to the general public by the good behaviour of its members, but also that some of the monks were in need of elementary instruction in conduct and behaviour.

The suggestion of using the two hundred and twenty-seven rules for monks, and the three hundred and eleven rules for nuns from the Suttavibhaṅga section of the Vinaya as a confessional formula came to the Buddha indirectly by King Bimbisāra of Magadha. The king had noticed that the non-Buddhist mendicants met regularly to recite their doctrine and that such meetings drew a considerable crowd of interested people. He recommended to the Buddha to hold similar periodical assemblies, and the Master immediately prescribed this for his monks (Mv 2.1). From then on the monks met on the fourteenth or fifteenth day of the lunar month (i.e. at full moon), as well as on the eighth day of the waxing and the waning moon, but sat in silence. The local population, however, scoffed at them for sitting there like 'dumb pigs'. Accordingly, Gotama ordered them to discuss Dhamma when they met (Mv 2.2). Later, he specified that they should recite the rules (Mv 2.3.1f.), but not more than twice a month

(2.4.2). Presumably the canon of rules was not yet complete, and therefore shorter than now.

The Buddha gave exact instructions for how these recitations were to be performed:

> The Order shall be informed by an experienced, knowledgeable monk, who shall say: 'Venerable assembly (*saṅgha*), listen to me. Today is the fifteenth (of the lunar month), and therefore an Observance day (*uposatha*). If the Order agrees, let it carry out the Observance and recite the confession-formula (*pātimokkha*).
>
> What is the Saṅgha's first duty? It is to ascertain that it (i.e. the assembly) is perfectly pure (i.e. that no one who does not belong to it has slipped in).
>
> I will now recite the *Pātimokkha*, while all those present listen properly and pay attention. If anyone has committed an offence, he should at once (when that offence is mentioned) reveal it. Whoever has committed no offence should keep silent. By their silence I shall know that the Venerable monks are pure (guiltless). Just as anyone who is individually asked gives answer, so any (guilty) monk, when the *Pātimokkha* has been recited in this assembly three times, should give an answer. Whoever avoids revealing an offence committed by him is guilty of an intentional lie. Intentional lying, your reverences, has been called by the Blessed One a hindrance (to emancipation). So whoever has committed an offence not yet revealed, and wants to be purified of it, should reveal it. To have revealed it will be a comfort to him.'
>
> (Mv 2.3.3)

After this introduction the formula of confession is recited, and everyone present is given an opportunity to admit to his fault. The practice of *pātimokkha* recitation is still observed in all Buddhist monasteries.

This periodical recitation of the confession formula is not the same thing as the meetings of the chapter, which are for the purpose of considering measures to be adopted. These assemblies are called for as required, and are purely administrative in character. On the other hand, the *pātimokkha* observances on *uposatha* days are ceremonies of solemn exculpation and disciplinary purification.

2 The life of a monk

Since the Buddhist Saṅgha belonged to the *samaṇa* movement that had established itself in the sixth century BC as an alternative to the Brahmanistic sacrificial cult, it stands to reason that it took on the characteristic features of the *samaṇa* way of life: celibacy, lack of possessions, homeless wandering, and support by alms-food. Rules had to be established, however, concerning those points which either were not clearly set out in the older *samaṇa* schools, or concerning which the Buddhist Saṅgha took a different line.

Instructions by the Buddha for the behaviour of the monks are contained not only in the Vinaya Piṭaka, but throughout the Pāli Canon. Right into his old age, Gotama was incessantly concerned to train his monks and nuns in the struggle against craving that is the cause of suffering, and to educate them in correct behaviour in public. Being convinced that a favourable public opinion was important for the Dhamma, he was always ready to change or abolish rules that caused unfavourable comment. One example is his instruction concerning the etiquette connected with sneezing. Once, when he was preaching, he sneezed, and was disturbed when the monks interrupted his discourse with the usual blessing: 'Long may you live!' So he forbade them to use this expression in future, or to reply to it. However, it soon turned out that lay followers who uttered a blessing for a sneezing monk thought he was rude not to reply. The Buddha therefore withdrew his instruction, and allowed the monks to reply to the blessing with the usual phrase of thanks: 'Long life to you!' (Cv 5.33.3). He was always ready to receive suggestions for new rules, from whatever side they came. In fact, besides the monks, various lay followers, including Bimbisāra, Jīvaka, Anāthapiṇḍika and Visākhā, helped to form the rules of the Order by making sensible suggestions.

At the suggestion of Jīvaka, the physician whom King Bimbisāra had appointed official medical officer to the Saṅgha, men who suffered from leprosy, boils, eczema, tuberculosis or epilepsy were not allowed to be admitted to the Order (Mv 1.39). In this way people with these diseases were prevented from joining in order to get free treatment from Jīvaka. Further grounds for refusing ordination were in the case of applicants who were eunuchs (Mv 1.61) or hermaphrodites (Mv 1.68), those who lacked a limb, were disfigured, lame, hunchbacked, dwarfed or who had a goitre or a crooked limb, who were senile, blind or deaf or who suffered from elephantiasis – the mosquito-borne filaria which is endemic in rice-growing areas (Mv 1.71). All these rules were meant to ensure that the Saṅgha did not become an asylum for the unfit.

Also excluded from ordination were soldiers on active service under the king, escaped convicts or those wanted by the police, those who had been scourged or branded, debtors and slaves (Mv 1.40–7). It was not exactly forbidden, but not considered desirable that an aged man should join the Saṅgha, because those ordained in old age seldom had the requisite qualities for a bhikkhu (AN 5.59–60).

Gotama did not pay any attention, in ordaining men, to the fate of their family, even if the ordinand was the breadwinner. He took it for granted that the greater family would look after the 'monk's widow' and her children. If not, the family had to put up with hardship. In his estimation the ephemeral hardships of the family did not count beside the eternal value of emancipation.

Typical of his uncompromising attitude is his praise for the Bhikkhu Sangāmaji (which later monks put into verse). Sangāmaji had come to Sāvatthi to see the Blessed One, and on hearing of this, his ex-wife also hurried to Sāvatthi with their little son. While the monk was resting under a tree at midday in Jetavana, she came to him and said: 'Look after me, *samaṇa*, and our little son!' But Sangāmaji did not stir. A second and a third time she spoke to him, with no effect. Angrily she set her son down at his feet, saying: 'This is your son, *samaṇa*, (at least) look after *him*!' Then she left, but when she turned round after going some distance, and saw that the monk had neither looked at his son nor spoken to him, she fetched the child back and went sadly away. The Buddha, who had heard of the 'improper behaviour' of the wife, remarked:

> 'She came, and he did not rejoice,
> She went, and he did not repine.
> A victor he, whose bonds are broken,
> Such a one I call a Brahmin.' (Ud 1.8)

A man who wanted to join the Order had to pay more regard to his parents than to his wife and children. This was the concession that Rāja Suddhodana had obtained from his son, the new leader of an Order, after Rāhula's ordination as a novice, that no one might be accepted into the Order without his or her parents' consent (Mv 1.54.6). The rule applied to men (Mv 1.76.1) and women. Women, if they were married, also had to obtain their husbands' consent (Cv 10.17.1).

Whereas at first the Buddha had ordained every applicant as a full monk with the words: 'Come, monk, the doctrine is well taught, lead a life of purity in order to realize the end of suffering' (e.g. Sāriputta and Moggallāna in Mv 1.24.5), he later ordered that the way of entry into the Order should be in two stages. By the ceremonial 'going forth' (*pabbajjā*), i.e. renunciation of the world, one was accepted into the ranks of the *samaṇas*, and became a novice (*sāmaṇera*) in the Buddhist Order; then, by the ordination proper, the 'attainment' (*upasampadā*) one gained the rights of a full monk (*bhikkhu*). For the 'going forth' the minimum age was fifteen (Mv 1.50), and for full ordination it was twenty (Mv 1.49.6), ages being reckoned from conception (Mv 1.75).

There is no particular prescribed interval between ordination as a novice and full ordination, according to the sources, except when the applicant was previously a member of a different school. Since it was assumed that such a person would need some time to give up his previous religious ideas and practices, a probationary period of four months was made obligatory in such a case (Mv 1.38), during which he was observed by the members of the Saṅgha to see if he was suitable. There was no probationary period if the applicant had previously been a matted-hair ascetic (*jaṭila*), or if he belonged to the Sakiya tribe (Mv 1.38.11). The favoured treatment of the *jaṭila* ascetics may have been because Gotama had once been their special guest, and was grateful to the leader of the *jaṭila* sect, Uruvela-Kassapa.

The procedure for ordaining a novice is simple: it is described in the Vinaya (Mv 1.54.3) as follows. The applicant shaves off his hair and beard and dons yellow robes, which are usually donated. Crouching at the feet of a monk, he puts his palms together in the attitude of greeting and recites the formula: 'I go for refuge to the Buddha, I go for refuge to the Dhamma, I go for refuge to the Saṅgha.' This is repeated three times. No reply is necessary from the older monk, since silence means consent. Ethical guide-lines for novices consisted, not of the whole catalogue of two hundred and twenty-seven rules according to the Pātimokkha, but just the list of ten prohibitions or negative rules. Soon it became customary for the novice formally to confirm his acceptance of these rules in the presence of the chapter.

The procedure for full ordination, *upasampadā*, is more ceremonious. It requires the presence of at least ten monks (Mv 1.31.2), all of whom must be 'elders' (*thera*), i.e. of ten years' standing. Outside of the 'middle country', where it was difficult to find a chapter of ten monks for an ordination, five were sufficient as witnesses.

A condition of ordination is that the novice has found an 'elder' as preceptor (*upajjhāya*) (Mv 1.25.7) who proposes him to the chapter for ordination. If they have indicated their consent by silence, the ordinand steps before them, crouches down with hands together, and says: 'Venerable sirs, I request the Saṅgha for ordination, may the Saṅgha raise me up out of compassion!' If at the third repetition no objection has been raised, one of the senior monks present says:

> 'Venerable sirs, let the Saṅgha hear me. This so-and-so (name) requests ordination from the Venerable so-and-so (president of the chapter), he asks for ordination through the Venerable so-and-so (preceptor). If it seems right to the Saṅgha, let the Saṅgha ordain so-and-so through the preceptor so-and-so. This is my motion.'
>
> (Mv 1.29.2f.)

In the early days of the Saṅgha it seems that if the motion was repeated three times without objection, this completed the ordination. Later the ceremony of acceptance was extended in such a way that the novice, who had previously already been questioned privately (Mv 1.76.3), had to confirm his suitability for ordination by publicly replying to questions. The president of the chapter asked him:

> 'Do you suffer from diseases such as leprosy, boils, eczema, tuberculosis or epilepsy?
> Are you a man (i.e. not a eunuch, and a human being, i.e. not a Nāga [serpent] in human form)?

Are you a free man?
Are you free from debts?
Are you not in the king's service?
Are you a full twenty years of age?
Have you an alms-bowl and monk's robes?
What is your name?
What is the name of your preceptor?' (Mv 1.76.1)

If the novice answered all these questions satisfactorily, his ordination as a full monk was valid. To this day, Buddhist monks are ordained in this way.

For a young bhikkhu it was very important to have a good preceptor, because he was subject to his spiritual guidance for at least five (Mv 1.53.4), but as a rule ten years (Mv 1.53.3). Less intelligent monks remained under a preceptor all their life (Mv 1.53.4ff.). The relationship between preceptor and pupil was like that between father and son; they should treat each other with courtesy and consideration (Mv 1.32.1). As long as they lived in a monastery, the young monk shared a cell with his preceptor and acted as a kind of monk-servant to him (Mv 1.25, 8–24). Ten years after his ordination he became an elder (*thera*), and could himself train young monks as their preceptor (Mv 1.32.1) and serve as a member of the chapter of the Order. After twenty years in the robe he became a great elder (*mahāthera*).

In contrast to the entry into the Order, which took place with the forms just described, leaving the Order occurred without ceremony. It was sufficient to take off the yellow robe. Some took this step as a protest, such as Sarabha, who was dissatisfied with the Dhamma (AN 3.64), and Sunakkhatta, who claimed that the Buddha had no superhuman knowledge and that his teaching was (not a revelation of existing facts, but) merely something intellectually hammered out and freely invented (MN 12.2; i, 68). Usually however the return to worldly life was for personal reasons. There was no social disgrace involved in leaving the Order, and an ex-bhikkhu was allowed to rejoin the Order, but for this a regular fresh ordination was necessary. It is said of the monk Citta that he joined the Order four times, having thus left it three times; still he became an Arahant and so gained the goal (AN 6.60+DN 9.56). However, it was not possible for those who had changed over from the Buddha's Order to another school to change their minds and rejoin the Saṅgha (Mv 1.25.3).

After ordination, the caste origin of a monk was of no further consequence: just as the great rivers Gaṅgā, Yamunā, Acirāvati, Sarabhū and Mahī lose their name and identity as soon as they flow into the sea, so too the members of the four castes lose their identity in the Buddha's Saṅgha, and are henceforth known as Sakiya Sons (AN 8.19). The monk was a member of a casteless monastic society.

All the same, his social origin was not always forgotten. The Pāli Canon mentions the names of many monks to which a reference to the owner's father's profession or his own former activity is attached: Citta, son of the mahout, Sāti, the fisherman's son, Tissa, son of the doorkeeper, Dhaniya the potter, Ariṭṭha the vulture-trainer, Suppiya the corpse-bearer, Sunīta the street-sweeper – a long list of such names can be made out. Often, but not always, these additions served to distinguish the bearers from other monks of the same name. But in no case did his humble origins prevent a monk from becoming prominent in the Order; for example, the expert in disciplinary law, Upāli, had been a barber. Monks from less favoured classes gained Arahantship as easily, or with the same difficulty, as those from well-to-do families. The conquest of greed, hatred and delusion demands different qualities from those one acquires at school.

Seniority according to protocol was determined by the age of ordination, which was reckoned by the number of rains retreats (*vassa*) a monk had spent in the Order. The junior monks had to salute their seniors and offer them the best seats and the best alms-food (Cv 6.6.4). However, order of seniority was disregarded in the queue for the latrines after a young monk, having made way for his seniors, fainted as a result of restraining his urge (Cv 8.10.1). Seniority was of no consequence in regard to the laity – all monks being outwardly equal.

An elementary precept for all *samaṇas* was that of poverty, but in the course of the years the Buddha made several concessions in this respect for his followers. As personal possessions the bhikkhu was originally allowed only eight items: three robes, an alms-bowl, a

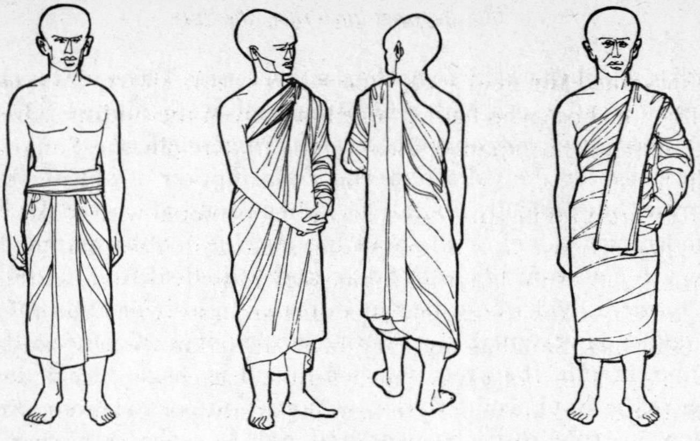

The three robes of a Buddhist monk.

razor, a needle, a belt and a water-filter. The robes – loin-cloth, shoulder-toga and outer robe – were originally to be made of rags that the monk had collected from dust-heaps and charnel-fields, and sometimes skin disease resulted (Thag 207). Later, Gotama allowed the monks to wear robes that had been presented (Mv 8.1.35). To this day the monks wear cloth that, in order to reduce its material value, has been sewn together out of square patches.

Footwear was not part of the original equipment of the monk, and at least in the early years of his mission the Buddha went barefoot. Later on, simple sandals were permitted (Mv 5.1.30). In addition, a woollen shoulder-cloth and a coverlet were allowed (Mv 8.1.36), finally too a mosquito-fan and, for as long as the bhikkhu was in the monastery precincts, a sunshade (Cv 5.23).

The Buddha also issued rules for personal hygiene. The bhikkhus made a pleasant change from some groups of ascetics who were characterized by the filth that hung about them, and who abstained from any form of bodily attention, seeing in this a religious observance which demonstrated their contempt for the world. The monks washed themselves just like layfolk, by daily pouring water over themselves. Bathing in ponds was permitted to them less often, probably owing to the lack of control that could so easily develop when young monks bathed together. For cleaning the teeth, a twig of the *nimba* tree

(Hindī *nīm*, *Azadirachta indica*, *Margosa*) was used. The end was chewed to form a small brush with which the teeth were rubbed (Cv 5.31). The bitter-tasting *nimba*-wood has an astringent effect.

The rules for the collection and consumption of alms-food were elaborate, but basically liberal. The alms-round always took place in the morning. Alone, or in small groups, the monks marched with downcast eyes from house to house and waited silently before every door to see if food would be put in their alms-bowl. Only prepared food could be accepted, not simply the makings of a meal. If there was not enough, the procession continued in single file to the next house. It was not permitted to leave houses out, or to favour streets in more prosperous districts: poor and rich householders were to be given an equal opportunity to gain kammic merit, and also the monks did not wish to give the impression that they favoured the houses of the wealthy because the food was better there. The idea which soon gained ground, that it was not the monk as the receiver of the food who benefited from the gift, but the giver who gained merit (*puñña*) thereby, had the effect of ensuring a plentiful supply, so that the Order seldom suffered from hunger. This idea also gave the monks a chance to show their displeasure at a lay follower who had misbehaved towards the Saṅgha, by simply 'inverting the bowl', i.e. not accepting his gift. In this way the Saṅgha deprived the person to be punished of the chance of making good *kamma* for himself by giving.

It is a sign of Gotama's practical common sense that he did not insist on his monks' being strict vegetarians. They only had to refuse meat or fish when they had reason to assume that the animal had been specially slaughtered or caught for them (Mv 6.31.14). The compassion that every follower of the Buddha's teachings must display to all beings demands that his consumption of meat should be kept to a minimum. On the other hand, it would have been difficult for the monks to observe a total ban on meat, because since they did not cook for themselves and the monasteries had no kitchens, they were dependent on what was offered them. A monk had to eat what was put in his alms-vessel. There is a story in the Canon concerning the bhikkhu Mahākassapa, who even ate the rotten thumb of a leper, which had dropped into his bowl (Thag 1045–56). Even if different donors gave him quite different kinds of food, a monk was bound to accept them all. It is not surprising that stomach troubles and dysentery were common in the Saṅgha, being practically an occupational disease. Nor was the sudden overloading of the stomach very good for health.

It was a relaxation of the bhikkhu life that Gotama accepted invitations from patrons and allowed his monks to do the same. In the house as well they ate from the alms-vessel. The meal had to be over before midday, because the monks were not allowed to eat later, and it usually ended with a discourse to the host. Whatever remained in the vessel was put out in a sandy place for animals, and the vessel was washed out in running water.

The daily routine for the monks permitted of few variations. Morning toilet was followed by the alms-round, often involving visits to particular houses by arrangement with the laity. The alms-round sometimes caused emotional irritations for the younger monks as the majority of donors were women and young girls. Accordingly, increased self-control was necessary when going the rounds, as the Master stressed:

> 'Here is a monk who has dressed in the morning, has taken his upper garment and his alms-vessel and now he goes into a village for alms. But his body, his speech and his thoughts are uncontrolled. There (in the village) he sees a woman, scantily dressed, scarcely covered, and his heart becomes polluted with desire. Therefore, monks, thus must you train yourselves: "Only with restrained body, restrained speech, restrained mind, practising mindfulness and with controlled senses will we enter a village for alms."'
>
> (SN 20.10, abridged)

On returning from the alms-round, the monks took their meal at the edge of the village, in the shade of a tree. It was their only meal of the day. After that they set off for another place, for the early Saṅgha took seriously the *samaṇa* tradition of wandering. When the midday heat made it impossible to continue on the move, a rest period ensued, which could be spent in meditation or sleep. In the afternoon the wandering continued till a place was reached near some settlement, and here the little group settled down for the night. The late afternoon was a period for conversations about the Dhamma and for the instruction of the monks, and the evening was given over to meditation.

During the monsoon period (June to September) the monks lived a settled life. By a decree of the Buddha's, which confirmed an old *samaṇa* custom, they had to keep the 'rains' (*vassa*) under a roof (Mv 3.12.6). They had the choice of building themselves a rain-hut or staying at an already existing monastery.

The rains retreat, which occupied three of the four monsoon months, generally began at the full moon of Āsāḷha (June–July), but it was allowable for any monk to start it one month later, at the July–August full moon (Mv 3.2.2). The ban on wandering ended with the third following full moon, Āssina (September–October) or, for those who had started a month later, Kattikā (October–November). Especially solemn *uposatha* confessional assemblies (*pavāraṇā*) concluded the rains retreat. Immediately afterwards the monks who were declared freed of their obligations set forth on their wanderings again.

Of course the custom of keeping the rains had not only traditional but also practical reasons. When the heavens burst open and the rivers flood their banks in gurgling brown streams, when the roads sink in mud and the unflooded patches serve as refuges of snakes and scorpions, wandering and camping in the open are next to impossible. Also, the steaming wetness of the monsoon created further health risks, and if a monk was ill, it was easier to tend him in a monastery than on the move.

The practice of keeping the rains was of benefit to the Saṅgha in various ways. During the months of wandering about on their own, it could happen that the one or other bhikkhu became too lax in his ways. The rainy period spent under the watchful eye of older fellow-monks forced the monks to pay attention again to etiquette, and made them toe the line. The *vassa* also strengthened the feeling among the monks of belonging to one great brotherhood. This living together in one place and joint study of the Master's words, the exchange of experiences and knowledge, led to the establishment of friendships whose educational value the Buddha rated highly:

> Truly this whole religious life together (in the Saṅgha) consists in the friendship of those who love the good, in their companionship, in their comradeship. A monk who is a friend of the good, a companion and comrade, may be expected to develop and cultivate this Noble Eightfold Path (for his companion's release as well as his own). (SN 3.18)

Not just half, but the whole of the disciplinary life of a monk, the Master told Ānanda (S 45.1.2) consisted in friendship with another monk who was striving towards the same goal. Even after cutting all bonds with the world, the monks were not without any human relationships: their world was the Saṅgha, and their neighbours were their fellow-monks. When Gotama once found a bhikkhu with dysentery, lying helpless in his own filth untended by anybody, he and Ānanda together took care of him. Then he called the local Saṅgha together and admonished them: 'Monks, you have no mother and father to look after you. If you do not take care of each other – who, I ask you, will do it? Monks, whichever of you would look after me (if I were ill), he should look after a sick fellow-monk' (Mv 8.26.3).

The rains retreat was also important for the monks' knowledge of Dhamma. In the monastic community they recited the *suttas* (discourses) of the Buddha and learnt fresh utterances of his. This exchange of knowledge by means of 'hearing' was not confined to the rains retreat, but it was favoured by the temporary togetherness of a larger group of monks in one place. The Dhamma would not have been transmitted to us in such a precise form if the monks had not had the chance, in the annual *vassa*, of recapitulating the Master's words and passing them on to the younger monks.

Naturally, the Buddha himself also kept the custom of the rains retreat. One commentary (*Manorathapūraṇī*, 2.4.5 ii p. 124) gives a list of the places where he spent the monsoons during the whole period of his mission (Table 1).

The list may not be entirely reliable, and in one case (year 7) it fills up a gap in knowledge with a piece of legend. For the historian of the Buddha's career it is nevertheless very useful as a guide, enabling him to give chronological order to some otherwise undated events.

Table 1

Year BC	*Year of mission*	*Rains retreat in*	*Notes*
528	1	Isipatana	Sārnāth near Benares
527–525	2–4	Rājagaha (Veḷuvana)	
524	5	Vesāli (only 8 days, the rest in Rājagaha)	
523	6	Mount Maṅkula	location unknown
522	7	'Heaven of the 33 Gods'	legendary
521	8	Suṁsumāragiri ('Crocodile Mountain')	City of the Bhaggas tribe in Kingdom of Vaṁsa
520	9	Kosambī	
519	10	Pārileyya	Village near Kosambī
518	11	Nālā	Village in Magadha, near Gayā
517	12	Verañja	south of Sāvatthi
516	13	Mount Cālika	location unknown
515	14	Sāvatthi (Jetavana)	
514	15	Kapilavatthu	
513	16	Āḷavī	85 km north of Benares (unidentified)
512	17	Rājagaha	
511–10	18–19	Mount Cālika	(see 516)
509	20	Rājagaha	
508–485	21–44	Sāvatthi	
484	45	Vesāli	

3 Monasteries

In the early days of the Order we can distinguish two types of monastery: settlements established by the monks themselves (*āvāsa*), which were pulled down again after the rains, and donated monasteries (*ārāma*), which were available to the bhikkhus throughout the year.

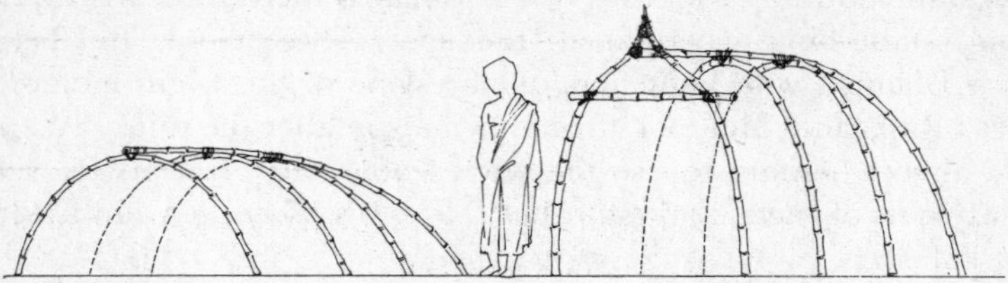

A few poles stuck in the ground at both ends and joined by roof-poles formed the skeleton of the original monk's hut, which each bhikkhu erected for himself for the monsoon period and then took down again. Later lay followers built and donated to the Saṅgha larger huts, made from the same material, that permitted standing upright. In this way they created the typical Buddhist building style with a gabled entrance, vaulted roof and round apse, which was subsequently executed in wood.

The *āvāsa* areas were established at the beginning of the monsoon. This was done by noting outstanding points in the landscape (hills, rocks, curious trees, roads, rivers, etc.) and connecting them by an imaginary line. The bhikkhus then agreed to regard the area delimited by this boundary (*sīmā*) as their (temporary) *āvāsa* (Mv 2.6). The circumference of this area must not exceed three *yojanas* (30 km) (Mv 2.7.1). The monks who built their huts in this area formed, for the period of the rains, a chapter of monks (*saṅgha*), and held their *uposatha* and consultative sessions together.

The site of such a seasonal monastery would be a spot not liable to flooding, and not too far from a village where alms could be collected. The huts, built by the monks themselves, were just high enough for squatting, and just long enough for lying down. A few flexible poles were bent over so that both ends could be stuck in the ground in a line. The arches were linked by longitudinal poles, and the resultant vaulting covered over with leaves, grass or mats; that was all. When the bhikkhu Dhaniya, who was familiar with clay from his former profession as a potter, built himself a hemispherical hut of clay and, by firing it from inside, created a solid brick igloo, the Buddha disapproved and ordered its destruction (Sv 2.1–2). He not only wanted to prohibit the practice of burning, which killed many small creatures, for the future, but he probably also wanted to stop Dhaniya, who had stayed there for nearly a year, from establishing a permanent residence. Those monks did better than Dhaniya who built huts on the slope of the Isigili mountain (near Rājagaha) and took them down again after the rains (Sv 2.1). We almost hesitate to use the word 'monastery' (*vihāra*) for such flimsy huts of leaves and mats, but that is precisely the word used in the Pāli texts.

The name of monastery seems more suitably applied to the groves (*ārāma*) that rich patrons gave to the Saṅgha by publicly dedicating them for monks' dwelling. The boundary of such monastic parks, sometimes of flowering trees, but usually of mangoes, was marked by a bamboo fence, a thorn-hedge or a ditch.

At first the donors of *ārāmas* seem to have merely given the land, and left it to the monks themselves to erect their rain-huts. Later the donors also had dwelling places and assembly halls built. Especially for the latter, they moved with the years to more stable constructions, using beams instead of bamboo, but keeping the vaulted roofing. We know what these looked like from the west Indian caves at Ajanta, Nāsik, Kaṇheri, Junnar, Kārla and Bhaja, which copied the vaulting of the early period and minutely imitated in stone the ribs of the now vanished wooden buildings. The caves at Nāsik and Kārla even reproduce in stone the clay vessels into which the wooden columns were originally set in order to protect them against the depredations of white ants.

As a result of the increasing construction of such solid buildings in the monastery groves, some monks stayed in the monastery after the end of the rains. The Buddha did not forbid this, although he was not pleased with such departures from the *samaṇas'* way of life. But he himself adopted another custom which crept in, namely to spend the rains retreat usually at the same place, and preferably in the same monastery. Apart from the year 484, when he spent the monsoon months in Vesāli, from 508 BC onwards he always took rain refuge in the *vihāras* of Sāvatthi.

These donated monasteries posed a problem in so far as the monks and the Saṅgha were pledged to poverty. The first monastery that the Order received, the Veḷuvana near Rājagaha, had been donated with a solemn ceremony by King Bimbisāra to 'the Order of monks with the Buddha at their head' (Mv 1.22.18). But Gotama, to whom the duties of possession were irksome, and who had learnt from

The western Indian rock-caves copied the ribbed structure of the early monastic buildings. The peaked frontal arch is reminiscent of the bamboo constructions of the early period. This cave at Bhaja, west of Poona (Pune) was carved out in the second century BC and remained in use until the sixth century AD.

experience, preferred in the case of the Jetavana at Sāvatthi that Anāthapiṇḍika should dedicate it to 'the Saṅgha of the four points of the compass, present and future', and with no ceremonial transfer of possession (Cv 6.9). Thus the Jetavana and other monasteries were permanent loans, the Order possessing the use, whereas the donor bore the costs of maintenance. Some donors employed numerous gardeners and artisans specially to maintain the grounds and buildings (Mv 6.15.4).

Some donors may have hoped the monks would at least help with the shaping of and care for the monastery park, but Gotama did not allow this. A park gardener must fight unwanted plants, but it is not fitting for a bhikkhu to undertake the cutting and killing of plants. Also, all garden work presupposes a hope of success, which binds the spirit to the world. The bhikkhu's job, however, is to devote himself to his emancipation from suffering and not be distracted by anything – not even by the joy of seeing the work of his hands flourish.

To the question of how many monasteries there were in the Buddha's time, we can only give an approximate answer. The statement of one commentator that at the end of the Master's life there were eighteen *vihāras* near Rājagaha alone, cannot be verified. With certainty there were ten permanent donated monasteries in the Middle Country. They are all in or near the main cities and almost all are known by the name of their donor.

Kingdom of Magadha
Rājagaha:
Veḷuvana ('Bamboo Grove'), presented by King Bimbisāra.

Jīvakāmbavana ('Jīvaka's Mango Grove'), donated by Jīvaka, physician in ordinary to the king and medical officer to the Buddha's Order.

Kingdom of Kosala
Sāvatthi:
Jetavana ('[Prince] Jeta's Grove') or Anāthapiṇḍikārāma ('Anāthapiṇḍika's Park'), bought at an excessive price by the merchant-banker Anāthapiṇḍika from Prince Jeta and placed at the disposal of the Order. The Buddha's favourite monastery.

Pubbārāma ('East Grove Monastery'), given by the faithful laywoman Visākhā.

Rājakārāma ('King's Grove'), a nuns' convent established by King Pasenadi for his sister Sumanā, who had become a bhikkhunī.

Kingdom of Vaṁsā
Ghositārāma ('Ghosita's Park'), given by a merchant of that name.

Kukkuṭārāma (Kukkuṭa's Park'), given by a merchant of that name, seldom visited by the Buddha, but often by Ānanda.

Pāvārikāmbavana ('Pāvārika's Mango Grove'): the donor was also a merchant, a friend of Ghosita and Kukkuṭa.

Badarikārāma ('Badarika's Park'), about 5 km from Kosambī, probably visited by the Buddha only once.

Republics
Vesāli:
Ambapālivana ('Ambapāli's Grove'), a gift of the courtesan of that name, shortly before the Buddha's death. Vesāli was the only republican capital that could boast a permanent Buddhist monastery.

With the aid of indications by the local population (long since Hinduized) and the work of archaeologists, the most important of these monasteries have been located. At Rājagaha (Rājgir), the Veḷuvana monastery can be visited, and the foundations of the Jīvaka monastery, near Sāvatthi (Maheth) we can see the Jetavana, and near Kosambī (Kosam) Ghosita's park – a moving experience of transitoriness. Where once the Buddha lived and preached and received visits of the kings, where for centuries there was a flourishing monastic life, today there is nothing but silence and solitude. Tended by the Archaeological Survey of the Republic of India, but with no religious life, the monastery sites of the Buddha's time lie abandoned and desolate in the sun.

4 The spirit of the Saṅgha

It was in the nature of Gotama's Dhamma that a rational and an intuitive wing of the Saṅgha should develop. A doctrine that sees one of the causes of suffering in ignorance (*avijjā*) must logically commend knowledge and understanding (*vijjā, ñāṇa*) as remedies against suffering. Knowledge, the Buddha was convinced, means liberation. It is therefore not surprising that intellectually gifted monks specialized in the gaining of knowledge, understanding and wisdom (*paññā*), seeking to gain the goal above all by rational means.

On the other hand, Gotama had taught his followers that suffering originated from craving, and instructed them to fight it by means of self-control, moral discipline (*sīla*), and meditation. Accordingly, many monks and nuns had specialized in exercises in self-restraint and absorption. They did not feel called upon to philosophize for themselves, because the Buddha had revealed everything necessary to emancipation, so that all that was needful was to follow his instructions.

The gap between these two attitudes was never so great as to threaten the unity of the Order; nevertheless it disturbed the bhikkhu (Mahā)Cunda, Sāriputta's younger brother, sufficiently to cause him concern. During a stay in Sahajāti he said it was regrettable that some bhikkhus who were devoted to the Dhamma, i.e. aimed at its rational understanding (*dhammayogā bhikkhū*) made fun of those who devoted themselves chiefly to meditative absorptions (*jhāyanti*). Rather, the 'rationalists' should praise the contemplatives, 'who abide having touched with the body the Deathless (i.e. have experienced Nibbāna in advance, in their meditation)'; likewise the contemplatives should praise the 'rationalists', who 'penetrate with wisdom a profound utterance and see it (with clarity)' (AN 6.46). Those who think and those who experience, Cunda thus made clear, belong together, and neither has any reason to feel superior to the other.

The more the Saṅgha grew, the more people joined it less from an inner calling than as a way of livelihood and support. The harm done by bhikkhus who misinterpreted the Dhamma like Ariṭṭha (MN 22.1; i, 132) and Sāti (MN 38.2; i, 258) was relatively slight. It sufficed that the Master gave them a talking-to or, in cases like that of Ariṭṭha, who was intractable, that the Saṅgha imposed a penalty on them. It was harder to deal with characters like the bhikkhu

Ujjhānasaññin, who was continually criticizing his fellow-monks, or the undisciplined Udāyin who boasted of knowledge he did not possess, or with the quarrelsome nun Candakālī. The nun Thullanandā too, must be mentioned here. She was an eloquent expounder of the Dhamma, but restless and given to intrigue, full of self-importance and too fond of men. Her positive qualities, which impressed King Pasenadi as well as some of the younger nuns, made her all the more effective as a bad disciplinary example.

The real threat to the unity of the Saṅgha came from whole local chapters, like that of Kosambī, which were divided by quarrels, or from monks joined together to form indoctrination cells with the intention of training young monks according to their own views. In Kīṭāgiri (between Sāvatthi and Āḷavi) it was the monks Assaji and Punabbasu, in Sāvatthi it was Paṇḍuka and Lohitaka, and in Rājagaha it was Mettiya and Bhumaja who attempted to undermine the *vinaya* in this way. Being threatened with a disciplinary punishment, Assaji and Punabbasu, the most active dissidents, finally left the Saṅgha, which took the heat out of the situation. The indoctrination of young monks with divergent ideas was also the method of Devadatta, who wanted to split the Order and put himself at the head of a part of the Saṅgha.

In one case a chapter of monks placed itself in danger through overreaction and psychosis. Gotama had preached to the monks of Vesāli on the impurity of the body, and had recommended them to meditate on the body's fragility and repulsiveness. He had thereupon withdrawn into solitude for his own meditation. On his return, he was astonished to find that the local Saṅgha had shrunk. Ānanda explained: several monks had become disgusted with their bodies after the Master's explanations, and had committed suicide. The Buddha immediately called a meeting of the monks and proffered them as an alternative the meditation-practice on breathing (SN 54.9). A parallel account (Sv 3.1) even mentions a 'false *samaṇa*' called Migalaṇḍika who made a speciality of cutting off the heads of those who wanted to commit suicide.

Suicide runs counter to Gotama's teachings in two respects. The desire for self-destruction which underlies suicide, he was convinced, necessarily prevents the doer from attaining liberation as liberation is freedom from desire. Moreover, suicide means throwing away a chance, because rebirth as a human being is rare (MN 129.19; iii, 169), and only man possesses the mental and ethical strength to achieve quickly liberation from suffering. The only excusable kind of suicide is in the case of an Arahant, who has overcome greed, hatred and delusion and will not be reborn, and who is suffering from an incurable disease. The Pāli Canon knows of three such cases: the monks Godhika, Vakkali and Channa.

The way in which the Buddha successfully overcame all subversive attempts and aberrations proves his great skill in guiding people. At the same time we must recognize the sound sense of the Saṅgha, whose members for the most part were seriously seeking liberation from suffering and did not allow themselves to be distracted from the Middle Way by solitary black sheep.

We can gain an impression of the atmosphere in the early days of the Order from the 'Hymns of the Elder Monks' (*theragāthā*) and the 'Hymns of the Elder Nuns' (*therīgāthā*). The enthusiasm which the Buddha inspired in his disciples, the optimism of the early community to be on the way to salvation, the enchantment of the encounter with the numinous, and the joy of liberatedness – all these are vividly recorded here. There are 264 poems (1279 verses) by monks, and 73 (522 verses) by nuns, each poem being ascribed to a particular member of the Order. No one would maintain that they all really go back to the author whose name they bear, or are all from the time of the Buddha. Nevertheless, they document that monks and nuns were filled with jubilation to such an extent that they felt urged to give lyrical expression to their state or realization (*aññā*). The following versions do not attempt to reproduce Pāli verse-forms but render the contents line by line. Torn between the life of the householder and that of the wandering mendicant was the monk Jenta, the son of a rāja. It was the perception of the impermanence of all things that finally decided him in favour of the life of a bhikkhu:

Hard is the homeless life
  And hard is life at home.
Deep is the (Buddha's) norm
  And hard is wealth to win.
The choice of either course

Is difficult to make.
Always do bear in mind
(The world's) impermanence.

(Thag 111)

As full-time seekers after liberation, some monks looked down on the lay followers who they assumed were bound to the world by desires. This is apparent in two verses by the monk Isidinna:

I know lay followers who praise the Law,
'All worldly joys are transient', they say.
Yet ornaments and jewels fill their hearts.
To wives and sons and daughters cling their minds.

They truly do not know the Dhamma's depth
When saying that all joys are transient.
They lack the strength to chop their passions off:
That is why children, wives and wealth keep them in bonds.

(Thag 187–8)

The hymns of the monks and nuns devote much space to the theme of the change from worldly life to that within the Order. The turning away was both outward and inward: the abandonment of professional and domestic life, and the rejection of the world of *Saṃsāra. The* monk Sumaṅgala from Sāvatthi sees the greatest advantage of the monk's life in the liberation from back-breaking work in the fields. He makes no claim to be near the goal of liberation from suffering, but spurs himself on to renewed endeavours:

I'm freed, I'm freed, I'm truly freed
From these three crooked things:
I'm rid of sickle, plough and stooping
My back when turning up the soil.

Those (drudgeries) are ours forever,
But *I* declare: 'Enough! Enough!'
Do meditate, Sumaṅgala,
And stay, Sumaṅgala, alert!

(Thag 43)

Likewise liberated from three 'crooked things' through joining the Order was the nun Muttā, who as a young girl had been married off to a hunchbacked Brahmin. In addition to her liberation from marriage and housework, especially crushing spices, she has also gained liberation from rebirth:

> I'm liberated well and freed
> From these three crooked things:
> From crush-stone and from rolling pin
> And from my hunchbacked lord.
> I'm free from (re)birth and from death,
> Shook off what bound me to the world.
>
> (Thīg 11)

The stanza by the nun Saṅghā is a paean at her release from craving and ignorance. The small poem is another proof that monks and nuns were permitted to describe their liberatedness in poetical form.

> Home I've left, gone forth to homelessness,
> Son I've left, and all my cherished herds,
> I freed myself from greed and also hate,
> And ignorance as well I have thrown off.
> Having defeated craving and its root
> I am composed, have reached Nibbāna's peace.
>
> (Thīg 18)

The monk Surādha also expresses joy at his deliverance:

> (Re)birth is now destroyed for me,
> The Victor's teaching is fulfilled.
> I have thrown off the so-called 'net';
> For me, becoming is annulled.
>
> The goal for which I wandered forth
> From home into the homelessness,
> That goal I have attained at last:
> All fetters have I cut by now.
>
> (Thag 135–6)

A similar note of triumph is found in dozens of other poems and other utterances in the Pāli Canon. This is understandable, for what can still oppress a person who has cut all social and intellectual bonds, who lacks nothing because he wants nothing, and who is convinced that whatever happens will not affect 'him'? Whoever holds such a view cannot be touched by anything, and has good reason to regard his condition as happy.

The contrast between life in the Saṅgha and their one-time worldly life often led monks and nuns to think back to their previous existence in the world. And so the group of 'before and after' poems in the collections of monks' and nuns' poetry is especially numerous. In the next example, the former prostitute Vimalā reflects on her past life. From her description, it seems that she was not one of the educated city courtesans, but a common prostitute of the streets:

> Conceited was I once of my complexion,
> My figure, beauty, popularity,
> I trusted that my youth would never dwindle –
> In short: I was unknowing and naïve.
>
> Having adorned with jewellery this body
> And with make-up, enticing for young men,
> I waited at the brothel door, desirous
> For victims, like a hunter setting snares.
>
> I showed myself when I put on my jewels
> And (shamelessly) revealed my hidden charms,
> In practising diverse tricks of seduction
> I had my fun with a great many men.
>
> Today I am bald-shaven, clad as nun
> And live on alms-food from my daily round.
> While sitting at a tree's foot (in the shadow)
> I reach the state where thought-conceptions cease.
>
> From all entanglements which bind the gods
> As well as men, have I cut free myself.
> With all the āsavas destroyed (forever)
> I rest in calm, have reached Nibbāna's peace.
>
> (Thīg 72–6)

Vimalā dwells with such pleasure on her former street-life that the hearer of her poem might have doubts about the destruction of the 'influences' (*āsava*). The thought of an insurance for her old age may have played at least some part in her desire to be ordained.

More moving – and perhaps more credible – is the account by himself of the Rājagaha street-sweeper Sunīta, whom the Buddha liberated from his miserable existence by accepting him into the Saṅgha. Like so many of his contemporaries, Sunīta was profoundly impressed by the Buddha's personality and his kindliness, and regarded him as a sort of saviour:

Born was I in a humble family
In poverty, and scanty was my food.
It was my lot to execute mean work:
I had to sweep away the withered flowers.

I was the scorn of everyone around,
Was disregarded, treated with contempt.
As I had given up self-confidence
I bent my head, servile to everyone.

And then one day I saw the Perfect One
Surrounded by a retinue of monks.
I saw him, the Great Hero, when he made
His entry into Magadha's chief town.

Having thrown down my carrying-pole I went
Towards him close to greet him with respect.
And then it happened that the Best of Men
Stood still out of compassion just for me.

I cast myself before the Master's feet.
Then to one side I stood, entreating him
That he, the Highest of all Beings, might
Accept me, granting me the *pabbajā*.

The Master whose compassion does comprise
The world, he felt compassion on me, too.
He said to me: 'Come, bhikkhu!' – Thus I had
Received my *upasampadā* as monk.

Alone I dwelt (from then on) in the forest.
Unfaltering and full of zeal I strove
To carry out the Master's word as he,
The Victor , had instructed me to do.

And so it happened in the first night-watch
That I beheld the Knowledge of past lives.
Then, while the middle watch of night elapsed
I (reached clairvoyance), gained the divine eye.
And in the last night-watch eventually
I pierced the cloud of ignorance – (was freed).

(Thag 620–7)

In four further (perhaps not genuine) stanzas, Sunīta describes how at sunrise the gods Indra and Brahma paid homage to him as an Arahant, and the Buddha declared that it was by good conduct and self-discipline that one became a true Brahmin (and not by birth).

The monk Nāgasamāla describes his awakening in a poem. A chance meeting was the spur that led to his becoming an Arahant:

Bedecked with jewellery and gaily clothed,
Garlanded, and made up with sandal-paste,
There, in the main road of the village, stands
A dancing-girl, and to the music turns.

Into the village I had come for alms,
And passing by, the maiden caught my eye:
Dressed up and tricked about, she was a snare
Like laid by Māra, by the lord of death.

So realizing, there arose in me
The penetrating thought of how things are,
The danger (of desire) was revealed,
Established was my disgust (at the world).

And thus my mind was set at liberty:
O see the Dhamma's fundamental truth!
The Threefold Knowledge had been gained by me,
And all the Buddha taught had been fulfilled.

(Thag 267–70)

Since the 'Hymns of the Elder Monks and Nuns' are religious poetry whose purpose is to inspire the hearer to take the path leading to the end of suffering, their main theme is man himself – and there is little mention of nature. Frequently, though, we hear of the great annual rains which compelled the monk to build himself a hut or withdraw into a fixed monastery to spend the 'rains retreat'. Impatience for the rains to begin is described by the monk Subhūti, brother of the merchant Anāthapiṇḍika. The little leaf hut that he built is ready, and he himself is inwardly firm. Boldly, he challenges the (Vedic) rain-god Parjanya to open the sluice-gates of heaven:

> Well-roofed and pleasant is my little hut,
> And screened from winds, so rain, god, when you like!
> My mind is well collected, and is free,
> And keen my mood – so rain, god, send your rain!
>
> (Thag 1)

All the poems quoted are in the I-form, none of them is in the we-form, and this is characteristic of the basic attitude of the Saṅgha. Since everyone must work out his own salvation, Buddhism is essentially individualistic. The Saṅgha is not a cult-community or a sacral fraternity, but a union of individuals who, each for himself, seek the same goal of emancipation by the same methods. When the Buddha lays so much stress on friendship among the bhikkhus (SN 3.18), one reason certainly is to prevent the monks from inner isolation.

The group-spirit, then, took second place in the Saṅgha to individualism. Nevertheless it did (and does) exist. This is shown in the following poem by the bhikkhu Kimbila. Born of Sakiyan stock in the Buddha's home town of Kapilavatthu, Kimbila uses the expression 'Sons of the Sakiyan', which denotes all ordained followers of the Buddha, in a double sense:

> Here in the Eastern Bamboo Grove we dwell,
> Sons of the Sakiyan, in close comradeship.
> No little wealth have we renounced for this,
> Contented with what alms-food fills our bowl.
>
> With energy and with determined minds
> We unrelentingly strive (for the goal).
> Love for the Dhamma, that is our delight:
> Delight in mundane things we have forsworn.
>
> (Thag 155–6)

Although every monk must gain for himself the victory over greed, hatred and delusion, as 'Sons of the Sakiyan' all monks are brothers. Their parallel striving forms a common bond of friendship and trust.

THE ORDER AND THE LAITY SOCIOLOGICALLY CONSIDERED

Entry into the Saṅgha abolished all distinctions of caste for the monk, just as all rivers lose their identity as soon as they enter the sea (AN 8.19). It might therefore be thought that especially the lower castes and the casteless would take advantage of ordination to escape from their restricted surroundings, and that the Order would form an asylum for people of the lower social classes. Such was not the case: the Buddha's Order attracted the upper levels of society more than the lower.

The Pāli Canon names 457 historical persons as contemporaries of the Buddha, who declared themselves followers of the Dhamma: 291 monks, 61 nuns, 74 male and 31 female lay followers. We cannot in all cases determine their caste. In the case of 92 monks and 22 nuns, their social origins are uncertain, and they are therefore unavailable for sociological analysis. The remaining monks and nuns are divided among the different castes as shown in Table 2.

Since it depended on various chance circumstances whether a name came to be preserved in the Pāli Canon or not, we cannot give much weight to the absolute number of monks and nuns. But the proportion of the castes, both for monks and for nuns, is significant, displaying as it does a preponderance of Brahmins. The caste of those who had been brought up to take a particular interest in religious questions also took the largest part in adopting the teaching of the Buddha, despite the fact that this teaching ran counter to the interests of the *professional* Brahmins who practised the rituals for a living. Brahmins were best equipped to appreciate the originality of the Dhamma, and most easily ready to leave house and home for its sake. A canonical list of 'pre-eminent disciples' (AN 1.14) mentions 41 prominent bhikkhus; 17 (=41.5 per cent) of these were of Brahmin stock. A similar result is obtained from the 259 monks whose poems are recorded in the Theragāthā; 113 (=44 per cent) of them were of Brahmin origin. However, the comparable figures for Brahmin-born nuns are considerably lower.

While khattiyas (Skt *kṣatriya*, the warrior nobility) and vessas (Skt

Table 2

	Monks		Nuns	
	No.	%	No.	%
Brahmins	96	48.2	15	38.4
Khattiyas	57	28.6	13	33.2
Vessas	27	13.5	10	25.8
Casteless	13	6.6	1	2.6
Suddas	6	3.1	—	0
Total	199	100	39	100

vaiśya, the bankers and merchants) take the second and third place in the Saṅgha, as might have been expected, one is surprised to find that the number of ordained casteless exceeds that of the suddas. Apparently a number of casteless really did seek to escape their poverty and socially conditioned disadvantages through ordination. That their share in the Saṅgha was not even greater has probably two reasons: the special frequency among them of diseases which prevented ordination, and fear of the unaccustomed intellectual effort that was associated with the monastic life. Casteless men who did join the Saṅgha often had difficulty, owing to their lack of elementary education, in grasping the Buddha's teaching. It is noteworthy that it was always monks of casteless origin whom the Master had to reprove for misinterpretation of the doctrine. This does not, of course, mean that simple origins were necessarily a hindrance to emancipation, because self-discipline does not demand any formal educational qualifications.

The smallest group among those ordained came from the suddas (Skt *śūdra*, the class of dependent workers and servants). There were special reasons for this. Suddas, because of their manual skills, were called up more frequently than others for forced labour for the king (*rājakariya*) and for the community, for specialized work such as digging wells, building dams and government buildings. In order to maintain this skilled work-force the royal officials tried to hamper members of the sudda caste from joining the Saṅgha, and sometimes may have

Table 3

	Male No.	*lay followers* %
Brahmins	18	34.5
Vessas	15	29
Khattiyas	11	21
Suddas	5	9.6
Casteless	3	5.9
Total	52	100

Table 4

	Female No.	*lay followers* %
Khattiyas	8	50
Vessas	3	18.8
Brahmins	2	12.5
Casteless	2	12.5
Suddas	1	6.2
Total	16	100

prevented their 'going forth' with threats of reprisals against their families. In so far as suddas made their living as servants, they had fixed contractual obligations from which it was difficult to escape. In addition, they were often indebted to their employers on account of wages paid in advance, and as debtors belonged to a category of people who were barred from joining the Order.

The social statistics for lay followers rest on a very narrow basis. Naturally fewer names of lay followers are recorded in the Canon than of ordained persons, so that the figures we have are too small for a reliable estimate. Of the seventy-four male and thirty-one female lay followers, contemporaries of the Buddha, who are mentioned in the Canon, we have no information about the caste of twenty-two males and fifteen females. The proportion of the castes for the remainder (fifty-two men, sixteen women) is different, so that two separate tables are required (Tables 3 and 4).

The only thing that clearly emerges from these narrowly based statistics is that the merchant class (vessas) were more strongly represented in the laity than in the Saṅgha, taking up not, as there, the third, but the second place.

From of old the merchant class had been accustomed to try to ensure success in business by having expensive Vedic sacrifices performed, and the professional Brahmins, as ritual specialists, had fully exploited this source of income. The Buddha's teaching made it possible to call for business success more cheaply. If gifts of alms to Buddhist monks made religious merit, the merchants considered, then they must also bring good luck in business. Those vessas who were moneylenders and who therefore always had considerable sums out on loan were also attracted to the new doctrine as it excluded debtors from ordination (Mv 1.46); the Saṅgha, unlike other Samaṇa groups, did not provide a refuge for those who sought to evade their creditors.

The merchants were also pleased that Gotama was favourably disposed towards economic activities – with the exception of trade in arms, living beings, meat, liquor and poisons (AN 5.177). He did not propagate ascetic renunciation of consumption which was bad for business, but only restraint and self-control. And he gave several sensible hints for the practical merchant and his commercial ethics. In sermons to his monks he explained (in parable form) that only a merchant who applied himself industriously to his business morning, noon and night could become rich (AN 3.19). A merchant needed a keen eye, namely knowledge of his goods and of the market, intelligence in buying and selling and the power of inspiring confidence, so that financiers would be willing to lend him money at interest for further investment (AN 3.20). The best way of employing one's wealth was to divide it in four, and to use one quarter to live on, half for business investments, and a quarter for reserve (DN 31.26).

The part played by the vessa caste in the social adoption and spread of Buddhism has hitherto scarcely been taken into account. The merchants more than anybody else, as well-to-do lay people, were in a position to donate monasteries, while as a much-travelled group it was they who carried knowledge of the Dhamma into distant parts. It was by means of the clumsy ox-carts of the trade caravans that Gotama's doctrine found its way to all points of the compass.

The merchants were the most influential group of Buddhist lay supporters, but not the most numerous. Lay followers came from all castes, for all were impressed by the eloquent preacher and thinker. His teaching attracted them also because it did not stamp lay followers as second-rate Buddhists. On account of his social ties the *upāsaka* found it more difficult than the monk did to gain inner detachment and release from suffering, but it was possible for him to do so. The

Pāli Canon (AN 6.119–39) lists the names of twenty-one householders who became Arahants without ever being monks. The list is neither complete as regards male Arahants, nor does it include female lay followers who achieved the goal. In Gotama's teaching, women were regarded as possessing the same capacity for liberation as men. It was no wonder, then, that the Saṅgha received so much devoted support from female lay followers.

It would be worth investigating what percentage of the population of the 'Middle Country' was converted to the teaching in the Buddha's lifetime. Unfortunately, the Pāli Canon does not provide sufficient evidence to answer this question. That the Buddhists comprised some 15 to 20 per cent of the population of the area, and that of these, about 2 to 3 per cent were monks and nuns, is merely an impression gained from reading the texts, and not a verifiable fact.

THE BUDDHA AND CASTE

Some older books praise the Buddha as a social reformer who fought against the caste system and its injustices. But is this description justified?

Gotama certainly did not accept the assertion of the Brahmins that they were born of the mouth of the god Brahma (Ṛv 10.90.12). Everywhere, he pointed out to the novice Vāseṭṭha, one could see Brahmin women who were pregnant or suckling their babies, and so it was clear that even the members of this caste were born into the world in the normal way (DN 27.3–4). Saying so he of course ignored the fact that the myth is intended to explain the origin of the Brahmin caste and not of every single Brahmin child.

But even though he denied the divine origin of the Brahmins, and thus of the entire caste system, he was nevertheless convinced that the caste system resulted from the mechanism of the world. Castes are conditioned by the natural law of rebirth and *kamma*, according to which deliberately intended acts determine the quality of existence in the next rebirth:

> Beings are owners of their deeds (*kamma*), heirs of their deeds, deeds are the womb from which they spring, they are kin of their

deeds and have their home in their deeds. *Kamma* divides beings into lower and higher (rebirth-forms and castes).

(MN 135.3; iii, 203)

Social inequality is the result of previous deeds; everyone has earned his social position by *kamma*. To rebel against the caste system would, according to Gotama's view of the world, be as pointless as it would be futile.

In addition, the people of the 'Middle Country' did not feel the caste system as particularly oppressive. The castes (*vaṇṇa*) and sub-castes (*jāti*) formed a hierarchy of estates and occupations which had arisen from the division of labour, and in which the intellectuals – who for historical reasons were largely the descendants of fair-skinned Indo-Aryan invaders – occupied the higher positions. The caste system grouped people according to their way of livelihood and their education, and a boy was expected to adopt his father's profession and, eventually, to marry within the caste. But no one was forced either to adopt his father's occupation or to enter into a caste-endogamic marriage. Nor was it impossible for members of the two lower castes to rise in society. Whoever accumulated wealth, or gained political influence, could rise above his origins and ensure, if not for himself at least for his descendants, recognition as members of a higher sub-caste or caste. The time of the Buddha was still far removed from the rigidity that the caste system assumed in the Hindu Middle Ages, and from the cruelty with which those engaged in dirty work were banished from society as 'Untouchables'.

That, of the four castes, that of the warrior-nobles (*khattiya*) was the highest, thus ranking above the Brahmins, was taken as a matter of course by Gotama and most of the inhabitants of the 'Middle Country'. Even many Brahmins did not hesitate to recognize the khattiyas as the highest class, although the struggle for supremacy between Brahmins and khattiyas had already begun and had further west already been decided in favour of the Brahmins. It is characteristic of the transitional period that the young Brahmin Ambaṭṭha, in speaking to the Buddha, referred to the hierarchy of castes from the top downwards as 'Khattiyas, Brahmins, Vessas, Suddas' and then, in the same breath, asserted that the other three castes existed in order to serve the Brahmins (DN 3.1.15).

How the Brahmins regarded themselves appears clearly from the words of the Brahmin-caste novice Vāseṭṭha, who told the Buddha of the abuses he had to endure when he joined the Saṅgha: 'The Brahmins say: "The Brahmin caste is the highest . . . Only a Brahmin is white, the others are dark. Only a Brahmin can become pure, and not the others. Only Brahmins are the children of Brahma . . ."' (DN 27.3). One of the arguments with which the Brahmins tried to prejudice their caste fellows against the *samaṇa* Gotama was that he recognized the purity of *all four* castes (MN 93.2; ii, 147).

It was not the caste system in itself that the Buddha opposed, but the false attitude of mind that people had towards members of another caste. His objection was to the conceit of the Brahmins and to the idea that one's caste allegiance had any relevance to one's worth as a person. Dozens of times, he stressed that the social differences between people were not due to any essential difference. All four castes had the same capacity for deliverance, just as from four fires, fuelled with different kinds of wood, the same flame shoots up (MN 90.24; ii, 129f.). Irrespective of caste, all men face falling into hell for evil deeds. Likewise, all are equally capable of developing benevolence and loving-kindness (MN 93.10; ii, 149ff.).

It was a clever move of the Buddha's to oppose the Brahmin caste's pride of birth, and at the same time to show respect for the spirituality of the Brahmin caste, by turning the notion of 'Brahmin' into an ethical concept. He declared that one was a Brahmin, not by birth but by worthy behaviour and ethical conduct. Whatever caste anyone belonged to – whoever had the necessary self-discipline deserved to be called a Brahmin. Once when he saw some advanced monks from the khattiya caste approaching, he cried: 'Here come Brahmins!' And at the question of a monk who was standing there (and who was a Brahmin by descent), he explained:

'Having banished evil things,
Treading mindfully the path,
Awakened and from fetters free –
Such in the world are Brāhmanas.'

(Ud 1.5)

5

Gotama – psychological aspects

HIS APPEARANCE

The Pāli Canon contains a description of the Buddha by the Brahmin Sonadaṇḍa. The Brahmin had not, it is true, seen the Master at the time of giving this description, he was merely repeating what he had heard, but later when he did meet him, he found that it was accurate:

> Indeed, the samaṇa Gotama is handsome, good-looking, inspiring trust, gifted with lotus-like complexion, in complexion similar to (the god) Brahma, radiant like Brahma. He is of no mean appearance . . . His voice is cultivated and so is his way of expressing himself, which is urbane, elegant, clear and precise. (DN 4.6)

The Buddha's fair skin was noticed by many of his contemporaries. He is often described as 'gold-coloured', and after a vigorous debate with the Jain layman Saccaka Aggivessana, the latter noted (MN 36.49; i, 250) that Gotama's complexion had remained clear. In a country like India in which people are so conscious of skin-colour, and where 'wheat-coloured' complexion is regarded as a sign of both higher caste (*vaṇṇa*, lit. 'colour') and a 'better-class' family, this remark implies not only praise of the Buddha's composure, but also a compliment to his ancestry.

Nevertheless it is not possible to draw conclusions as to Gotama's racial origins from his colour. The inhabitants of the Sakiya republic were partly Indid – many of them of Indo-Aryan stock – who had immigrated from the south and west, and partly Mongolid, having come down from the north along the river valleys. In the Buddha's time these two races – brown Indids and yellow-brown Mongolids –

were already mixed up in the Sakiyan region, so that there were many transitional types and people of all possible shades.

One indication that the Buddha probably belonged more to the Indian than to the Himālayan race was his height. People of the Mongolid race are squat and wiry, and shorter than the Indians, and it is recorded that Gotama, even when travelling among the Indid peoples south of the Ganges, was seen as a physically majestic and imposing figure.

THE DEVELOPMENT OF HIS PERSONALITY

If Suddhodana, the Rāja of Kapilavatthu, had hoped that his eldest son would turn out as a robust man of action, taking interest in the world and being politically ambitious, he was disappointed. Not attracted by jolly group games and military exercises, the young man had become a loner, far too much inclined to philosophical speculations and spiritual contemplations. Instead of enjoying the pleasures of his position, he had developed his own standards and, therefore, was dissatisfied with the world and suffering from its inadequacies. At the same time, he meditated on how, subjectively, to transcend the world. In short, he was in psychological terms a sensitive, habitually introverted intellectual type. It was hardly surprising that household and married life did not satisfy him, and that he seized the opportunity to renounce the world as a *samaṇa*.

We must see in Gotama's enlightenment (*bodhi*) experience of 528 BC the key event which not only gave the doctrine to the world, but also turned the predominantly introvert Siddhattha Gotama into the periodically extrovert Buddha. How great was the force with which the experience of Bodhi drove towards expression! It compelled the young Buddha to seek people to whom he could reveal his discoveries, and to whom he could pass on the spiritual treasure that he had found.

Throughout the forty-five years of this missionary activity we can observe Gotama swinging between introversion and extroversion. Periods in which, teaching with great success, he moved from one populated centre to another, are clearly distinguishable from others in which, tired of people, he sought solitude and quiet. He loved to wander alone (AN 6.42, SN 22.81) 'like the rhinoceros'. His teaching was suitable for the solitary, not for those who delight in society, he declared (AN 8.30). Nevertheless, he only yielded within limits to his inclination for solitude, because even a propagator of a philosophy of withdrawal, if he wants any converts, has to turn outwards and move among people. Later on, a distinction was made between a *Pacceka-Buddha* (one 'enlightened for himself'), who regards his discoveries as private property and keeps silent about them, and a *Sammā-Sambuddha*, a 'fully-enlightened Buddha', who proclaims his discovery of the path to salvation to the world. The ideal of the Fully-Enlightened Buddha is a higher one, for a wise man with lofty insights does not think only of his own good, but also of that of others (AN 4.186.4).

With growing age, Gotama's introvert phases grew longer. As far as the spreading of the Dhamma was concerned, he was satisfied with the success of his mission and did not feel any longer the elation that a speaker enjoys when listeners hang on his lips; he was tired of fame (AN 5.30). Although he was at eighty still in full possession of his mental powers (MN 12.62; i, 83), and a good speaker, his imagery had lost something of its freshness and colour, and his sermons had developed a certain stereotyped manner. Accordingly, he contented himself more and more with instructing the monks, only addressing the laity when he was asked to do so. As for the rest, the Saṅgha, which had developed into a broad-based organization with outstanding propagandists for the Dhamma, had by now largely taken over the task of presentation (DN 29.15).

To these reasons for the reduction in Gotama's missionary activity, another important one was added. From about his sixtieth year, his health compelled him to spare himself.

The Buddha had always been health-conscious, and as a *samaṇa* too he observed certain elementary rules. During the hottest last month of the Indian summer he allowed himself some sleep after the midday meal (MN 36.46; i, 249), and he dispensed altogether with an evening meal, in order to maintain his 'health, freshness, buoyancy, strength and living in comfort' (MN 70). Apart from occasional digestive troubles, unavoidable in a mendicant, and which he cured with oil-massage and laxatives (Mv 8.1.30f.), by drinking molasses in hot water (SN 7.2.3) or with gruel of three ingredients

(Mv 6.17.1), he suffered with advancing years from back trouble, probably a slipped disc. Long standing gave him back pains (AN 9.4), and although when he visited Kapilavatthu he sat in the new council hall with his back to a pillar, his spine gave him so much pain that he had to lie down and ask Ānanda to continue with the talk (MN 53). Warmth was good for his back, and this probably led to the Master's frequent bathing, when in Rājagaha, in the hot springs there. One *sutta* (SN 48.5.1) describes how the aged Buddha sits in the Eastern Grove Monastery with his bare back to the evening sun, while Ānanda massages his weak limbs and indulges in speculations about the decay of the body in old age. Shortly before his death, the Master remarked that his body was only kept going by being bandaged up (DN 16.2.25).

HOW THE BUDDHA REGARDED HIMSELF

As mentioned before the enlightenment that took place in the thirty-five-year-old Sakiyan nobleman was not only an act of understanding, but also of a change of personality. Moved to his depths through his *bodhi*, Gotama was convinced that as a Buddha he no longer belonged to any worldly category, but rather himself represented a special category of being (AN 4.36). 'Do not address me (with the old familiarity) as "brother",' he said to his former companions in asceticism, when he met them again after his enlightenment. 'I am (now) an Arahant, a Fully-Enlightened Buddha' (Mv 1.6.12).

Distinguished alike by Buddhahood, noble birth, good education and high intelligence, Gotama saw no reason for bashfulness. With kings and rājas of the 'Middle Country' he spoke upright and without inhibitions, and conversed on an equal footing with the most learned Brahmins of his time. Countering the arrogance of some of the Brahmins, who had once shown their scorn in rude fashion (DN 3), he made a point of not being treated by them as inferior. When one of them reproached him for not saluting high-ranking professional Brahmins, not rising for them or offering them a seat, the Master replied that he saw nobody in the world to whom he owed such respect (AN 8.11). He just wanted to dispute like with like, and nothing more. An Arahant, he once declared, felt neither better nor worse than anyone else (AN 6.49).

Comparative religion distinguishes among founders of religions between prophets and mystics. The prophet is the extrovert fanatic who, obsessed by his religious experience, tries to persuade his fellow-men into obedience to God, and seeks to improve the world according to God's will. He makes converts with promises of bliss and threats of damnation, does not avoid the struggle and, when he comes into conflict with traditionalists, often suffers a violent death.

The mystic, on the other hand, starts from the position that deliverance is not to be realized in the external world or through the intervention of a god, but that it can only be found within – through plunging deep into one's own being. The wise man lives at peace with the world. His basic attitude is one of tranquillity, of inner distance, of self-repose.

The Buddha represents the type of the mystic. Since he denied the existence of a self and an absolute, his experience of awakening took the form, not of the *unio mystica*, but of a breakthrough in understanding. It consisted in the insight that the world with all its suffering (*dukkha*) can be overcome, and that it is possible, by one's own efforts, to break out of the round of rebirths (*saṃsāra*). His experience of the transcendental, from which he derived his lofty status, was the realization of liberation through 'quenching' (*nibbāna*). Whoever met him felt that this man was still *in* the world but not *of* it, that a transcendental insight had immunized him against the world of changing phenomena.

> 'Monks, the Perfected One (i.e. Gotama himself) has perfectly understood the world and freed himself from it. He has understood the origin of the world (and of suffering), and freed himself from it. He has understood the cessation of the world and realized it (for himself), he has understood and taught the way to the cessation of the world. Whatever beings in the world have (ever, as liberating knowledge) seen, heard, felt, recognized, realized, sought or considered, that the Perfected One has understood. Just for this reason he is called the Perfected One.' (AN 4.23, abridged)

> 'Monks, I do not quarrel with the world, it is the world that quarrels with me. No proclaimer of the Dhamma quarrels with anyone in the world.

Whatever (views) are denied among the wise, I too deny. Whatever (views) are acknowledged among the wise, I too acknowledge . . .

As a blue or white lotus is born in the water, grows up and (because of its grease-covered leaves) is unpolluted by the water, so too the Perfected One has grown up in the world, has risen above the world, and stands unpolluted by it.'

(SN 22.94, abridged)

No mystic could have characterized himself more appropriately.

Gotama's statement that he acknowledges only views recognized by the wise (or educated) deserves closer examination. It is based on his conviction that the Dhamma was no dreamt up philosophy but was derived from the insight of direct experience and represented objective truth. He had no doubt that anyone who should penetrate to a deeper understanding of the world would confirm the Dhamma as being *the* true reality pure and simple.

With such a conviction, it is not surprising that he regarded differing viewpoints as mere fantasies and baseless assertions (DN 1.1.29). Speculative metaphysical problems, such as whether the world is eternal or not (DN 1.2), what the ego (whose existence he denied) might be like and whether it survived death (DN 1.2.38; DN 1.3), or what the future might hold – all such questions he dismissed as pointless. Only one kind of knowledge was essential: the knowledge of emancipation (DN 1.3.30).

Others would have attacked theories they considered wrong, and entered into a debate with those who held them, but not so the Buddha, who reacted in a way typical of the mystic 'who quarrels with none'.

Some people speak with evil minds,
Some others speak intent on truth:
In any case the sage is not
Concerned, and therefore unobliged.

(SNip 780)

He who is pure shuns preconceived ideas
About (the world's) becoming and decay.

He has cast off delusion and conceit.
Who, then, can grasp him? He can not be reached.

Concerned with things one cares what people talk,
But how to reach the unconcerned with words?
Accepting not and not rejecting, too,
He here already washed all views away.
(SNip 786–7)

The word rendered 'ideas' or 'views' (*diṭṭhi*) denotes theoretical views of the world not supported by experience.

The Pāli Canon contains many instances that Gotama, whenever a discussion was tending towards the speculative, brought the subject back to the practical path to liberation. In matters of religion he was a pragmatist, as he made clear to the monk Māluṅkyaputta with the parable of the arrow. Māluṅkyaputta had thought of all kinds of speculative questions which he posed to the Buddha. The Master replied:

'(Asking like this, Māluṅkyaputta) is like the case of a man who is struck by a heavily poisoned arrow. His friends call a doctor, but (the wounded man) says: "I won't have this arrow pulled out until I know the name and family of the archer, whether he is tall or short, with a swarthy, brown or golden skin, where he lives, what the bow and the string are like, exactly what the arrow is made of and what bird's feathers are used for the shaft." Māluṅkyaputta, that man would be dead before he could find out all the answers.' (MN 63; i, 429, abridged)

The advice to proceed pragmatically, making utility for emancipation the criterion, was given by the Buddha in Kesaputta, a small place in the kingdom of Kosala, also to the members of the Kālāma clan. They had asked him how one could distinguish truth from falsehood when *samaṇas* and Brahmins taught contradicting things. The Buddha told them:

'Kālāmas, do not be guided by hearsay and tradition, nor by the common opinion and the authority of scriptures, nor by speculations and conclusions, nor by attractive theories and favourite ideas, nor by the impression of personal merits (of the teacher in question), and not by the authority of a master! But rather, when you yourselves discern: "These things are unwholesome, to be rejected, are blamed by the wise, and lead, when realized, to misfortune and suffering" – then, Kālāmas, you should reject them . . . And when you yourselves discern: "These things are wholesome, acceptable, are praised by the wise and lead, when realized, to good fortune and happiness" – then, Kālāmas, you should adopt them.' (AN 3.65)

The sole criterion of a doctrine is its effectiveness for leading to emancipation: its value lies in its result. But if its liberating value has been established, one should keep to it.

The Buddha was equally pragmatic about presenting his own discoveries, confining himself to the revelation of those that were relevant to the goal. Once, as he was resting near Kosambī under a group of *siṃsapā* trees – the Asoka tree (*Saraca indica*) with its wonderful blossoms – he took a few fallen leaves in his hand.

The Buddha 'What do you think, monks, is the greater, this handful of *siṃsapā* leaves I have here, or the number of leaves in the trees above us?'
The monks 'Lord, there are only a few leaves in your hand, there are many more leaves up in the trees.'
The Buddha 'In the same way, monks, there are far more things that I have found out than I have revealed; there are only a few things that I have revealed. And why have I not revealed those things? Because they are of no profit, do not serve the holy life, do not lead to revulsion, dispassion, calm, understanding, wisdom, Nibbāna.' (SN 56.12.4.1, abridged)

If some Indian teachers claimed to be able to deliver the whole world, Gotama was clear that only those could be emancipated who, through favourable kammic disposition, had 'ears to hear'. He saw himself as a guide to liberation, who could not compel those to whom he pointed out the way to tread the path.

'Only a few disciples, taught by me, gain the highest goal, Nibbāna.

Others do not gain it . . . There is Nibbāna, there is the way leading to Nibbāna, and I am there as pointer out of the way. But of my disciples, taught by me, some gain the goal, others do not. What can I do? I only point out the way.'

(MN 107; iii, 4f. abridged)

EMOTIONAL DISPOSITION

The Buddha opposed the convictions of his own caste when he taught that warriors who fell in battle would suffer an adverse kammic future. Owing to the feelings of hatred that he develops for the enemy, a professional soldier who is killed fighting can expect rebirth in the Sārājita Hell, he declared (SN 42.3). Though a hero's death might benefit one's country, it brought a bad rebirth for the one who fell.

Gotama's unconditional pacifism appears clearly in three stanzas of the Dhammapada, in which he describes non-resistance as the means to bring enmity and hatred to cessation:

'I was abused and was done harm,
I was defeated and was robbed' –
In those who harbour thoughts like these,
Their enmity will never end.

'I was abused and was done harm,
I was defeated and was robbed' –
In those who harbour no such thoughts,
Their enmity will be appeased.

For enmity can at no time
Through enmity be made to cease:
Non-enmity stills enmity –
This is a timeless truth (of life).

(Dhp 3–5)

When the native Indian religions were being persecuted by Islam in the eleventh and twelfth centuries, several thousands of bhikkhus allowed themselves to be murdered without resistance. Tibetan sources have preserved the memory of their heroic self-discipline.

Non-enmity is a high but cold ideal, which needs to be complemented by loving-kindness (*mettā*). Even if robbers and murderers were to cut off a monk's limbs with a tree-saw, the monks were not supposed to allow any hostility to arise in them. Even in such a situation they should be controlled, and tell themselves:

> Our minds will remain unaffected, and we shall not utter one bad word. We shall abide kind and compassionate with a mind of loving-kindness, without hatred. Having suffused that person with a mind of loving-kindness, we shall abide (in that state) . . .
>
> (MN 21; i, 129)

The Buddha had loving-kindness in plenty, and directed it towards all spheres of the living world. Professions which cause suffering to people or animals, such as the 'cruel occupations': butcher, fowler, trapper, hunter, fisherman, robber, executioner or prison warder (MN 51; i, 343) – he regarded as objectionable, and incompatible with right livelihood. He abhorred the sacrifice of animals and even felt compassion for plants, as when he rejected the destruction and damaging of seeds and plants (DN 1.1.10f.).

Loving-kindness was the essential trait in the Buddha's character, the physician Jīvaka declared in a conversation with him (MN 55; i, 369), but this too the Master kept under control, not allowing it to pass beyond a certain level: he did not let himself wallow in pity. Mental balance and stability of feelings was the most important thing with him, and had become part of his nature through self-discipline.

Accordingly, attacks bounced off him without affecting him. Even his philosophical opponents admitted that the *samaṇa* Gotama could be neither provoked nor shaken. The Jain layman already mentioned, Saccaka Aggivessana, declared at the end of a discussion (MN 36; i, 250) that Gotama's complexion had remained clear, i.e. that he had not turned red in the face; other religious teachers, in such disputations would avoid questions by prevarication, and become angry.

Equanimity (*upekkhā*), combined with a ready wit, was shown in the Buddha's dealings with the Rājagaha Brahmin Bhāradvāja. Being displeased that a relative had been converted to the Dhamma, the Brahmin abused the Buddha with expressions like 'thief, crackpot, camel, donkey'. Calmly Gotama let Bhāradvāja curse and then suddenly asked him if he sometimes invited friends home to dine. On receiving an affirmative answer, he next inquired what happened to dishes that the guests did not eat. They were for himself, the Brahmin replied. 'It is just the same with abuse,' declared the Buddha. 'I don't accept it, and it returns to you!' (SN 7.1.2).

During a discourse to the monks in the Jetavana at Sāvatthi, the Master described his imperturbability, and urged the monks to strive for similar equanimity:

> 'If, monks, others revile, abuse and annoy (me), the Perfect One, then I bear no resentment, distress or dissatisfaction . . . And if others revere, esteem and honour (me), the Perfect One, I feel no joy, gladness or elation.' (MN 22; i, 140)

Dozens of episodes in the Pāli Canon confirm this self-characterization.

There were, however, cases when the Buddha did not simply accept what was said, but made a sortie from his bastion of equanimity and went over to the attack. This was the case when it was a question of defending the teaching against misunderstanding and wrong interpretations by his own disciples. The Dhamma was his great discovery, his life's work and his gift to the world; he did not tolerate in the Saṅgha, whose task it was to hand the message down to later generations, the presence of bhikkhus who misrepresented it through carelessness or ill-will. When the monk Sāti interpreted the Dhamma in the sense that consciousness (*viññāṇa*) survived the body and took on a new form of life, thus constituting an immortal soul, the Master sent for him and asked him if that was his opinion. When Sāti confirmed that it was, Gotama cried:

> 'From whom have you heard, you foolish man (*moghapurisa*) that I have explained the Dhamma in that way? Foolish man, have I not in many ways declared that consciousness is dependently arisen (and therefore perishing at death)? . . . You, foolish man, have not only misrepresented me by your wrong grasp, but have also done yourself (kammic) harm!' (MN 38; i, 258)

And he went on to seek confirmation from the monks present that Sāti the fisherman's son had no glimmer of understanding of the

Dhamma. We can almost pity the wretched monk who, as the Sutta describes it, sat down silent, dismayed, with drooping shoulders, brooding and speechless.

The monk Ariṭṭha, a former vulture-trainer, fared no better. He had understood the Dhamma to mean that actions described as stumbling-blocks by the Buddha did not in *all* cases lead to tribulation. He too was upbraided by the Master as a foolish man (MN 22; i, 132). It is noteworthy that in both cases the Canon mentions the humble origins of the monks so blamed. It seems that Gotama expected men of no education to have ethical qualities, but not much power of understanding.

At first sight surprising is the Buddha's negative attitude towards the arts. Perhaps, as a rāja's son, he had had more than enough of music and dancing displays. More probably, however, his objection was to the seductive quality of all the arts. The function of art is to move the emotions and carry them away, to evoke a response, and to distract the mind from self-observation. It tends towards arousing the passions whereas the Dhamma serves to calm them. The artist creates an enticing world of the imagination, but the Dhamma seeks to penetrate the real world. As head of a religious order the Buddha was therefore bound to be inimical to the arts: 'Like a wailing, monks, singing is regarded in the discipline of the Noble Ones, like madness is dancing, and childishness is laughter showing the teeth' (AN 3.103). That Gotama despite his rational rejection of music had a feeling for artistic quality emerges from one *sutta* of the Dīgha Nikāya, though a legendary one. Having heard a love-song from the heavenly musician (*gandhabba*) Pañcasikha, he praises the performer for the harmony between song and strings – and also because in the song the Buddha, the Dhamma and the Arahants are mentioned (DN 21.1.6).

Gotama was equally opposed to theatrical performances, which in ancient India were a cross between pantomimic dance and lofty or comic declamation. Near Rājagaha there was a theatre director named Talapuṭa, who maintained a travelling theatre with a large company of performers and assistants. On meeting the Buddha, Talapuṭa asked the Master if it was true that actors who made the audience laugh and delighted them with stage effects were reborn in the realm of laughing gods. The Buddha was tactfully silent, in order not to embarrass Talapuṭa with an unfavourable answer. But when Talapuṭa persisted, he explained that those who created illusions in people through their deluding arts would be reborn in hell or among animals (SN 42.2).

One should avoid theatrical productions, Gotama explained to the young Sigāla, because it not only cost money to attend them, they also captivated the mind with the continual desire for more plays, songs, music, recitations, clapping and drum-music (DN 31.10). Addiction to the arts is a hindrance to enlightenment.

GOTAMA'S DEALINGS WITH LAY FOLLOWERS

Within a very few years of the beginning of his mission, Gotama was famous as a speaker in the 'Middle Country', and whoever was able took the opportunity to hear him. He spoke audibly, calmly, with an elegant and urbane style and a rich vocabulary. Often he gave to a verb or an adjective that in itself would perhaps have been too colourless one or more synonyms, which did little to make the idea more precise, but gave the listener more time to take it in. And he illustrated his themes with imagery drawn from life. More than eight hundred similes have been counted in the Pāli Canon, drawn from all spheres of Indian life and from nature. We see the goldsmith at work, and the ivory-carver, the arrow-maker and the potter; the butcher cuts up the cow, who was not yet sacred in the Buddha's time, the merchant manipulates the scales slightly to his advantage – there was not an occupation he did not draw on for a parable. He likewise drew images from nature: the lion (which was frequent in western India) and the elephant; the nervous greed of the monkey, the gracious shyness of the gazelle, the cunning of the crocodile – all these are referred to as well as the world of plants: lotus and banyan, mango and palm. The Buddha's imagery reflects the subtropical world.

Some Buddhist scholars have seen proofs of humour in Gotama's utterances, but whether rightly or wrongly is hard to say. His descriptions based on Indian popular mythology (DN 11.81; SN 11.3.2), the parable of the long-suffering housewife Vedehikā who, when put to the test, finally got in a rage and hit her maid over the head with the door-bolt so that she bled (MN 21) – it is possible that this, and some other such things, were neither meant humorously by Gotama nor, in the cultural milieu of India, were taken as such. The Buddha did not consider laughter as helpful to liberation. Probably he recognized that laughter reconciles one with existence, whereas in his view the whole point was to break free from the world.

Gotama was not a preacher of fiery eloquence. Rather he set forth an unemotional display of arguments and recognitions. He acted on the principle of not persuading his listeners but convincing them. He never pressed anyone to accept the Dhamma, knowing well that insight does not come suddenly but must first ripen – just as the sea becomes gradually deeper, with no abruptness like a precipice (AN 8.19). In fact, if anyone declared his conversion too quickly, he even warned him against over-hasty change, as in the case, among others, of the Jain-follower Sīha, the general of the Licchavīs of Vesāli. And when Sīha, in spite of Gotama's warning to think again over his conversion to the Dhamma, insisted on accepting the Buddha's teaching, the Master told him to continue giving alms to the Jain monks (Mv 6.31.10f.).

One of the Buddha's special gifts was his ability to inspire confidence in people. King Bimbisāra remained faithful to him for thirty-seven years till his death, and Bimbisāra's son Ajātasattu, who was by no means an admirer of the Buddha, went so far as to confide in him how he had murdered his father (DN 2.99). Closest of all was Gotama's relationship with King Pasenadi, who valued him as a partner in philosophical discussions and also sought comfort from him after various blows of fate.

But he did not make things out to be prettier than they were. He gave consolation by telling the truth, even though this might seem cruel. When the aged householder Nakulapitā requested: 'May the Lord cheer me up and edify me!', the Master replied:

> 'It is true, householder, that your body is feeble and vulnerable. Anyone who carries such a body around and claims, even for a moment, that it was healthy, would be foolish. Therefore, householder, thus should you practise: "Though my body is sick, my mind shall not be sick!"' (SN 22.1)

With the sick bhikkhu Vakkali Gotama made no attempt to arouse false hopes and deny the approach of death. He prepared Vakkali for dying. He gave him a discourse on the impermanence of the body and, soon after, when his condition worsened, sent him a message that he would have a good death (SN 22.87). However, he did not foresee Vakkali's suicide.

The Buddha's relationship with women was ambivalent. Women had repeatedly tried to discredit him and the Saṅgha; for instance Sundarī who, egged on by jealous *samaṇas*, posed as Gotama's mistress (Ud 4.8), or Ciñcā who pretended to be pregnant so as to denounce him in front of a large gathering for not having made any preparations, as a father-to-be, for her confinement (Thag Commentary). There had also been difficulties from women of the Gotama family, such as his former wife and his foster-mother Mahāpajāpati, who had persuaded him to found the order of nuns. All these experiences were sufficient cause for Gotama to fight shy of women.

There were other reasons as well, because the proximity of women was a constant threat to monastic discipline. Greed, hatred and delusion were the forces that caused rebirth, and which it was therefore necessary to overcome in order to achieve liberation. Even the briefest encounter with a woman might arouse sexual desire in a monk who had not yet attained to perfection, and could set him back on his path to liberation. It was therefore inevitable that the Buddha, as the head of a celibate Order, should warn against these seductive and disturbing creatures:

> 'Monks, I know of no other form that so captivates the mind of a man, than the form of a woman. I know of no other voice, no other scent, no other taste, no other contact, that so captivates the mind of a man as the voice, the scent, the taste, the contact of a woman.' (AN 1.1)

Women arouse desire in a sage (*muni*), it says in one text (SNip 703). Especially on the daily alms-round, when he often meets scantily dressed women and girls, should a bhikkhu be on his guard (SN 20.20). And when Ānanda asked the eighty-year-old Buddha how a monk should behave towards women, the Master said:

'He should not look at them, Ānanda.'
'But if we see them, what should we do?'
'Do not speak to them, Ānanda.'
'But if they speak to us, Lord, what should we do?'
'Be on your guard, Ānanda.' (DN 16.5.9)

The fact that many men left home and family against the wishes of their wives in order to become bhikkhus, sometimes led 'monks' widows' to try to entice their husbands back into worldly life by cunning, intrigue or seduction. This was the reason why Gotama sometimes used harsh words about women: 'Monks, there are three things which work in secret, not openly: the ways of women, the chanting of the Brahmins, and wrong view' (AN 3.129, abridged). Women are cunning, liars, secretive, fond of intrigue, and unfaithful, we read in the Pāli Canon, a judgement which is exemplified in the Jātakas with hair-raising stories (e.g. Jāt 62 and 192).

Still, it would be quite wrong to assume from all this that the Buddha was a misogynist. If he had considered women to be ethically thoroughly weak, he would have had to deny that, in their present existence, they could gain liberation. On the contrary, he expressly confirmed that they were capable of reaching Nibbāna (Cv 10.1.3). The Canon is full of mentions of nuns and female lay followers who attained the goal. Arahantship is open to women as well as men, but not Buddhahood, which can only be realized by a man (AN 1.15).

In order to see Gotama's judgement of women in a proper light, we must balance his negative utterances with the positive ones. Of the virtues of women he spoke in a conversation with King Pasenadi, who was depressed because Queen Mallikā had borne him a daughter instead of the hoped-for son (SN 3.16). Gotama consoled him by saying that a woman, if she is clever and virtuous, honours her mother-in-law and is faithful and devoted to her husband, is more valuable than a man. And he congratulated the householder Nakulapitā of Sumsumāragiri on having such a good wife as Nakulamātā, who had promised her husband, when he appeared to be mortally ill, that she would support the family, educate the children and live virtuously (AN 6.16). The Aṅguttara Nikāya (1.24) gives a list of outstanding disciples of both sexes. Beside forty-one monks and eleven male lay followers it names twenty-three women: thirteen nuns and ten female lay followers. In another place (8.91) the same book lists the names of twenty-seven prominent *upāsikās*.

All the accounts in the Pāli Canon of meetings of the Buddha with women prove that he regarded them as the equals of men. The fact that there were quarrelsome and bad women, and that women could entice bhikkhus away from the path, did not prevent him from admitting that women have a high capacity for understanding, and that many of them surpass men in warmth of heart and self-sacrifice. He also knew that it is usually the women who determine the religious climate of the family and teach their children ethical principles. The fact that there were so many women among the supporters of the Dhamma is in large measure due to the fact that – unlike other teachers of his time – Gotama recognized women as responsible and fully capable of gaining emancipation. For this, touched and delighted, they showed themselves grateful.

THE MASTER

Apparently the Buddha did not like to occupy himself much with monks at the very beginning of their training, especially if they did not know how to behave. One group of young monks who made as much noise 'as fishermen hauling in their catch', he sent away (MN 67) and only allowed them to approach him when they had learnt proper monkish behaviour and had even gained Arahantship (Ud 3.3). He preferred to converse with more advanced disciples with whom he could assume some knowledge and concentrate on some particular point of doctrine. The more perfected a pupil was in knowledge and self-discipline, the closer he was to the Master.

To hear a discourse from the lips of the Buddha was something for which the bhikkhus would undertake long journeys on foot. If the meeting did not take place spontaneously, it was often Ānanda, the Master's attendant and adjutant, who established the contact, and he sometimes managed this so skilfully that the Buddha scarcely noticed his guiding hand (e.g. MN 26). A standard formula (generally rendered too feebly) in the Canon describes the all-embracing effect the Buddha had on his listeners: 'He instructed them through a

Dhamma discourse, made them accept it, inspired them (with enthusiasm) and made them glad' (DN 4.27 etc.). This phrase makes it clear that the Buddha not only conveyed contents, but appealed also to the feelings of the listener. His charisma gave everything he said an air of something special and turned any meeting with him into a moving experience.

In addition, he gave his supporters a method of mental discipline with the aid of which they could work on themselves: meditation (*samādhi*). In accordance with the Dhamma, which aims at calming the passions and conveying liberating knowledge, two basic forms of meditation can be distinguished (AN 2.32). Meditations for calm (*samatha*) are those that cause the meditator to withdraw his mind and senses from the world and, in the experience of calm, to give him a foretaste of Nibbāna. They tend to the destruction of desire and make the mind receptive for higher insights. The second type of meditation, that for penetration or insight (*vipassanā*), serves to combat delusion and ignorance. It is always directed to an object: one's own body, the psychic-mental functions, a thought, a physical object or a point of doctrine. The purpose is to penetrate the object analytically, i.e. to come to recognize the things of the world by direct observation, without ego-reference or evaluation, as impermanent, painful and without substance, and to comprehend their interrelation and their conditioned existence. In this way understanding (*ñāṇa*) and wisdom (*paññā*) arise. If the meditation-object is a particular aspect of the Buddha's teaching, the purpose is to transform the intellectually understood content into a living experience of realization, so as to make it truly one's own.

But meditation is by no means an end in itself. Was it for the sake of dwelling in meditation, Mahāli asked the Buddha on a visit to Vesāli, that monks undertook the religious life? The Master replied: 'No, Mahāli, the monks do that for the sake of higher and sweeter things, namely the destruction of greed, hatred and delusion' (DN 6.12f.). Meditation is an aid to liberation, nothing more. It creates favourable mental conditions for understanding, but it can neither bring about liberation by compulsion, nor is it absolutely essential. The Pāli Canon contains many examples of people who had never meditated, and yet gained enlightenment and liberation.

The Hindu god Brahma, who looks in all directions with his four faces, gave his name to the four 'Abidings in Brahma' (*brahma-vihāra*). If the meditations described above direct the mind inwards or to a particular theme, the Brahma-vihāras are directed outwards into the world and society. The term 'meditation' therefore appears only partly appropriate for them; they are better described as irradiations. How they should be practised was explained by the Buddha to the young Brahmin Vāseṭṭha. The monk seats himself in the meditation posture in a solitary place, and calms his mind so that it is no longer affected by external influences. In this way he experiences feelings of happiness and concentration. So tuned, he then 'radiates with a mind full of loving-kindness (*mettā*) first one direction, then a second, a third and a fourth, then upwards and downwards – he irradiates the whole world with thoughts of loving-kindness, with a mind that is wide, free, boundless and empty of hostility or hate' (DN 13.76). In the same way he irradiates the various directions with compassion (*karuṇā*), sympathetic joy (*muditā*) and equanimity (*upekkhā*). The irradiations are not only regarded as beneficial to the monk who practises them, but also have an observable effect in the world. Once, when Gotama was attacked by a bull-elephant, we are told that he radiated loving-kindness towards the great beast and so calmed him (Cv 7.3.12).

India is a land of belief in miracles, and even in his own lifetime exaggerated tales were spread about the '*samaṇa* Gotama'. It is therefore not surprising that many regarded him as omniscient. Since, as an Enlightened One, he had destroyed ignorance, the idea of his omniscience was a plausible conclusion. On being asked about this, the Master replied:

> 'Whoever says, the *samaṇa* Gotama knows and sees everything, claims to possess omniscience and omnivision, whether walking, standing, sleeping or waking, whoever says that, misrepresents me . . . But if anyone were to say: "The *samaṇa* Gotama possesses the Threefold Knowledge (i.e. of previous lives, of the working of Kamma, and of the destruction of the *āsavas*)", he would state the position correctly.' (MN 71, abridged)

He did not claim to have spontaneous knowledge of everything that happened in the world, but only to know what was important for liberation from suffering. It was only in questions relevant to liberation that he was omniscient.

The Buddha did not deny possessing magic powers (*iddhi*), which according to Indian belief automatically developed in every genuine religious as a result of self-discipline. The Saṁyutta Nikāya (51.7.2.1) lists the following powers: to multiply oneself, to pass through solid objects, to sink into the earth as if into water, to walk on water, to sail cross-legged through the air and to touch the sun and the moon with one's hand, to hear the voices of distant gods and men, to recall past existences, and, with divine, paranormal vision to observe the passing away and kammic re-arising of beings. Once Ānanda asked the Master whether he was able by means of supernatural powers to reach the Brahma world. The Master replied: 'When the Tathāgata concentrates body in mind and mind in body, he abides in the feeling of bliss and lightness . . . With little effort his body rises in the air. Then he enjoys the various forms of magic power' (SN 51.7.3.2). We are surprised that Ānanda asked the question, because according to various passages he had been present when the Master performed miracles (e.g. Ud 7.9). We may conclude from this that the tales of miracles in the Canon were added later by editors.

This is all the more likely because the Buddha, while not denying his ability to work miracles with regard to the masses who were always seeking a miracle, nevertheless had a poor opinion of such capabilities, and allowed them no place in his system. He regarded them as by-products of the search for enlightenment, which proved nothing about the correctness of a doctrine, and could lead people astray because some might believe they were the goal of religious striving. He accordingly expressly described them as dangerous, unpleasing to him, and to be rejected (DN 11.5). Monks were forbidden to perform miracles before householders (i.e. lay people), even for the sake of conversion, and he imposed a penalty for infringement of this prohibition (Cv 5.8.2).

What was the relation of the monks to the Buddha? What were their feelings for him? We can scarcely say that they 'loved' him. A teacher who untiringly preaches that suffering arises from every kind of love, and who philosophically depreciates all intimate links, can scarcely become the object of deep emotional attachment, and would have discouraged this. To the mortally sick monk Vakkali, whose heart's desire had been to see the Master, he said: 'Enough, Vakkali. What use is the sight of this vulnerable body? Whoever, Vakkali, sees the Dhamma, sees me, and whoever sees me, sees the Dhamma' (SN 22.87.13). He demanded the deference that is due to an Enlightened One, but rejected emotional manifestations of devotion. Such devotion was contrary to the Dhamma, which he regarded as being alone of importance, and behind which he as a person receded.

Also, his mental superiority and his inner detachment commanded respect, but scarcely aroused close affection. Only people with a strong personality like Bimbisāra and Pasenadi, with a full understanding of the Dhamma like Sāriputta and Moggallāna, or with naïve spontaneity like Ānanda and the laywoman Visākhā, were able to enter into a cordial relationship with him. The mass of the bhikkhus and the laity kept at a distance. They felt his loving-kindness, but realized that it was directed to all beings and did not favour any individual. He was, in fact, 'The Master' (*satthar*) – a designation that expresses both the greatness of the one so titled and the respect which is his due, but at the same time indicates the gap between him and the ordinary disciple.

6

Later years

RIVAL PHILOSOPHIES

Between about 515 and 500 BC there were in the 'Middle Country' among the great numbers of *samaṇa* teachers seven who had particular influence. Omitting the Buddha, the Buddhist sources (DN 2.2–7) give a list of them:

1 Pūraṇa Kassapa.
2 Makkhali Gosāla.
3 Ajita Kesakambalin.
4 Pakhuda Kaccāyana.
5 Sañjaya Belaṭṭhiputta.
6 The Nigaṇṭha Nātaputta.

They were all 'aged and venerable' (DN 2.2ff.) – but we must bear in mind that the average expectation of life of an Indian in the sixth-fifth century BC was about twenty-two, so that anyone over fifty was considered very old.

1 Pūraṇa Kassapa claimed to be omniscient (AN 9.38), and so his name is probably to be explained as Pūraṇañāṇa, 'having complete knowledge'. All we learn about his origin is that he was of humble birth and went around naked – 'dressed in the garment of virtue', as this condition was termed. Jain sources mention a 'foolish ascetic' called Pūraṇa from Bebhela; this may be our Pūraṇa. He is supposed to have fasted to death after twelve years of asceticism, and to have died in Sāvatthi. But according to a late Buddhist Sanskrit text (Divyāvadāna) he fastened a pot full of earth to his neck and drowned himself.

Just enough of Pūraṇa's teaching is preserved to enable us to see its philosophical outlines. King Ajātasattu, who had had a conversation with Pūraṇa, reported on it to the Buddha as follows:

> Pūraṇa Kassapa said to me: 'Your Majesty, by the doer or instigator of a thing, by him who mutilates, burns, causes grief and weariness, agitates, takes life and robs . . . no evil is done. Even if with a razor-sharp discus he were to make the beings of this whole earth one single mass and heap of flesh, there would be no evil as a result of that, no evil would accrue . . . And if he were to give alms and sacrifices . . . there would be no merit as a result of that, no merit would accrue. In generosity, self-control, and telling the truth there is no merit, and no merit accrues.' (DN 2.17, abridged)

In conformity with this, one of Pūraṇa's pupils sums up his master's teaching with the words: 'Kassapa sees nothing evil in mutilating and killing, in cheating and deception. Nor does he believe in any merit for oneself' (SN 2.3.10). And Mahāli the Licchavī reports to the Buddha Pūraṇa's statement: 'There are no conditions or causes for the impurity of beings. They become impure without cause or condition. There are no conditions or causes for the purity of beings. They become pure without cause or condition' (SN 22.60).

Pūraṇa thus held that good and bad deeds have no effect on the doer: he denied the law of *kamma*. Since liberation is without presuppositions it cannot be realized by one's actions. In other words, beings can contribute nothing to their liberation, but have to accept their fate and passively await their salvation. Pūraṇa's fatalist teaching bears a strong resemblance to that of the consolidator of the Ājīvika position, Makkhali Gosāla.

2 The Jain scripture, *Bhagavatīsūtra* gives Makkhali's name, in its Ardha-Māgadhī form, as Maṅkhaliputta Gosāla. He was therefore the son of a street singer (*maṅkha*), an occupation which he probably followed himself. He was born in a cowshed (*gosāla*) in Saravaṇa, hence his name.

Makkhali met the Nigaṇṭha Nātaputta (Mahāvīra), the subsequent founder of Jainism, when the latter was in the third year of his ascetic practice (524 BC). Fascinated, Makkhali begged Mahāvīra to accept him as a pupil, but Mahāvīra walked silently away. After some time, Makkhali decided, like Mahāvīra, to give up all clothes and to spend his life from then on as a naked *samaṇa*. Not far from Nālandā, in Paṇiyabhūmi, he met Mahāvīra again, and repeated his request to be accepted as a pupil. This time, Mahāvīra agreed, and for a full six years the two stayed together, sharing all the discomforts of the homeless life.

It was during this period that Makkhali developed a belief in the determined nature of all that happens. He was deeply impressed by the fact that his mentor prophesied various occurrences which could then not be prevented. Once, for instance, Mahāvīra predicted that Makkhali would on a particular day be given a false coin when on his alms-round, and although Makkhali did everything he could to prevent it, it happened precisely as Mahāvīra had prophesied. Makkhali concluded that, 'What must be, must occur so and not differently.'

It was partly owing to his philosophy and partly through his boastfulness that Makkhali repeatedly landed himself and his mentor in tricky situations. More than once he was beaten up by the crowd. Sometimes it seems as if he took insidious revenge on those who refused to give him alms, for it occurred suspiciously often that he prophesied to people who did not give him anything that their house, or even the entire village, would be destroyed by fire – and so it in fact happened!

Because Mahāvīra once did not help him against his attackers, Makkhali left his mentor, only to find soon that without the latter's protection he would have difficulty in surviving without harm. Six months later he rejoined him, but he had learnt nothing from his experience and continued to behave in a provocative and roguish manner. On one occasion, when a marriage procession passed by, he commented that bride and groom were both remarkably ugly. After a thrashing from the bridal party, he realized that his words were not in the best of taste.

The final breach with Mahāvīra was due to another of his tricks. On the road through Magadha, Makkhali pointed to a sesame plant and asked if this particular plant would bear fruit. Yes, said Mahāvīra, abundantly. When they continued their journey Makkhali stayed behind a little and, unnoticed by Mahāvīra, pulled the plant out of the ground. Some time later they came to the same place again and saw that the plant, though pulled out, had not perished. A shower of rain had caused it to take root again, and it had even produced seed-panicles. Although Mahāvīra was thus proved right with his prediction Makkhali's experimental prank was sufficient reason for him to chase away his cranky disciple.

Left to his own devices, Makkhali made great efforts to gain magic powers and knowledge, goals which he is said to have attained within six months. This can probably be dated 517 BC. Till his death Makkhali lived as a wandering *samaṇa*, but always kept his rains retreat in Sāvatthi in the house of a woman potter. In the course of time he succeeded in gaining a considerable following of lay people and disciples. He must have had some personal charisma for he even impressed Pasenadi, King of Kosala and friend of the Buddha.

The Jain books give details of Makkhali's life once again for the twenty-fourth year of his wanderings, which was the year of his death (501 BC). In that year he gathered his six main disciples around him in order to codify his doctrine. When Mahāvīra, his former mentor, heard of this assembly, he remembered Makkhali's follies from the time of their life together, and frankly told his monks all about them. The story spread like wildfire – to Makkhali's great annoyance.

Angry at being made a fool of, he appeared before Mahāvīra, declaring that he was no longer the old Makkhali Gosāla from the past: several spiritual rebirths had made a new man of him. When Mahāvīra scornfully rejected this argument, Makkhali completely lost his temper. 'You are bored through by my magic power!', he shouted at Mahāvīra. 'In six months you will die of fever!' Mahāvīra, however, was unshaken: magic could not affect him and would recoil on its user: 'In seven nights from now, you yourself will die of fever!'

And indeed, the Jain sources go on, Makkhali, who had returned to the pottery at Sāvatthi, began to sicken. He fell into a feverish delirium, danced and sang and smeared his body with cooling potter's clay. To an admirer who saw him in this condition he spoke confused words. A little later on he gave his followers instructions for his cremation, which was to be performed with pomp.

If we may believe the (no doubt prejudiced) Jain books, Makkhali in the seventh night after the duel of curses made a confession of his infringements of the ascetic code, admitting to his followers that he was not a perfected one but a swindler, and was therefore dying of his own curse. Withdrawing his previous funeral instructions he directed that his body should be dishonoured, the monks should spit three times in his face and then put a rope round the left foot of the corpse, drag it through Sāvatthi, and cast it away somewhere.

The disciples only symbolically performed the desecration. They drew the plan of the city of Sāvatthi on the floor of the potter's hut and dragged the body over this, after which they cremated him with full ceremony.

Of the contemporary teachers, the Buddha despised Makkhali Gosāla most of all. 'I know of no one,' he declared, 'who has brought so much harm, damage and misfortune to so many people as Makkhali, the madman' (AN 1.30). 'Among the doctrines of all the many *samaṇas* and Brahmins, that of Makkhali is the worst. For Makkhali, this madman, proclaims and maintains that there is no (law of) *kamma*, no (kammically efficient) action, and no strength of will (to achieve liberation)' (AN 3.135). And in a dialogue with the wandering Brahmin Vacchagotta he declared that no Ājīvika had ever gained liberation from suffering; only one of them had been reborn in heaven, but he (was not a proper Ājīvika, because he) had believed in *kamma* and action (and thus had made some merit for himself) (MN 71; i, 483).

The Pāli Canon gives a summary of Makkhali Gosāla's doctrines from his own lips. King Ajātasattu reported his words, allegedly verbatim, to the Buddha:

> There is no cause or condition for the defilement of beings, they are defiled without cause or condition. There is no cause or condition for the purification of beings, they are pure without cause or condition. The attainment of any form of existence does not depend on self-power or other-power or effort . . . All beings, all living things, all creatures, all souls (*jīva*) attained (their form of existence) not through will-power or strength, but have ripened as a result of fate (*niyati*), (parental) begetting (*saṅgati*) and development (*bhāva*) to a life in the six classes of rebirth where they now experience pleasure or pain . . . After 8,400,000 aeons (of *saṃsāric*

> wanderings) fools and wise alike will find the end of suffering . . . One should not think: 'By this discipline or practice or penance or holy life I will bring my unripened *kamma* to fruition, and will get rid of my *kamma* that has matured.' Neither of these things is possible. Pleasure and pain are apportioned and neither shortening nor extending of *saṃsāric* wandering is possible. Just as a ball of string when thrown runs till the string is fully unwound, so fools and wise alike will reach the end of suffering when they have completed their circle of rebirths. (DN 2.20, abridged)

The central conception of this philosophy is that of fate (*niyati*) which determines every being's path through the chain of rebirths. Fate is his fixed life programme. It cannot be influenced, and therefore deeds, good or bad, are of no consequence for the quality of rebirth. In the same way, religious observances are valueless, and even being an Ājīvika does not speed up the process of liberation. Ājīvika *samaṇas* are monks because fate has assigned that role to them, not from any hope of improving their future lot. However, one motive common with them was to learn the art of prediction. If the fate of every being is predestined, so they thought, it must be possible to get to know at least the near future.

As everyone's course through *Saṃsāra* is programmed, the amount of happiness and suffering he gets is preordained by fate. Therefore, the only sensible attitude is to take everything as it comes and put up with it without complaint. Liberation will take place automatically, as soon as a being has passed through 8,400,000 aeons. There was an Ājīvika saying:

> To heaven there's no gate – just live down your fate.
> Joy and sorrow come to you, all as fate decrees.
> The cycle of rebirths at last makes all men pure,
> Be not too keen to know whatever's coming next.
>
> (Jāt 544, VI, 229)

Especially the soldiers felt drawn to this fatalism, but many another, too, will have remembered some Ājīvika saying when things went wrong.

With the disappearance of the Ājīvika school (in the second century

BC in North India and the fourteenth century AD in the South), all its books disappeared too; our knowledge of the Ājīvika philosophy is derived from quotations in the writings of opponents. Some fundamental questions, such as to the nature of the soul (*jīva*) that forms the link between different existences, and the nature of liberation at the end of the long path mapped out by fate, are, therefore, without precise answer.

3 There are no biographical details preserved about Ajita Kesakambalin, beyond the fact that he was much older than the Buddha. His cognomen indicates that he wore a cloak (*kambala*) of human hair (*kesa*), a garment which, as the Buddha remarked (AN 3.135) was singularly inconvenient: cold in cold weather, hot in the heat, ill smelling and scratchy. Why he wore this penitential garment is obscure, since, as he denied the value of ascetic practices, he could not expect that it would do anything towards his liberation.

Ajita's nihilistic-materialistic doctrine is identical with that of the Lokāyatas, Cārvākas or Nāstikas, and (according to Ajātasattu) was summarized by him as follows:

> There are no alms or sacrifices or offerings (that might be of value for emancipation), there is no fruit or result of good or bad deeds (*kamma*), there is not this world or the next (but only what meets the senses). There is no mother or father and there are no spontaneously arisen beings. There are in the world no *samaṇas* or Brahmins who have attained (the goal), who are perfect and proclaim this world and the next after having realized them by their own superknowledge. Rather, this human being is composed of the four elements. When he dies his solid part returns to earth, the liquid part to water, the temperature to fire, the breath-part to air, and the faculties pass away into space. The five of them, i.e. the four bearers and the corpse on the bier as fifth, march to the cremation ground, and the bearers sing praises until they reach there. There the bones whiten, and the offerings become ashes. Only fools propagate gifts. When people say they are useful, this is nothing but false talk. Fools and wise, at the breaking-up of the body, are destroyed and perish, they do not exist any more after death.
>
> (DN 2.23)

It is difficult to suppose that Ajita, who offered neither a hope of an afterlife nor a way to salvation, could have had any monks as his disciples. Presumably he appeared as a lone speaker and had his followers among householders.

4 An atomistic theory, from which he drew scurrilous conclusions, was put forward by Pakudha Kaccāyana, of whom we only know (from his name) that he was a member of the Brahmin caste. He recognized seven basic factors (*kāya*) belonging to various quite distinct categories, of which everything was composed. They were uncreated, had always existed, and were immutable. These seven elements or basic factors are: earth, water, fire, air, pleasure, pain and the soul (*jīva*).

> There is neither slain nor slayer, neither hearer nor proclaimer, neither knower nor causer of knowing. Whoever cuts off a man's head with a sharp sword does not deprive anyone of life. He just inserts the blade in the intervening space between the seven basic factors (without harming any of them). (DN 2.26)

That the seven basic factors, if combined to an empirical totality, might comprise something more and greater than their mere sum, had obviously not dawned on Pakudha. Historically, he is important as the first Indian atomist. His seven basic factors were later taken over by the southern Ājīvika school, so that he is sometimes described as an Ājīvika.

5 The Buddhist sources give a somewhat blurred picture of Sañjaya Belaṭṭhiputta, who is probably identical with the Sañjaya of Rājagaha who had once been the teacher of Sāriputta and Moggallāna. In discussion with King Ajātasattu he described himself as a sceptic and agnostic, who rejected all theories that could not be established by observation or experience. Perhaps his philosophy had some positive content, but if so this has not survived the two and a half thousand years since his time.

6 The Nigaṇṭha Nātaputta ('the scion of the Nāta family who joined the Nigaṇṭhas') bore the personal name of Vardhamāna, and was the son of the politically influential warrior-noble Siddhārtha

and his wife Triśalā. He was born in 557 BC in Kuṇḍagrāma (now Basukuṇḍ) near Vesāli. He is better known under his honorific titles Mahāvīra ('Great Hero') and Jina ('Victor'). The name of his religion, Jainism, is derived from the second of these.

Vardhamāna grew up in prosperous conditions, receiving the usual education of a khattiya. When he grew up he married and had a daughter. His parents followed the teachings of Pārśva(nātha), a probably historical teacher, said to have come from Benares, who lived in the eighth century BC and whose followers were called *nigaṇṭha* ('freed from fetters'). They took this very ascetic religion so seriously that, in order to purify themselves of old *karman* (Pāli *kamma*) they starved themselves to death. Following in the footsteps of his parents, besides Vardhamāna, his elder brother Nandivardhana was a Nigaṇṭha, too. After his father's death Nandivardhana took over his political functions, using his influence in Vesāli to make propaganda for the Nigaṇṭha religion.

Two years after his parents' fast to death, Vardhamāna, at the beginning of the Indian winter, left his home in order to take up the life of a *samaṇa*. At that time (527 BC) he was 30. Since he followed the commandments of Pārśva, he did not need to look for a teacher, but simply lived according to Pārśva's rules. At first, as an ascetic, he wore a single robe, but after thirteen months he gave this up and lived henceforth 'dressed in the air', i.e. naked – a practice which was taken over by his one-time pupil Makkhali Gosāla, the Ājīvika.

Vardhamāna subjected himself to strict rules, and is said to have erected a high wall round himself in order to meditate in its shelter. For two years and two months he remained at the same spot in this way, and then set forth on his wanderings, which led him eastwards from the 'Middle Country' into the modern West Bengal, and possibly to the sea. His encounters with the population of eastern India were not altogether happy, as the people there considered nakedness shameless and did not understand the mendicant way of life. They sometimes set their dogs on the naked *samaṇa*.

Vardhamāna led a life of extreme austerity, though he does not seem to have indulged in any form of self-torture. His enlightenment, which is supposed to have made him omniscient, dates from twelve years after his adoption of the homeless life, i.e. 515 BC. The scene was a *sāla* tree near Jrimbhikagrāma. Through his enlightenment, Vardhamāna became the Jina ('Victor'). With this, the period of rejection by the populace was over: the Jina was treated with respect.

After a thirty-year mission and a successful career as head of his school, Mahāvīra died at Pāvā (now Pāvapurī) near Patna in 485 BC at the age of seventy-two. Like his parents, he had fasted to death. He left behind him a community of monks, nuns and lay followers, less numerous than those of either the Buddhists or the Ājīvikas, but well organized. The Nigaṇṭha doctrine as revived by him, which came in course of time to be known as Jainism, maintained itself in India and has today about 2 million followers there, especially in Bombay.

The sketch of the Jain teachings we find in the Pāli Canon (DN 2.29) misses the main point of the system. Fortunately we do not have to depend on this, as the Jains themselves have an extensive sacred literature which was committed to writing in the fifth century AD. It is preserved in Ardhamāgadhī (Mahāvīra's own language), Apabhramśa and Sanskrit. In addition, the secular literature of India owes much to the Jains. Their school considers it a meritorious act to preserve important old books, which in the form of palm-leaf manuscripts generally perish after about a hundred and fifty years, by copying them by hand or printing them.

The Jains did not, like the Buddhists, believe in periodic evolutions and involutions of the world. The world as such has always existed and is imperishable, although all sorts of changes take place in it and conditions are constantly altering. Everything happens by a natural causal law, and there is no divine supervisor of the mechanism of the world. External interventions in the natural law are impossible.

The totality of the world consists of the inanimate and the animate, which are sharply distinguished by the Jains. The realm of the inanimate (*ajīva*) embraces five categories, modes and substances, namely space, movement, rest, time and matter (*pudgala*). Matter (i.e. earth, water, fire and air) is composed of atoms (*anu*) which cannot be further broken down. The atoms join together with other atoms, and out of this union the manifold manifestations of perceptible matter are born. Shade and light, sounds and notes are also regarded as matter.

Opposed to the realm of the inanimate is that of the animate (*jīva*).

To this belong the infinitely numerous individual souls (*ātman*), which are eternal, endowed with consciousness, omniscient, free from sorrow and perfect, so long as they are not, through external pollution, degraded to *jīvas* or 'incarnate souls'. The terms *ātman* and *jīva* both denote the same soul, according as it exists in a pure state or in that of incarnation. All *ātmans* are alike, whereas the *jīvas*, on account of their embodiment, are different.

The degradation of the *ātman* to a *jīva* is caused by the deposit of a fine-material kind of impurity, invisible to the eye, on the *ātman* in the same way as grains of dust settle on an oily surface. In this way the *ātman* acquires, first a mental, then a physical body, which first conceals and finally encrusts the primary qualities of the *ātman*. Thus the *ātman* becomes a *jīva*, a physical living being that is bound to the cycle of rebirths (*saṃsāra*) and so endures ever-renewed suffering. All suffering arises from the binding of the soul to matter. *Jīvas* are not only human beings and animals, but also plants, the earth, running water, fire, wind, even rocks and stones. The latter possess a collective soul. In the Jain view, then, wide areas of existence are animate, which other schools of thought would class as inanimate. This belief accounts for the special care the Jains take not to harm their surroundings.

The binding (*yoga*) of souls to the realm of matter, and to the cycle of rebirths, has existed since time immemorial. It is caused by the actions (*karman*) of mind, speech and body of a being. Every act, whether good or bad, whirls up karmic grains of dust – *karmans* (plural) in Jain terminology – which soil the *jīva* as the doer: these *karmans* are regarded as physical fine-material 'guilt-substances'. Acts of cruelty and selfishness cause more karmic dust than others, and bind the more firmly to *saṃsāra*.

The aim of Jainism is to liberate the soul from rebirth. Emancipation, i.e. changing the *jīva* back to a pure *ātman*, is possible by living out the old *karmans*, which are thus cancelled out, and by creating no fresh ones. The way to this goal leads through numerous rebirths, and is long and painful. The Jains therefore assume that only a few beings tread the path to the end, and that many are destined to eternal rebirth. In order to annihilate their old *karmans* as fast as possible, many Jains practise rigorous observances up to and including fasting to death. Death from austerity is permissible, though ordinary suicide is branded as cowardice. In order to prevent the arising of new *karmans*, they regulate their lives in a very strict way.

For all Jains, lay folk as well as monks, there are five basic rules (*vrata*), which are interpreted loosely for the laity, but with extreme strictness for the monks: not to harm any *jīva* (*ahiṃsā*), not to steal or to lie, to use sexual restraint, and not to have excessive possessions. The path to salvation for the laity is divided into eleven stations (*pratimā*). Because of the impossibility of avoiding harming tiny beings living in the earth, lay people are forbidden, among other occupations, to practise agriculture. The Jain lay community therefore consists for the most part of merchants, many of whom have become rich through dealing in gold and precious stones. Gold and jewels are inanimate, and therefore in handling them one does not harm any *jīva*.

Perfection (*siddhi*) and liberation (*mokṣa*) can only be gained by monks. This consists in the setting free of the soul, in the restoration of the purity of the *ātman*. Those who are liberated (*kevalin*) dwell after death in a paradise above the universe. There they exist as incorporeal spirits in a condition of inactive, omniscient bliss which is free from joy and sorrow.

This in brief is the Jain system; though one or the other point may have been categorized in later times, it is nevertheless considered certain that the essential ideas go back to Mahāvīra or even Pārśva.

The Pāli books give no hint that the Buddha ever actually met any of the great teachers of his time personally. He avoided such meetings on principle (SNip 828; 912), although the chances are that he would have been victorious in any such discussion. He was considered a formidable opponent. 'The *samaṇa* Gotama is tricky, he knows the enticing (*or* converting) trick by which he draws in the disciples of other schools' – thus the Jain monk Dīghatapassin reported to his teacher Mahāvīra, after disputing with Gotama (MN 56; i, 375). Mahāvīra could easily have formed a personal opinion of 'the *samaṇa* Gotama', for at the time both were staying near each other in Nālandā (MN 56; i, 371). On the other hand, Gotama as well had no interest in making Mahāvīra's acquaintance.

In the first two decades of his mission, the Buddha's successful conversions were relatively easily made. His enthusiasm was still fresh and infectious, and the philosophical opposition was weaker. Serious competitors for popular favour, and trained dogmatic opponents arose only in the course of time, first among the Ājīvikas, later among the Jains. In the last decade of his life it was almost only the Jains who were his philosophical opponents.

Although the Buddha never personally met any of the heads of other schools, it was quite common for the pupils of such teachers, especially of Mahāvīra, to visit him. The Pāli Canon gives reports of several such visits, such as the following:

Once the Lord was staying at Nālandā, in Pāvārika's mango-grove (monastery). Then Asibandhakaputta, the village headman, a follower of the Unclothed (Mahāvīra), came to see him. As he sat down at the (left) side of the Lord, the Lord said to him: 'Headman, what is the nature of the doctrine that the Unclothed son of the Nāta (family) teaches his disciples?'

'Lord, the Unclothed son of the Nātas teaches this: "Whoever kills a living being – they all go on the downward path, to hell. Whoever takes what is not given, whoever misbehaves in respect of sensual passions, whoever tells lies – they all go on the downward path, to hell. According as a man habitually lives, he goes to his destiny." That, Lord, is what the Unclothed teaches his disciples.'

'You say, headman, "as a man *habitually* lives, he goes to his destiny." (But) if that is so, then nobody goes on the downward path, to hell. For what do you think, headman? If a man occasionally kills, which is the more habitual with him: the time when he is killing, or the time when he is not killing?'

'Lord, surely the time when he is not killing is the more habitual.'

'But you said: "as a man habitually lives, he goes to his destiny." Therefore, according to the teaching of the Nāta son, *no one* goes on the downward path, to hell. (And the same applies to the other actions disapproved of by Mahāvīra.)

'Now, headman, another teacher teaches (the exact opposite of what Mahāvīra declares), and his followers too put their trust in him. He thinks: "My teacher declares that whoever kills a living being – they *all* go on the downward path, to hell. I too have killed a living being, so I too must go on the downward path, to hell." And since he holds firmly to this conviction, and does not abandon it, he really does go to hell.

'But now, headman, there arises in the world a Perfect One, a *Buddha*. He (too) censures most strongly the taking of life, stealing, sexual misconduct and lying. His disciple, who believes in him thinks: "I too have killed living beings. That was not proper, it was not good. Bearing in mind that the evil deed cannot be undone, let me be remorseful." And thinking thus, he refrains from killing in future, and thus he overcomes the evil Kamma . . . and develops (in time) right view, self-control, concentration and kindness . . . Just as a conch-blower penetrates to all four quarters, so he (penetrates the four quarters) with (loving-kindness), compassion, sympathetic joy and equanimity.'

At these words Asibandhikaputta the village headman said to the Lord: 'Excellent, Lord, excellent! . . . May the Lord accept me from this day forth as long as life shall last as his lay follower who has taken refuge with him!'

(SN 42.2,8 abridged, last part paraphrased)

The *sutta* is interesting, not only as the description of an intersectarian discussion, but also on account of the didactic technique employed here by Gotama, which can be called, the 'method of limitation'. Having described Mahāvīra's *kamma* theory as Extreme A ('occasional evil deeds do *not* lead to a kammic descent'), and that of another teacher as Extreme Z ('*all* evil deeds lead to a kammic descent'), he presents his own *kamma* doctrine as the reasonable middle way M: 'The kammic results of an evil deed can be overcome by remorse and the development of virtues.' Both in the matter and in the logical method, Gotama here demonstrates his middle way.

The Buddha had no high opinion of either Mahāvīra's teaching ability or his doctrine. The Jain doctrines, he told the monks, were unsatisfactory from any point of view. For, if the joy and sorrow of beings was determined by actions in a past existence, then the Jains, who (because of their strict observances) had to endure so much suffering, must have been evil-doers in the past. Or, if one assumed that joy and sorrow depended on a creator, or on chance, then the Jains must either have been made by an evil creator, or be the result of an unfortunate mischance (MN 101; ii, 220ff.).

Gotama's lively intelligence allowed him to refute opposing philosophies by exposing their inner contradictions. One example is the dialogue with the Jain village headman just quoted, and another is his conversation (MN 74) with the wandering mendicant Dīghanakha Aggivessana, a son of Sāriputta's sister. Dīghanakha, who visited the Buddha on the Vultures' Peak near Rājagaha, held the opinion 'nothing pleases me'. Gotama replied that if everything (*sabbam*) displeased him, this must include his own philosophy. Under pressure, Dīghanakha had to admit that this was so. Then the Buddha explained that such internally contradictory ideas hindered the calming of the mind. The goal of liberation could only be gained by giving up all philosophical speculations, through insight into the basic fact of life, that the body is impermanent, painful and empty (i.e. without a self that survives death). This recognition would lead to a turning away from obsessive feelings, to dispassion, to liberation, and to the end of (one's own) rebirth. Overcome by this explanation, Dīghanakha joined the Buddha's community as a lay follower.

GOTAMA THE WANDERER

Although it says in the Pāli Canon that the life of a householder is full of hindrances, and the life of a *samaṇa*, on the other hand, like the open sky, still the existence of a wandering mendicant was not without problems. The nights of the winter months (December–January) were mercilessly cold for the homeless *samaṇa*, and the summer with temperatures (in May–June) rising to 40 degrees C, was utterly exhausting. When even in the early morning, the sun is felt like fire, the air is shimmering in the heat and the fields lie grey under the pale bright sky, the road ahead of the wanderer seems endless. His eyes sting from the sweat that runs down his forehead into them.

In the Buddha's time, with its still sparse population in the subcontinent, towns and villages were further apart than they are today, so that the overland journey of the bhikkhus was not without danger. There were very few pleasant gardens, groves, fields and ponds, and many more cliffs and gorges, almost impassable rivers, areas of heavy undergrowth and insurmountable mountains, the Buddha stated in a simile (AN 1.33). And the animals too, which included tigers and bears, did not always give the yellow-clad monks a friendly welcome. Even in the cities, the wanderer was not safe from mad cattle: four cases of death from raging cows are recorded in the Pāli Canon.

Once the monk had reached his goal for the day, on the edge of a settlement, he had to find out what was the attitude of the inhabitants towards his alms-round the following morning. Many places disapproved of the mendicant way of life. The citizens of Thūṇa in the Malla republic, for example, even blocked the well with straw, in order to dissuade the *samaṇa* Gotama and 'the whole shaven-headed bunch of *samaṇas*' from slaking their thirst and stopping there (Ud 7.9) – a truly shocking step as it is part of the Asiatic code of decent behaviour never to refuse water to the thirsty. The father of the devotee Rohinī from Vesāli, who could not understand his daughter's enthusiasm for the Saṅgha, summed up his opinion of the monks in this verse:

> Work-shy they are, a lazy bunch
> Who live on other people's gifts,
> Sweet-toothed and parasites they are –
> How *can* you like the *samaṇas*?
>
> (Thīg 273)

Many of his contemporaries agreed with him, and let the bhikkhus stand in vain on their doorsteps waiting for alms. Fortunately, these were in a minority. Our sources do not mention that any bhikkhu died of hunger.

Gotama's missionary successes took place in the 'Middle Country', which is only vaguely defined by means of places not all of which can now be identified (Mv 5.13.12). Presumably it was never, even in the Buddha's day, geographically precisely defined. Probably the expression denoted simply the cultural province that was felt to be intellectually in the lead. The Gaṅgā (Ganges), between about the present-day Kānpur in the west and Sāhibgañj in the east, formed its central axis. Other 'great rivers' known by personal observation to the Master were the Yamunā, Aciravatī (Rāpti), Sarabhū (Ghāgara) and the Mahī, a tributary of the Gandak (Cv 9.1.3). Strangely, the mighty Soṇa is not mentioned. This comes from the south and at that time joined the Ganges at Pātaligāma (Patna), but has since then shifted its mouth further west.

A glance at the physical map of India shows that the area of the Buddha's activity is confined to the parts marked green, i.e. the plains, and that it ends to north and south just where the brown colouring, for mountains, begins. The highest mountains climbed by him appear to have been those surrounding Rājagaha. Since the other leaders of schools also confined their activities to the plains, the reason is to be sought in the political situation. A wandering mendicant needs freedom of movement, which at that time was only guaranteed where kings and rājas kept order. The power of the kings ended in the mountainous regions of northern India, where the local tribes were fiercely independent. A *samaṇa* who ventured into the mountains was not only exposed to natural dangers – he could also be taken for a spy and roughly handled.

As regards the boundaries of Gotama's wanderings, Kosambī on the Yamunā (25 km south-west of Allāhabād) was the most westerly, and Campā (40 km east of Bhāgalpur) the easternmost point of his travels. From north to south, his knowledge of places extended from his home-town of Kapilavatthu (95 km north-west of Gorakhpur) to Uruvelā (south of Gayā), the scene of his ascetic practice. Thus, the holy land of Buddhism covers an area of 600 by 300 km.

The main centres of the Buddha's activity were the cities; there in particular he found the cultivated people he wished to appeal to, as he considered the Dhamma as 'intelligible only by the learned (*paṇḍita*)' (MN 26; i, 167). As the Saṅgha enjoyed the patronage of the kings of both Kosala and Magadha, it is not surprising that Gotama visited the royal capitals of Sāvatthi and Rājagaha especially frequently. Most of the smaller places where he gave talks are on or near the trade routes that connect the capitals. That he never undertook any direct journeys from west to east was due to the absence of a corresponding road. The west–east transport of goods was by sailing boat on the Ganges: a road parallel to the river existed only between

Payāga (Allāhabād) and Benares. For longer west–east journeys the river provided the only connection. But we never hear of the Buddha's having undertaken any longer journey by water.

Since the Master and his disciples used the same roads as the trading caravans of creaking ox-carts, the indications of routes given in the Pāli Canon are of interest for the economic geography of the area. The great north–south-west trade route, coming from the north-west via Takkasīla, reached the 'Middle Country' near Sāvatthi, where the road forked, and continued southwards to Sāketa (Ayojjhā) and to Kosambī, which lies between the Ganges and the Yamunā. Thence it went in a south-westerly direction via Vedisa (30 km north-east of Bhopāl) and Gonaddha to Ujjenī (now Ujjain), one of the two capital cities of the kingdom of Avanti. From there there was a connection to the river Narmada and across this to the port of Bharukaccha (now Broach) on the Gulf of Cambai on the Arabian Sea.

The route from the north to the south-east branched off from the south-west route at Sāvatthi, proceeding eastwards to Setavyā and Kapilavatthu, where it turned south-eastwards through Kusinārā, Pāvā, Hatthigāma and Bhandagāma towards Vesāli. At Pāṭaligāma (Patna) the Ganges had to be crossed, and then the road continued towards Nālandā and Rājagaha. There was, naturally, traffic in the other direction as well. The principal exports from Rājagaha consisted of iron goods.

Gotama was scarcely in any hurry on his wanderings. He took sixty days for the 600 km from Rājagaha to Kapilavatthu. Assuming that he stopped nowhere for more than one night, this works out at 10 km a day, or barely three hours of leisurely walking.

A DECADE OF CRISES

In 493 BC the Buddha was seventy years old. He was weary, and it occurred more and more often that he bade his disciples Sāriputta, Moggallāna and Mahākassapa deliver the addresses that were expected of him. His fame, which led to his being frequently invited to speak at opening ceremonies – as when the Mallas of Pāvā (DN 33.1.2) or the Sakiyas of Kapilavatthu (MN 53) inaugurated new council halls, or Prince Bodhi(rāja), the son of King Udena of Vaṃsā, inaugurated a new palace at Suṃsumāragiri (MN 85) – was becoming a burden to him. It was obvious that sickness and age had battered and bent the Master's body, even if his mind had retained its mobility and precision of expression (MN 12; i, 83).

Sadly the aged Buddha observed how his influence over the monks, especially the younger ones, was waning. Formerly he had not needed to issue any instructions, he told the monks in Sāvatthi: he had merely needed to demonstrate a way of behaviour before the monks of those days, and immediately they would adopt it (MN 21; i, 124). He was also concerned that the strict observances of the early days of the Saṅgha were more and more falling into disuse. In a conversation with Mahākassapa he remarked that once many senior monks had lived as forest hermits, supporting themselves entirely by the alms-round (without accepting invitations); they had worn robes of rags and practised restraint and solitude, which had inspired the younger monks to imitate them. But nowadays the younger monks only respected their elders according to how well-known they were and what amount of alms they received (SN 16.8). And he agreed with Mahākassapa that the younger generation of monks showed a lack of faith, self-control, zeal and insight, and showed signs of retrogression (SN 16.7).

His weakening grip on the Saṅgha was noticed not only by the Master himself, but also by the monk Devadatta, his cousin and brother-in-law, whom he had ordained with six other Sakiyas in 527. Carefully, Devadatta watched the Master's ageing, and decided to take over the control of the Order as his successor.

In order to realize this ambition and to secure to himself a powerful ally, Devadatta approached Prince Ajātasattu, the son of King Bimbisāra of Magadha, and won him over with a display of magic powers (Cv 7.2.1). This alliance of the ambitious monk and the prince eager to rule produced a dangerous combination. It was Moggallāna's attendant Kakudha who first noticed this. Moggallāna reported the matter to the Buddha, who however made light of it (Cv 7.2.2.4). He also disregarded the warning of other monks, that Prince Ajātasattu was looking after Devadatta too generously and showing him all honours, saying that Devadatta would perish as a result of his own ambition like the banana tree that is killed by its own fruit (Cv 7.2.5).

Devadatta had the courage not to pursue his aim solely by intrigue, but to proclaim it openly. Once, when the Buddha was preaching the Dhamma before a large congregation including the king, Devadatta got up, bowed to the leader of the Order, and said: 'Lord, you are now old, worn-out, an aged man, you have lived your allotted span and are at the end of your existence. Lord, may you be content to live in this world henceforth unburdened. Hand over the Order to me – I will lead the Saṅgha!' The Buddha declined, but Devadatta repeated his plea a second and a third time. This obstinacy stirred the aged Gotama to a rebuke: 'I would not even hand over the Order to Sāriputta and Moggallāna, still less to you, Devadatta, a common lickspittle!' Cut to the quick by this insult before so many witnesses and referring to his role with the prince, Devadatta took his departure. By his sharp reaction, the Buddha had made himself an enemy with whom he would have to reckon in future (Cv 7.3.1).

He was not satisfied with humiliating Devadatta. Thinking in legal terms, he arranged for the chapter of the Saṅgha in Rājagaha to pass a vote of no confidence in Devadatta, and instructed Sāriputta, with other monks, to proclaim this decision in the city. This task was very embarrassing for Sāriputta, because he had once publicly praised Devadatta on account of his magic powers. However, the Buddha insisted, so there was nothing for it for Sāriputta but to announce everywhere that the Order had withdrawn its confidence from Devadatta, who henceforth, in whatever he did or said, would be acting not in the name of the Buddha, the Dhamma and the Saṅgha, but purely as a private individual (Cv 7.3.2–3).

As for both Devadatta and Ajātasattu, one man stood in the way of their ambitions for leadership, and their friendship soon assumed a conspiratorial character. The Pāli Canon declares that Devadatta egged the prince on to murder his father, but in reality the idea lay in the air. In any case, one night Ajātasattu armed himself with a dagger and sneaked, trembling but brutally determined, into Bimbisāra's rooms in order to stab him in his sleep. The guards were suspicious, seized the prince and forced a confession from him, in which he blamed Devadatta as the author of the plot.

The council of ministers, acting as a court, were too frightened to pass sentence on the prince, and placed the matter before the king. He decided that in view of the vote of no confidence passed by the Saṅgha chapter against Devadatta, no guilt could attach to the Buddha and the Saṅgha. But he also refused to punish Devadatta and Ajātasattu. Weary of rule and full of dark suspicions that further murder attempts would be made in the future, he reacted in a surprising way. He declared that, if Ajātasattu was so anxious to rule the Kingdom of Magadha, he should have it – and abdicated (Cv 7.3.4–5). The year of Ajātasattu's accession was probably 492 BC.

As soon as Ajātasattu had become King of Magadha, he got rid of his father, to whom he owed his life and the throne, in brutal fashion. He had him cast into a foul prison and refused him all food. Of Bimbisāra's three (official) wives only one, Ajātasattu's mother Kosaladevī, a sister of King Pasenadi of Kosala, had the courage to smuggle food into her husband's prison, but her visits were soon stopped. Bimbisāra died of starvation (491 BC), and Kosaladevī died a few months later of grief, deeply mourned by her royal brother in Sāvatthi.

Ajātasattu had got what he wanted, but Devadatta had not. The monk, therefore, talked the young king into trying to kill the Buddha. Although Ajātasattu had no sympathy for the old peace propagator who hindered his plans of conquest, he did not want to risk such a deed. Accordingly, he ordered a group of his soldiers to obey Devadatta's instructions, so that, if the instigator of the murder should be sought, Devadatta would be exposed as the guilty party.

Devadatta's plan sounds like fiction, but is related as a historical event in the Canon. He ordered one soldier to watch for the Buddha, kill him and return by a certain path. On this path he posted two further soldiers with orders to kill the man who should approach them. These two murderers were to be slain by four others, the four by eight, and finally the eight by sixteen others, so that the cause of the whole bloodbath would be forgotten in the avalanche of killings.

The plot failed, because the soldier, when he approached the Buddha with sword and bow, was petrified with terror. 'Come closer, friend, don't be afraid!' the Master addressed him, whereupon the soldier fell at his feet and revealed the murder plan. Gotama advised him to go back a different way from that which he had been ordered to take. Thus each saved the other's life (Cv 7.3.6–7).

The Vinaya Piṭaka ascribes two further attempts on the Master's life to Devadatta. Whether they are historical events or cases which have been transferred to Devadatta's account cannot be established. One of these attempts took place on the way up to Vultures' Peak. According to the text, Devadatta caused a huge stone to roll down the mountainside, intending it to kill the Buddha, but in fact only injuring his foot (Cv 7.3.9). The injury may be historical, and may have given rise to the story of the attempt. Falling stones are a frequent occurrence on Mount Chatha, the south slope of which must be ascended to reach the Vultures' Peak.

The third attempt on the Buddha's life – if it was one – took place within the city of Rājagaha. The Pāli Canon reports that Devadatta bribed with promises certain mahouts to let the working elephant Nālāgiri loose against the Buddha. The mighty bull-elephant, which had already killed one person, stormed through the streets on the exact path along which the Buddha was coming on his alms-round. With raised trunk, ears spread out and tail stretched behind him, the brute rushed at the yellow-robed *samaṇa* who, unafraid, radiated loving-kindness (*mettā*) towards him. Suddenly the mighty elephant stopped, lowered his trunk, and allowed Gotama to stroke him. Then he picked up dust from the ground, blew it over his head and backed away, keeping his eyes fixed on the Buddha, and finally trotted back to his stall (Cv 7.3.11–12). At least the story of the working elephant that broke out and endangered the Buddha has some historical probability.

The failure of such attacks led Devadatta to consider other means. If he could not gain control of the whole Order, he would split it and become the leader of one half. He knew that the Buddha rejected strict asceticism, but that there were in the Saṅgha others who favoured more rigid rules: These he wanted to win over for his plans. In spite of all that had happened between them, Devadatta appeared before the old Master and proposed that he should make the rules stricter in five points: (1) The monks should in future live only in the forest; (2) they should eat only alms-food (i.e. accept no invitations); (3) they should dress in robes made from rags they had collected themselves; (4) they should no longer sleep under a roof (even during the monsoon), but under trees; and (5) they should be strict vegetarians. The Buddha replied that every bhikkhu was free to keep the first three observances, but that he saw no reason to make them obligatory. As for points 4 and 5, it remained that the monks could sleep under trees for only eight months of the year (but that they should spend the rains in a *vihāra*), and that meat and fish were not forbidden them, provided the animals were not specially killed for them (Cv 7.3.14–15). This was the answer Devadatta had expected, and which enabled him to drive a wedge into the Saṅgha. He publicly declared that the Buddha had rejected the five points, but that he, Devadatta, regarded them as binding. He succeeded in creating the impression in some quarters that Gotama was fond of easy living and did not take the monastic self-discipline seriously. Although the Buddha warned him that schism was an offence that created evil *kamma* and prolonged suffering, he continued his polemics (Cv 7.3.16). One morning, meeting Ānanda on the alms-round, Devadatta told him that in future he would keep the *uposatha* (full-moon) day without regard to the Buddha and the Saṅgha (i.e. in his own way), and that (with a chapter of his own monks) he would conduct legal acts for the Order (*saṅghakamma*). The Master was indignant when Ānanda told him the news (Cv 7.3.17; Ud 5.8).

Devadatta did as he had said. A number of newly ordained bhikkhus from Vesāli, who were not yet firmly established in the *vinaya* rules, followed his lead and supported the five points, without realizing that this was a breach of the Buddha's code of discipline. With these, now 'his' monks, Devadatta made for Mount Gayā Head at Gayā, which he chose as the headquarters of his new Order.

The news of Devadatta's successful schism reached the Buddha through Sāriputta and Moggallāna. He at once ordered these two to follow in Devadatta's tracks and fetch the young monks back. The two of them set out, and were welcomed by Devadatta, who took it for granted that they wanted to join him.

The night had commenced, and Devadatta had gone to sleep when Sāriputta and Moggallāna addressed themselves to the young monks. With instruction in the true Dhamma of the Buddha, they succeeded in inspiring the bhikkhus, and when the two great disciples declared that they were now returning to the Master, the majority joined them. When Devadatta woke up and realized that he had been deserted by most of 'his' monks, he was so upset that 'hot blood burst forth from his mouth' (Cv 7.4.1–3). He is said to have been ill for nine months afterwards.

However, Devadatta's Saṅgha did not cease to exist with the defection of the young monks. Mount Gayā Head (now Brahmayoni) near the city of Gayā remained Devadatta's headquarters, and King Ajātasattu established a monastery there for Devadatta (Jāt 150) which the schismatic never left. Since it was amply supported by state funds, it once happened that one of the monks faithful to the Buddha slipped in to share in the food – an action for which the Buddha, naturally, severely rebuked him (Jāt 26). Devadatta did not live much longer: he soon was 'swallowed up by the earth' (490 BC?). His Saṅgha outlived him for a long time. The Chinese pilgrim Fa-hsien, who visited India about a thousand years later, in the fifth century AD, reported that he had met monks who claimed to be followers of Devadatta.

With Ajātasattu's accession, a new political style developed in the kingdom of Magadha. Even Bimbisāra, who pursued no imperialistic aims, had established a professional army which took the oath of loyalty to himself. Ajātasattu enlarged this army and drilled it hard, making it into an instrument for conquests. This cost money, and compelled the young king to find new sources of income. He increased taxation, and made the system of registering and collecting taxes more efficient. Thus there came into being a bureaucratic administration, with numerous officials.

Already in 490 BC the Magadhan army was put to the test. It was just a year since Bimbisāra had starved to death in his dungeon and his widow Kosaladevī, Ajātasattu's mother, had died of grief. The dead queen's brother, King Pasenadi of Kosala, grieved by her death and that of his brother-in-law, resolved to give his unscrupulous nephew Ajātasattu a lesson. He remembered that his sister, when she married Bimbisāra, had brought as a dowry the income from the taxes on a village near Benares (Kāsi) (Jāt 239). Pasenadi now demanded this dowry back from Ajātasattu, and occupied the village with his troops. At once Ajātasattu mobilized his well-trained army, and a battle was fought near the disputed village. Ajātasattu was victorious, and the plump old king Pasenadi fled headlong back to his fortified capital Sāvatthi. The Buddha heard with regret that the unjust had defeated the just. Two further battles took place, but Ajātasattu was victorious in both. In a fourth battle Pasenadi took good advice, and cunningly enticed Ajātasattu into an ambush (Jāt 282), not only defeating him, but taking him prisoner.

Once again, Ajātasattu owed his life to the gentle disposition of another. Pasenadi kept Ajātasattu's elephants, horses, chariots and infantrymen as booty, but did not harm his nephew (SN 3.2.4–5). Ajātasattu had to swear with the holiest of oaths never in future to make war on the kingdom of Kosala, and in order to seal the pact, Pasenadi gave his nephew his daughter Vajirā in marriage. As her dowry, she received the taxes of the very village the war had been fought about. Quite quickly, a friendly relationship established itself between the two kings. We even hear mention of a magnificent cloak which Ajātasattu sent his uncle as a present (M 88, II, p. 116).

Ajātasattu's one and only meeting with the Buddha came about through a romantic mood of the king's. A brilliant full-moon night of the month of Kattikā (October–November) awakened in him the wish to hear an edifying discourse (DN 2.1). Various *samaṇas* were mentioned, till finally Jīvaka, the old court physician and a follower of the Dhamma, suggested to the king that he visit the Buddha, who was at the time staying in the mango-grove monastery in Rājagaha that Jīvaka himself had founded. Mounted on his elephant, the king set out (DN 2.8), not without being overcome with fear on the way that Jīvaka might have laid a trap for him in order to deliver him into the hands of his enemies (DN 2.10).

The king greeted the Buddha, who, in order to spare his weak back, was sitting leaning against the central pillar of the monastery hall, and sat down on the ground, aside from the monks. He then asked the Master: 'Is there any fruit of the life of a wandering mendicant to be gained in this very life?' (DN 2.14). The Buddha replied in the affirmative, and explained the advantages of the monastic life to the king with various parables (DN 2.36–98). The conversation ended with Ajātasattu's repentance at having murdered his father (DN 2.99).

In 484 BC Ajātasattu took it into his head to make war on the eight republics and tribes that formed the Vajjī federation – the most important of them being the republics of the Licchavī, with their capital at Vesāli, and that of the Videhas with their capital at Mithilā. He claimed that they were getting too powerful (DN 16.1.1); it is more probable that he simply wanted to incorporate their territory in his own kingdom. Most kings considered it a matter of course to enrich themselves at the expense of a neighbouring country (MN 82; ii, 71f.).

Knowing that the Buddha was familiar with the Vajjī territory and friendly with the inhabitants, Ajātasattu sent his chief minister, the Brahmin Vassakāra, to him to seek his opinion (DN 16.1.2). The Buddha explained to the minister that there are seven conditions for a stable (republican) state: regular and well-attended council meetings, decisions by consensus, holding fast to traditions and laws, care for the aged, protection of women and girls, maintenance of sacred places and making proper provision for visiting Arahants. As long as these conditions should hold for the Vajjīs – as indeed they did – no decline could be expected for them. Vassakāra acknowledged these statements, saying that if the Vajjīs could not be defeated in open warfare, it would be necessary to overcome them by skilful propaganda and by sowing discord among them (DN 16.1.4–5). And in fact Ajātasattu sent agents and political agitators into the republics.

Round about the same time, Ajātasattu found it advisable to move his capital from Rājagaha northwards to the Ganges. The good defence possibilities which Rājagaha offered through its surrounding mountains and its cyclopean wall, seemed to him dispensable now that he had better protection from his strengthened army. Not only was the old city not favourably situated as regards transport and trade, it also had an unhealthy climate owing to the wind-barrier; moreover its sanitary arrangements were terrible: the foul smell of Rājagaha was proverbial. Accordingly, Ajātasattu gave orders that the village of Pātaligāma, which lay in the angle between the river Soṇa and the Ganges, be developed into his new capital of Pāṭaliputta (now Patna), and be fortified against the Vajjīs. He entrusted the planning and supervision of the work to his ministers Vassakāra and Sunīdha (DN 16.1.26).

By about 481 BC when the new capital was sufficiently advanced and the strength of the Vajjī federation had been sufficiently undermined by Ajātasattu's subversive agents, the king with his army crossed the Ganges to conquer the region. By this time the Buddha was already dead. He would probably have reproached himself had he lived to see the effects of his words to Vassakāra, which he had meant quite differently, and to see the fall of the Vajjī republics and tribes, and their merger in the kingdom of Magadha.

So much for the events in the Magadha kingdom. Meanwhile time had not stood still in the kingdom of Kosala either. Three years after Pasenadi had defeated Ajātasattu and tamed his nephew, he was driven off the throne by his son Viḍūḍabha. The key role in this putsch was played by the general Dīghakārāyana ('tall Kārāyana').

Kārāyana's hatred for Pasenadi had causes that reached far back. Kārāyana's uncle Bandhula had been a fellow-student of Pasenadi's at the university of Takkasīla, and on acceding to the throne, Pasenadi had put him in command of his army. While Bandhula was once away with his sons putting down a frontier conflict, Pasenadi's ministers had suggested to the king that Bandhula was aiming at the throne. Pasenadi thereupon had Bandhula and his sons beheaded without trial, but soon afterwards realized that the charges against the general were baseless. He regretted his action, and as an act of repentance appointed Bandhula's nephew Kārāyana as the new general. Kārāyana, however, could not get over the murder of his uncle (Jāt 465; IV, p. 150f.).

His chance for revenge came in 487 BC, when Pasenadi visited the Sakiya republic, which was subject to him. In Naṅgaraka the king heard that the Buddha was in Medaḷumpa, and, in order to see his old friend again, he set out to that place with his bodyguard, which was under Kārāyana's command. When he arrived at the house where the Buddha stayed, Pasenadi removed his badges of royalty, the ceremonial sword and turban, and gave them to Kārāyana to look after. The Buddha opened the door, the king entered, and after a hearty greeting the two old gentlemen had a long conversation (MN 89).

When Kārāyana, waiting outside the house, found himself in possession of the two most important items of the five royal insignia, he realized his chance to take revenge on Pasenadi. Leaving behind a horse and a maidservant, he rode off with the bodyguard to Prince Viḍūḍabha and invested him with the symbols of sovereignty. By the defection of the elite army unit to his side, and by the possession of the insignia of a ruler of Kosala, Viḍūḍabha entered Sāvatthi as the new king.

As soon as Pasenadi, having finished his conversation with the Buddha, discovered that he had been deserted, and when the maidservant confirmed Kārāyana's treachery, the heavy old man mounted the horse and rode to Rājagaha, in order to persuade his nephew Ajātasattu to undertake a punitive expedition against Viḍūḍabha. By the time he reached Rājagaha it was night, and the city gates were shut. Tired out after the long ride, and beaten by wind and sun, the seventy-six-year-old man lay down to rest in a shed outside the city wall. He died the same night from exhaustion. Ajātasattu gave him a magnificent funeral (Jāt 465; IV, p. 151f.).

The possession of sovereignty over Kosala and its army, which had come his way so easily, gave Viḍūḍabha the means to carry out a long-cherished plan of revenge. This was against the Sakiya republic, which had once practised a deception on his father Pasenadi. Many years before, when Pasenadi had let the Sakiyas of Kapilavatthu know that he wanted to have one of their daughters as a wife, in order to establish blood-bonds with them, they had sent him, instead of a full-caste girl of the warrior caste, a half-caste, Vāsabhakkhattiyā, the beautiful daughter of Mahānāma, a warrior-noble and cousin of the Buddha, and a slave-girl. Knowing nothing of all this, Pasenadi had married her and made her his chief queen. Within a year, she had given birth to Prince Viḍūḍabha.

Viḍūḍabha was seven when he noticed that other children received presents from their maternal grandmothers, but he did not. At the age of sixteen he travelled to Kapilavatthu to find out why. The Sakiyas received him coolly, and made derogatory remarks behind his back. Finally, by chance, the prince learnt the truth about his mother, and he swore to take bloody revenge on the Sakiyas when he got the chance, for so wickedly deceiving his father (Jāt 465; IV, p. 145f.).

The time had now come. At the head of an army Viḍūḍabha set out eastwards, but refrained from attacking Kapilavatthu when the

Buddha begged him to spare the people. Allegedly, the aged Master managed to restrain Viḍūḍabha a second and third time, but then the king could not be held in check any longer. He took Kapilavatthu, and had the citizens of military age executed. Finally he set fire to the city in which the Buddha had spent his youth (the modern Tilaurakoṭ in Nepal). The destruction of Kapilavatthu probably took place in 485 or 484 BC, shortly before Gotama's death.

Understandably, many Sakiyas had fled before Viḍūḍabha's approach and taken refuge with the neighbouring tribes of the Moriyas and Mallas. When they heard that Viḍūḍabha had finished his work of destruction and regarded his revenge as complete, they returned from their exile. Since not much was left of the old Kapilavatthu (Tilaurakoṭ in Nepal = Kapilavatthu I), they settled in another place (Piprāvā in India = Kapilavatthu II). They called the place *Mahā*-Kapilavatthu ('Great Kapilavatthu'), and it was here, after the Buddha's cremation, that they deposited in a stūpa their share of his relics.

483 BC

7

The great return home

LAST JOURNEYS

As had been his custom for more than twenty years, the Buddha spent the rains of 485 BC in Sāvatthi. He did not consider that the anger of King Viḍūḍhaba against the Sakiyas concerned him.

While staying at Anāthapiṇḍika's Jetavana monastery, the Master received the news that his principal disciple Sāriputta had died of a sickness in Nālagāmaka, not far from Rājagaha. It was Cunda(ka), Sāriputta's younger brother, who brought the news, and also the dead monk's legacy: his alms-bowl, his outer robe, and, knotted in the cloth used as a water-strainer, his ashes (SN 47.3.2.3).

When the rains had ended the Buddha started his wanderings again, this time towards the south. As he stopped in the village of Ukkācelā (or Ukkāvelā) on the Ganges, it seems that the news of the death of his second main disciple, Moggallāna, reached him. Moved, he declared to the monks that the Saṅgha was now the poorer. Just as in a great and healthy tree individual branches die off, so Sāriputta and Moggallāna had died away from the Saṅgha. But how could it be that anything that had come to be should not perish? (SN 47.3.2.4).

A jātaka (No. 522) gives details about Moggallāna's death. According to this, the great disciple was murdered near Rājagaha, at the Black Stone on Isigili ('Seer's Hill' – the modern Udaya Hill?). As he had attracted so many followers away from other *samaṇa* schools, they had hired a robber, who killed him. The day of Sāriputta's death is given as the full moon of Kattikā (October–November), and that of Moggallāna as the following new moon (Jāt 95). According to this, then, both disciples died in 486 BC.

The post-monsoon months of the year 485 saw the aged Buddha in Rājagaha, where the minister Vassakāra took the opportunity to ask him about the Vajjīs. Soon after this, he left for the north, accompanied by Ānanda and a train of monks. The story in the Dīgha Nikāya (DN 16.1.16–17) that he met Sāriputta near Nālandā must have slipped into this context by mistake, because at the time Sāriputta had been dead for a whole year.

The next stop was Pāṭaligāma, where the Master observed the work in progress on the new Magadha capital and fortress of Pāṭaliputta. Among other things, he was here guest of the ministers Sunīdha and Vassakāra, who were supervising the building works. They named the gate by which he left the city 'Gotama Gate' in his honour. The Ganges, which at Patna can reach a width of 2.5 km, was still in flood, but the Buddha crossed it without difficulty (DN 16.1.19–34).

The year 484 had long since started when the yellow-robed monks, having passed through Koṭigāma and Nādika, reached Vesāli (now Vaishāli), the capital of the Licchavī republic, where they stayed in the mango-grove of the ageing but still attractive town courtesan Ambapālī. Ambapālī had had a son by the former King Bimbisāra, called Vimalakondañña, who had become a bhikkhu. As soon as she heard that her son's teacher was camping out in her grove, she hastened to him and invited him to a meal for the following day. Gotama accepted by silence.

Other citizens of Vesāli also wanted to entertain the Master, and were very disappointed to learn that Ambapālī had stolen a march on them. The courtesan rejected their offer of money to yield up the meal for the honoured guest to them. Next morning, she gave a splendid meal to the Buddha and his bhikkhus, and afterwards presented her grove (Ambapālīvana) to the Master and the Saṅgha as a monastery (DN 16.2.11–19) – partly no doubt in the hope that her son might spend the rains there. In her prime she had charged 50 kahāpaṇas, the price of five milch-cows, for a night of love, so she was well able to afford expensive gifts. Subsequently, she joined the order of nuns and is even supposed to have reached sainthood (Thīg 252–70).

As far as Vesāli, the Master had travelled with a following of monks, but the rains (of 484 BC) he wanted to spend alone, accompanied only by the faithful Ānanda, devoting himself to meditation. Hence, when the rain began to fall, he requested the bhikkhus to find *vihāras* for themselves in the surroundings of Vesāli, while he himself would stay for the rains in Beluva (now Basarh), a southern suburb of the city (DN 16.2.22).

It was a bad time. The aged Teacher became very ill and had severe pains. However, he retained his clarity of mind and overcame his sickness by strength of will. When he could get up again and sit in the shade of the hut, Ānanda described how worried he had been about him. It had been a comfort to him, he said, to think that the Tathāgata would not enter Parinibbāna before making provision for the Order (DN 16.2.24). The Buddha, however, would have none of this:

> 'Ānanda, why does the Order of monks expect this of me? I have taught the Dhamma, making no distinction of "inner" and "outer": the Tathāgata has no "teacher's fist" (in which certain truths are held back). If there is anyone who thinks: "*I* shall take charge of the Order", or "the Order is under *my* leadership", such a person would have to make arrangements about the Order. The Tathāgata does not think in such terms. Why should the Tathāgata (= I) make arrangements for the Order? I am now old, worn out, . . . I have reached the term of life, I am turning eighty years of age. Just as an old cart is made to go by being held together with straps, so the Tathāgata's body is kept going by being bandaged up . . . Therefore, Ānanda, you should live as islands unto yourselves, being your own refuge, seeking no other refuge; with the Dhamma as an island, with the Dhamma as your refuge, seeking no other refuge . . . Those monks who in my time or afterwards live thus, seeking an island and a refuge in themselves and in the Dhamma and nowhere else, these zealous ones are truly *my* monks and will overcome the darkness (of rebirth).' (DN 16.2.25–26, abridged)

Thus the Buddha appointed, not a teacher but the Teaching (*dhamma*) as the future leader of the Saṅgha. A few days after these words to Ānanda he was sufficiently restored to health to resume his almsrounds in Vesāli (DN 16.3.1).

Like everyone who has returned to the world after a dangerous illness, the aged Buddha saw it with fresh eyes. On an expedition to the Cāpāla Shrine, he spoke in almost romantic terms of the beauty of Vesāli and its surrounding shrines (DN 16.3.2). And when, some time later, he left Vesāli with the premonition that he would never see it again, he had a melancholic glance back at the city from some distance (DN 16.4.1).

By slow stages the journey proceeded through Bhaṇḍagāma, Hatthigāma, Ambagāma, Jambugāma and Bhoganagara, always in a north-westerly direction. Apparently he wanted to wait for his death, which he felt to be near, in one of the monasteries of Sāvatthi. Not having appointed any monk as his successor and head of the Saṅgha, and having declared the Dhamma as the highest authority over the Order, he spent some time on the way in considering how the Saṅgha should behave towards any monk who might claim to have heard this or that doctrine from the Master's own lips. In such a case, he instructed the monks at Bhoganagara, the words of that monk were to be judged according as they could be verified from a discourse (*sutta*) and were in harmony with the discipline (*vinaya*). Only if this could be established with certainty could such words be recognized as being the word of the Tathāgata (DN 16.4.8). The statement shows that Gotama was sure his discourses would be borne in the memory of his monks and passed on by them.

THE GREAT PASSING

In Pāvā (probably the modern Fazilnagar, 16 km south-east of Kasia), the Master and his group were invited to a meal for the following day by the smith Cunda. In order to put something special before the venerable guest, Cunda had, among other dishes, prepared *sūkara-maddava*. What exactly this was still remains uncertain. Some writers think it was pork, others think of tender bamboo-shoots such as grow near a pig-sty, others again some kind of fungus, possibly truffles. But, whatever it may have been, the Buddha viewed this food with suspicion, and asked Cunda not to offer it to the other monks. He himself, however, partook of it, in order not to disappoint the well-meaning smith (DN 16.4.13–19).

This concern for the donor was a mistake. The Buddha became sick with dysentery, and suffered from painful attacks of colic. Weak and exhausted as he was, he still left Pāvā behind and headed for Kusināra. Again and again he was forced to turn aside to relieve himself and rest by the wayside.

The colic and dehydrating diarrhoea was accompanied by thirst. When he begged for water, Ānanda pointed out that the nearby stream had been fouled by the passage of ox-carts and would only yield dirty water unfit to drink – better continue to the river Kakutthā (now Bādhi or Barhi) which was not far away. But the Master persisted and drank water from the stream, which meanwhile had settled and was clear again (DN 16.4.20–5).

At this moment, a man from the Malla tribe came along. His name was Pukkusa. He addressed the Buddha and it turned out that Pukkusa was a follower of Āḷāra Kālāma, under whom Gotama had studied before his enlightenment. When Pukkusa saw the dirty robes of the sick old man and his assistant, he quickly sent a servant to get two robes, which he presented to the Buddha and Ānanda (DN 16.4.26–35).

As soon as Pukkusa was out of sight, the little group continued its march and reached the river Kakutthā, where the master drank, bathed and rested at the other bank where the novice Cundaka had spread out his outer robe on the ground under the mango trees. Cundaka's presence recalled the smith Cunda to the Buddha, in whose house he had suffered the food-poisoning, and he impressed on Ānanda that the Order should not reproach the smith, whose intentions had been of the best (DN 16.4.37–42). As soon as he had regained a little strength, the journey continued. The exhausted Teacher waded the Hiraññavati (now Little Gandak) with his monks, and reached Kusināra, the second capital of the Mallas, which he knew from previous visits (MN 103, AN 10.44).

As he declared that he was tired and must lie down, Ānanda prepared a resting-place for him under the sāla trees in the Upavattana wood at the southern edge of the town. The sāla trees (*Shorea robusta*) were in bloom, which, contrary to tradition, which puts the Master's death in Vesākha (April–May), points to the months of March–April. Lying on his right side, perhaps contracted with pain, he tried to rest. Because the cold sweat that is associated with colic and intestinal troubles made him feel cold, he sent the bhikkhu Upavāṇa, who was fanning him, away (DN 16.5.1–4).

He now no longer doubted that from this place in the sāla grove near Kusināra he would not rise again. Clear-headedly, he instructed Ānanda about what was to be done with his body. The monks were not to concern themselves with his funeral, but only strive for their own liberation. There were plenty of people who had faith in the Tathāgata, and they would do all that was necessary (DN 16.5.10). Weeping, Ānanda went aside and gave way to grief: 'Alas, I am still only a learner, I still have much to do (in working on myself), and now the Master who took pity on me is about to enter Parinibbāna!'

When the Buddha noticed that his faithful servant was not there, he sent for him and comforted him:

> 'Enough, Ānanda, do not weep and wail! Have I not always told you that we must part with all things that are dear and pleasant to us, that we must say farewell to them, that nothing can remain eternally as it is? That something that is born, become, conditioned (by the *kamma* of previous existences and, therefore, is) destined to perish – that such a thing should not pass away, that cannot be. For a long time, Ānanda, you have been in the Tathāgata's presence and have with patient kindness looked after my wellbeing. You have gained much merit by that. Make the effort, and you will soon destroy the influences!' (DN 16.5.14, end abridged)

It was presumably on the alms-round next morning, and allegedly on the Buddha's instructions, that Ānanda made the Master's sickness known in Kusināra. Thereupon, numerous citizens of the town made their way to the sāla grove to see the venerable head of the Order, of whom they had heard such wonderful things for the last forty-five years. Ānanda did everything he could to prevent the exhausted old man from being disturbed. Subhadda, a *samaṇa* of another school, who came in the evening to see the Master, was sent away, but the Master, who had overheard the conversation, told Ānanda to let the visitor in. At the end of his conversation with the Buddha Subhadda requested the Master to ordain him in the Saṅgha, and Ānanda gave him the 'going forth' (*pabbajjā*). Subhadda was the last person to be accepted as a novice into the Order in the Buddha's lifetime. Later, after the conclusion of the usual waiting-period for *samaṇas* of other schools, he also received the bhikkhu ordination (*upasampadā*) (DN 16.5.19–30).

To prevent any monk from laying claim to the leadership of the Saṅgha was so important to Gotama that, shortly before his death, he once again stressed the guiding function of the Dhamma for the Order:

> 'Ānanda, it might be that some of you think: "The Master's instruction has vanished, now we have no Master!" It should not be seen like this, Ānanda. What I have taught and explained to you as Dhamma and Discipline (*vinaya*) will, at my passing, be your Master.' (DN 16.6.1)

This presupposed that there were no unclear points that might lead to differences of interpretation. Therefore, the Buddha gave the monks a last opportunity to question him:

> 'It may be, monks, that some monk has doubts or uncertainty about the Buddha, the Dhamma or the Saṅgha, or about the (eightfold) path or the practice (for gaining liberation). Ask, monks, lest you afterwards feel remorse, thinking: "We sat face to face with the Master, and yet we failed to ask him personally."' (DN16.6.5)

But the bhikkhus remained silent. Then the Buddha gave them a last chance: if they did not dare to speak out of respect for him, they should ask through a fellow-monk. Again the monks remained silent. There was no unclarity anywhere. The night was far advanced, and it was quiet between the trees when the dying teacher addressed the bhikkhus once more:

> 'Now, monks, I declare to you: all elements of personality (*saṅkhāra*) are subject to decay. Strive on untiringly!' (DN 16.6.7)

These were the Buddha's last words. Thereafter he fell into a coma, which Anuruddha declared to the monks was a meditational state, and, without recovering consciousness, the eighty-year-old teacher passed into Parinibbāna, the state of liberation from suffering after abandoning the body (DN 16.6.8–9). The majority of historians of India date this event at 483 BC.

THE CREMATION

The most composed was Anuruddha, a cousin of the Buddha and Ānanda's half-brother, who consoled the monks, some of whom were weeping, repeating to them the words of the deceased Master about the transitory nature of all life. Towards the morning he told Ānanda to go to Kusināra to announce the Tathāgata's death to the citizens. Willingly as ever, the aged Ānanda carried out this mission. He reported the decease of the teacher in the assembly hall, where the Mallas were just in session. At once the assembly ordered ceremonies for the funeral (DN 16.6.11–13).

The canonical account of the cremation conveys the impression of utter confusion. As the little group of monks, consisting of Ānanda, Cundaka, Anuruddha, Upavāna and possibly one or two others, had received instructions from the Buddha to leave his funeral arrangements to his lay followers who, however, were apparently not numerous in Kusināra, nobody felt really responsible. Tokens of mourning in the form of flowers and incense came in plenty, but it seems no one was prepared to bear the cost of the wood for the pyre. The cremation was postponed from one day to the next, it is said for a week.

Further, there was confusion about the form of ritual to be used. The dead man was a Sakiya and a khattiya, but also a *samaṇa* and an opponent of Brahmin ritualism – so what form of ceremonial was suitable for him? Should he be cremated to the south or to the east of the city? Finally they decided on the latter, and bore the cloth-wrapped corpse in through the North Gate and out again through the East Gate to the Makuṭa-bandhana, by which is probably meant a mortuary, open at all sides, at the cremation place (DN 16.6.13–16).

In the meantime the monk Mahākassapa or 'Kassapa the Great' was on his way to Kusināra with a company of bhikkhus, presumably intending to spend the coming rains in Sāvatthi. Mahākassapa was, after the deaths of Sāriputta and Moggallāna, the most prominent monk in the Saṅgha, and if the Buddha had nominated a successor, the choice would probably have fallen on him. He was a Brahmin from the Magadha village of Mahātittha. The Buddha had, many years previously, personally accepted him into the Saṅgha on meeting him between Rājagaha and Nālandā. Within a week thereafter, Kassapa had gained the highest understanding (SN 16.11.16–23), thus becoming an Arahant.

Mahākassapa was the proud wearer of the Master's threadbare outer robe. This honour had, it is true, been his by accident. When the Buddha once wanted to rest from wandering under a tree, Kassapa had folded his own outer garment and offered it to the Master to sit on. Gotama accepted and, being sensitive on account of his painful back, found that the cloth was especially soft. Kassapa therefore gave it to him, receiving the Master's worn rag robe in exchange. On this basis he claimed to be a true 'son of the Blessed One, born of his mouth' (SN 16.11.24–30), who was fitted for special tasks.

The Buddha had always esteemed Mahākassapa highly, had visited him when he was ill (SN 46.2.4), and had praised him to younger monks as a bhikkhu whose life was exemplary and who was content with little (SN 16.1). All the same, he was not unaware of Kassapa's difficult character, and the way he demanded the utmost discipline from the young monks, without always showing sufficient understanding or making any allowances. One novice, driven to desperation, had even set fire to Mahākassapa's leaf-hut just erected for the rains (Jāt 321), which did nothing to increase Kassapa's sympathies for the younger monastic generation. More than once he roundly refused the Buddha's request to address the young monks (SN 16.6; 16.7; 16.8).

It was, then, this Mahākassapa who together with other bhikkhus, was on the way from Pāvā to Kusināra, and who was just resting under a tree when an Ājīvika monk came along. The following dialogue ensued:

Mahākassapa 'Brother, do you know our Master?'
The Ājīvika 'Certainly I do. Today it is just a week since the *samaṇa* Gotama attained Parinibbāna. (DN 16.6.19)

This was sad news which only the advanced monks in Kassapa's group were able to accept philosophically; the rest burst into tears. One exception was Subhadda – not to be confused with the novice of the same name to whom the Buddha, on the eve of his death, had granted the going forth. This Subhadda, a former barber from the village of Ātumā, who had only gone forth into homelessness at an advanced age, declared: 'Enough, brothers, do not weep and wail! We are well rid of the Great Samaṇa. We were always bothered by his saying: "You are allowed to do this, you are not allowed to do that!" Now we can do what we like, and not do what we don't like!' (DN 16.6.20). Mahākassapa made no reply to these words, but was soon to have occasion to remember them.

Instantly he hastened forward with his group to Kusināra, reaching the cremation place just in time to find the pyre of the Buddha not yet lit. The small quantity of wood that had been collected is clear from the fact that the wrapped-up feet of the corpse were still visible.

After Mahākassapa and the other monks had circumambulated the body three times in a clockwise direction, and had paid homage by bowing with palms together, the wood was set alight. When the pyre had burnt down, the embers were quenched with water. Of the Buddha's body, only a few fragments of bone remained. They were buried in an earthen pot at the cremation place, and the Mallas marked the spot by planting spears in the ground all round (DN 16.6.22–3).

It seems not to have occurred to any of the Kusināra Mallas that any other tribes might lay claim to relics of the Buddha. They were therefore very surprised when messengers arrived in Kusināra from all directions, requesting a share of the Buddha's relics. At first they were unwilling to give away any part of the bones, but finally heeded the advice of the Brahmin in charge of the cremation, Doṇa, who pointed out that a selfish attitude to the relics would lead to trouble, besides being contrary to the teachings of the deceased, who had always stood for peace (DN 16.6.25). Accordingly, Doṇa divided the bone remains into eight parts, of which one part each went to:

King Ajātasattu of Magadha in Rājagaha,
the Licchavīs of Vesāli,
the Sakiyas of Kapilavatthu (i.e. *New* Kapilavatthu),
the Bulīs of Allakappa,
the Koliyas of Rāmagāma,

The inscription, in Brāhmī letters, on the lid of the urn from Piprāvā is the oldest preserved inscription in India. Translation: 'This urn with relics of the exalted Buddha of the Sakiya (clan) was donated by Sukiti and his brothers, together with sisters, sons and wives.'

a Brahmin from Veṭhadīpa, and
the Mallas of Pāvā.
The Mallas of Kusināra kept the remaining eighth.

When the bone relics had already been thus distributed, a messenger arrived from the Moriyas of Pipphalivana asking for a share. He had to be content with some ashes from the pyre. Doṇa took for himself the clay pot in which the relics had been kept between the cremation and the distribution (DN 16.6.24–6). All ten recipients of relics or souvenirs buried their share in stūpas (DN 16.6.27).

So far, two of these relic-urns have been discovered and examined by archaeologists. The small spherical urn with a votive inscription on the lid which the Sakiyas buried in what is now Piprāvā (= Kapilavatthu II) is in the Indian National Museum in Calcutta, but without the ashes, which were presented decades ago to the king of Siam (Thailand). The covered bowl in which the Licchavīs buried their share of the relics was unearthed in Vesāli in 1958. It contains remnants of bone, ashes and other things and is today in the custody of the Department of Archaeology and Museums of the State Government of Bihār in Patna.

KUSINĀRA – THE ARCHAEOLOGICAL SITE

According to Ānanda, the Mallas' city of Kusināra was 'a miserable

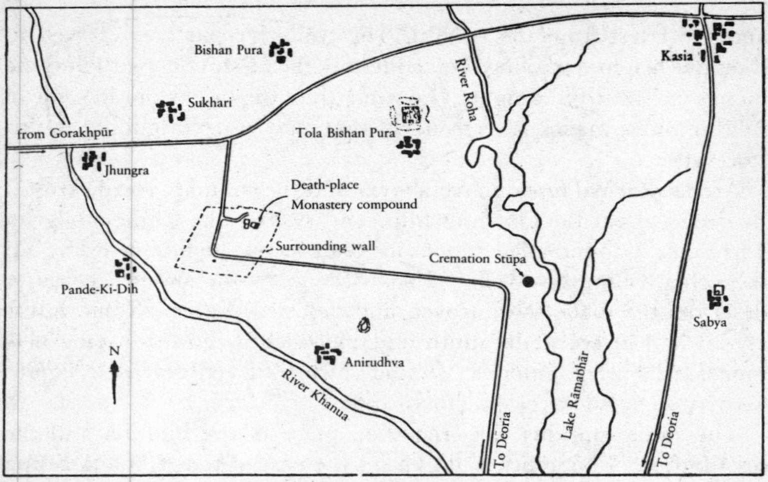

Kusināra (Skt Kuśinagara), overall plan.

little town of wattle-and-daub, right in the jungle in the back of beyond' (DN 16.5.17). Today, no trace of it can be found. The name Kusināra denotes simply the archaeological monuments of the site of the Great Passing, which can be most conveniently reached from Gorakhpur by car or bus. The distance is 55 km, the direction due east. Two kilometres before the village of Kasia we turn to the south and come to the site of the Buddha's death, the sāla grove, after 500 m. The attempt of the Indian government to reafforest the region with sāl trees is still in its infancy, but promises success.

The most striking monument on the spot is the Nibbāna Stūpa, some 20 m high, the original core of which, enclosed in repeated cladding, probably dates from the third century AD. The stūpa was restored to its erect hemispherical form in 1927. Its original height is estimated at about 45 m. In front of it and sharing the same rectangular platform is the Nibbāna Temple, reconstructed in 1956, a hall with tunnel vaulting after the model of the early rib-vaulted *vihāras*. It contains a 6.20 m-long sandstone sculpture of the dying Buddha, lying on his right side, which dates from the fifth century.

To the west, north and north-east of these two monuments are the remains of several monasteries, the oldest from the third century AD, and the latest from the twelfth. The walls are partly preserved to shoulder height, enabling one to identify the inner courtyard and the monks' cells surrounding it. The strength of the brickwork in some of the buildings makes it seem likely that they were originally multi-storeyed.

Archaeological research has shown that the complex was destroyed by fire in about the fourth or fifth century AD. The Chinese pilgrim Fa-hsien still found a few monks in residence in the fifth century, but the other Chinese traveller, Hsüan-tsang, in the seventh century, describes the place as destroyed and deserted. Later it came to life again, and between the ninth and the twelfth centuries some new monasteries were founded. In the thirteenth century all religious activity seems to have come to an end.

The stūpa marking the cremation place of the Buddha and the distribution of his relics is 1.5 km to the east of the Nibbāna Stūpa and is called by the local inhabitants either by the Sanskrit name of Aṅgārastūpa ('Stūpa of the Ashes'), or, in Hindī, Rāmabhār-ṭila ('Rāmabhār Hill'), after the Rāmabhār Lake to its east. It stands on a flat base and has a diameter of 34 m. Its original height cannot be judged, because treasure-hunters and brick-robbers have over the centuries removed more and more of the upper part. Archaeologically speaking, the stūpa is of no great significance, but for any visitor familiar with the story of the Buddha's life it is a moving memorial.

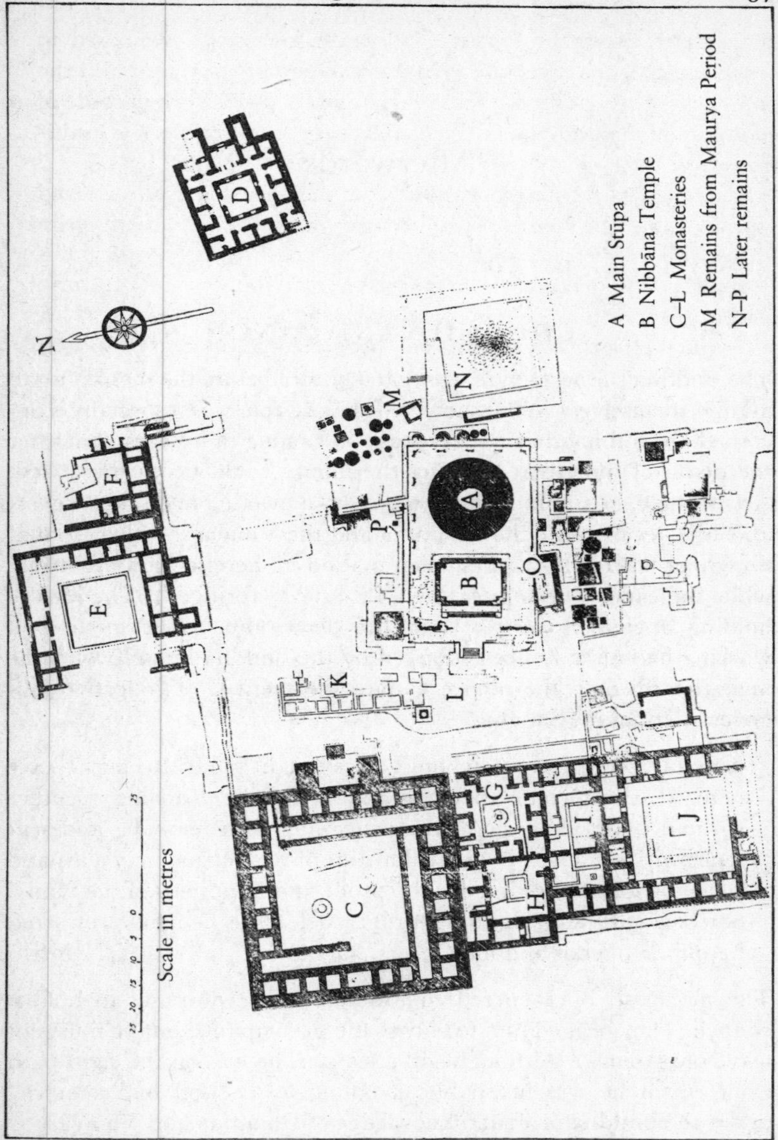

Kusinārā (Skt Kuśinagara), site of the Buddha's Parinibbāna.

8

Afterwards

COUNCILS AND CANON

The Buddha's funeral pyre was scarcely cool before the monks began asking themselves: What now? Mahākassapa was especially concerned, for Subhadda's remark was still ringing in his ears, that after the death of the Great Samaṇa the monks could do as they liked. Accordingly, he summoned the monks to a meeting and said: 'Venerable Sirs, let us recite the Dhamma and the Vinaya together, so that no wrong teachings or rules creep in, and no heretics become strong while the experts become feeble' (Cv 11.1.1, abridged). The idea of holding a council (*saṅgīti*) and the description of its method of working had already been supplied by the Buddha himself, when he once described to the novice Cunda the method of collective self-government of the Saṅgha:

> 'Cunda, those of you to whom I have taught the truths that I have realized, must come together and recite the teaching together without quarrelling, comparing meaning with meaning and sentence with sentence, in order that this pure doctrine may exist and continue for a long time for the profit and happiness of the many, out of compassion for the world and for the benefit, profit and happiness of gods and men.' (DN 29.17)

The monks at once agreed to Mahākassapa's proposal to hold a council. They begged him to choose the participants, but he must not leave out Ānanda. Although still a learner, he was on the right path from which he was incapable of falling away, and had acquired under the Buddha profound knowledge of Dhamma and Vinaya.

The especial commendation of Ānanda as a member of the council had a particular reason. It was well known in the Saṅgha that there had been repeated differences of opinion between the uncompromising Mahākassapa and the soft-hearted Ānanda. Because Ānanda occasionally instructed the nuns, Kassapa suspected him of emotional involvement and once had even threatened him with a disciplinary investigation by the Order (SN 16.10.13). On another occasion, because some of the novices under Ānanda's care had left the Saṅgha, Kassapa had addressed the aged Ānanda, in the hearing of some nuns, as 'laddie' (*kumāraka*) (S 16.11.7). On the other hand, Mahākassapa could not deny that Ānanda had heard and remembered more discourses of the Buddha than any other bhikkhu. In the interest of the cause, therefore, he included him in the list of members of the council. The list is supposed to have embraced 500 monks, all 'elders' (*thera*) (Cv 11.1.2), i.e. monks of at least ten years' standing.

It was probably still in Kusināra that the Order agreed to Mahākassapa's list, and decided on Rājagaha as the venue for the synod. The date was fixed for the forthcoming rains (483 BC). No other monks, apart from these five hundred, were to be allowed into Rājagaha for the monsoon, so that the council might meet undisturbed.

Arrived in the Magadha capital, the monks spent a month building themselves rain-huts and restoring ruined older lodgings. The fact that after the long journey from Kusināra to Rājagaha they still had so much time before the outbreak of the rains (usually mid-June) is a further indication that the Buddha's Parinibbāna must be assumed to have taken place in March or April 483 BC.

Eventually everything and everyone was ready for the council to begin – all except Ānanda, who had not yet become an Arahant. Ashamed, he meditated almost the whole night through, until in the early morning before the beginning of the council, when he wanted to take a little rest, suddenly, 'between lifting his feet off the floor and laying his head down on the bed', he achieved 'the destruction of the influences (*āsava*) and liberation from rebirth' (Cv 11.1.3–6). Now he too was a Holy One, an Arahant, which naturally increased the standing of the council. Perhaps it was for the sake of giving the council greater authority that the members decided to ascribe Arahantship to the aged bhikkhu, who had been in the robe for forty-four years without attaining liberation, so shortly before the council began.

According to the commentaries, the codification session of the five hundred took place in the Sattapaṇṇi Cave of Mount Vebhāra (now Vaibhāra), the most north-westerly of the mountains surrounding Rājagaha. The information is not contained in the canonical account. If it is correct it raises doubts about the number of participants (which in any case is not to be taken literally), because five hundred bhikkhus would have room neither in nor in front of the cave.

In the course of the following seven months, Mahākassapa asked the bhikkhu Upāli about the rules of the Order (*vinaya*) and the bhikkhu Ānanda about the Buddha's discourses (*sutta*) (Cv 11.1.7–8). If the assembly remained silent, the statement of the Master, as conveyed by Upāli or Ānanda, was considered to be reported correctly and was thus recognized as canonical. Each monk present was encouraged to make objections or additions, or to declare any utterances of the Buddha that he remembered, for the record. The canon so established was not written down but committed to memory. In ancient India writing was used only for legal agreements and contracts, i.e. for relatively short-lived documents not considered worth memorizing. Texts which served for acquiring a mastery of life were learnt by heart so as to be ready for recitation at any time. They were passed on to younger generations of monks by recitation and repetition exercises.

The differences between Mahākassapa and Ānanda threatened to break out once again when, during the council, Ānanda quoted the Buddha's words (DN 16.6.3) to the effect that after his, the Buddha's, death the monks might, if they wished, abolish the minor disciplinary rules (*sikkhāpadāni*). At once, Kassapa inquired: 'Ānanda, did you ask what rules those are?' 'No, I did not,' Ānanda was forced to admit. Then a discussion arose as to what could be considered minor rules. Finally, Kassapa proposed to the assembly that they should retain all the rules, so that the laity should not think the Order had grown lax after the Founder's death. The synod accepted this proposal by silence (Cv 11.1.9). Ānanda's lapse, of course, gave food for talk for some time, and led, as always in such cases, to other mistakes of the old monk's being recalled. For the sake of peace, Ānanda made a formal confession of guilt (Cv 11.1.10).

The language used by the Rājagaha council, and in which it canonized the word of the Buddha, was Pāli, an elevated form of Māgadhī, avoiding dialect forms and with its vocabulary enriched through expressions borrowed from related Indian languages. Pāli was a supra-regional *lingua franca*, spoken only by the educated, but understood also by the common people. The Northern Indian rulers used it as the language of administration and of the courts, so that Siddhattha Gotama the rāja's son was familiar with it from youth. Upāli and Ānanda, too, presumably spoke it fluently.

The council had just ended and the original form of the Pāli Canon had been established when the bhikkhu Purāṇa with a group of friends came to Rājagaha to collect alms. Proud of the task they had achieved, the monks from the council asked him to agree to the text as they had codified it. Purāṇa replied: 'The elders of the Order have well recited and canonized the Dhamma and Discipline. But I prefer to remember them as I myself heard and received them from the Blessed One' (Cv 11.1.11). This does not necessarily imply that there were any factual differences between his conception of the Dhamma and those of the synod. Probably Pūraṇa's words just mean: 'Why should I, who have heard the Master speak and who am still under the immediate impression of his personality – why should I accept a second-hand literary fixation of his words?'

One hundred years after the First Council, in 383 BC, a Second Council undertook a revision of the original Canon. The occasion of this council was disagreement in regard to the discipline (*vinaya*). After much toing-and-froing, a committee had decided against the acceptance of ten proposed innovations, and in order to confirm this decision the Canon in the course of eight months was once again recited by a synod of seven hundred *theras* in Vesāli, under the chairmanship of the bhikkhu Revata (Cv 12.12.8–9). In order to make clear their adherence to tradition, the participants in the council called themselves Theravādins, i.e. 'supporters of the Doctrine of the Elders'. The innovators, who claimed to be in the majority, called themselves Mahāsaṅghikas, i.e. 'members of the Great

Community'. Out of the Mahāsaṅghika there developed, about the beginning of the Christian era, the Mahāyāna or 'Great Vehicle'.

If the First Council had seen its task as to establish faithfully the words of the Buddha and codify them for the Community of the future, the Second Council sifted – or rather 'heard' – this great mass of texts according to certain editorial principles. In spite of the Buddha's statement (MN 90; ii, 127): 'No one knows everything', the synod was concerned to prove Gotama's omniscience, which in their opinion he had acquired at his enlightenment (*bodhi*) that had made him a 'Buddha'. They therefore endeavoured to cut out of the original Canon all references to any later findings and recognitions of the Master's, and to harmonize all statements made in the earlier and later stages of his life. Fortunately, they were not always careful about doing this, so that Indologists still have some clues to the progress of Gotama's intellectual development. In order to make the Buddha's omniscience clearer, they made some fairly crude additions to the text, so as to show that the Master already knew what he was about to be told. For instance, when the physician Jīvaka prescribed a medicine for him, Gotama already knew what it would be, but still waited for the prescription.

Further, the Vesāli council under Revata was responsible for the inflation of the canonical text. Owing to a hundred years of memorization and oral repetition, many passages had become ossified to 'word-blocks'. When the Canon was repeated, these blocks were inserted wherever they seemed relevant to the subject-matter, even if they made nonsense of the train of thought. Finally, too, the Second Council expanded the Canon by the inclusion of material that had been passed on outside the textual mass of the original Canon.

A Third Council was held at Pāṭaliputta (Patna) in 253 BC under the patronage of the great Indian Buddhist emperor Asoka Moriya (Skt Aśoka Maurya). This assembly of a thousand monks was presided over by Moggaliputta Tissa. In nine months' work the Council once again reviewed the Theravāda Canon, and added to the existing two collections of *Vinaya* and *Sutta* a third, scholastic work. With the addition of further scholastic books, in the course of the next two centuries there finally arose the third collection, known as the *Abhidhamma*. The three collections of texts are referred to as 'baskets' (*piṭaka*), and the Pāli Canon is therefore often called the 'triple basket' (*tipiṭaka*).

It is due to the successful missionary activity of Asoka (ruling as sole ruler 269–232 BC) that the Pāli Canon has been preserved to us. It was Asoka who, through his son Mahinda, converted the island of Ceylon (Lanka) to Buddhism, thus assuring to the Buddha's teaching a home in which it survived all historical crises. In the monasteries of this island, the Pāli Canon was preserved in the memories of the monks until, in the first century BC, they wrote it down on the dried leaves of the *talipot* palm (*Corypha umbraculifera*) (Dv 20.20f.; Mhv 33.100f.). The rock-monastery Aluvihāra (P Ālokavihāra), where this was done, lies 3 km north of Matale. When the visitor to Sri Lanka journeys by car northwards from Kandy he should not fail, after passing Matale, to cast a thankful glance to the left at the great rock of Aluvihāra, where, two thousand years ago, the timeless doctrine of the Buddha was put into writing.

Bibliography

All the most important works of the Pāli Canon have been translated into English, mainly by the Pāli Text Society ('Sacred Books of the Buddhists', later 'PTS Translation Series'). Apart from these, a new translation of the Dīgha Nikāya by M. O'C. Walshe appeared in 1987 under the title *Thus have I heard – The Long Discourses of the Buddha* (London). A translation of the Majjhima Nikāya, by the late Ven. Ñāṇamoli, will appear shortly. See also: Russell Webb, *An Analysis of the Pāli Canon*, BPS, 1975.

ANCIENT BIOGRAPHIES OF THE BUDDHA

Apart from the biographical information contained in the Pāli Canon, there are four Indian biographies, all of which contain much legendary material:

1 *Nidānakathā* (=Introduction to the Jātakas), transl. from Pāli by T. W. Rhys Davids in *Buddhist Birth Stories*, 2nd edn, PTS, 1925.

2 *Mahāvastu*, transl. from Sanskrit by J. J. Jones, 3 vols, London, 1949–56.

3 *Lalita Vistara*, French transl. from Sanskrit by P. E. Foucaux, 2 vols, Paris, 1884–92; partial English transl. (15 chapters) by R. L. Mitra, Calcutta, 1881–6.

4 *Buddhacarita* by Aśvaghoṣa, English transl. from Sanskrit by E. B. Cowell, in *Sacred Books of the East*, vol. 49, Oxford, 1894.

MODERN BIOGRAPHIES

A. Bareau, *Le Bouddha*, Paris, 1962.

E. H. Brewster, *The Life of Gotama the Buddha, Compiled Exclusively from the Pāli Canon*, 2nd edn, London, 1956.

M. Carrithers, *The Buddha*, Oxford, 1983.

A. Foucher, *The Life of the Buddha According to the Ancient Texts and Monuments of India* (abridged transl. from French), Middletown, Conn., 1963.

D. Ikeda, *The Living Buddha, an Interpretive Biography*, New York-Tokyo, 1976.

Ven. Ñāṇamoli, *The Life of the Buddha as it Appears in the Pāli Canon*, BPS, 1972.

M. Pye, *The Buddha*, London, 1979.

H. Saddhatissa, *The Life of the Buddha*, London, 1976.

E. J. Thomas, *The Life of the Buddha as Legend and History*, 6th edn, London, 1960.

K. D. P. Wickremesinghe, *The Biography of the Buddha*, Colombo, 1972.

GEOGRAPHY

B. C. Law, *Geography of Early Buddhism*, 2nd edn, Varanasi, 1973.

B. N. Puri, *Cities of Ancient India*, Meerut-Delhi-Calcutta, 1966.

SOCIAL CONDITIONS AND DAILY LIFE IN ANCIENT INDIA

J. Auboyer, *Daily Life in Ancient India from 200 B.C. to 700 A.D.*, London 1965.

A. L. Basham, *The Wonder that was India. A Survey of the Culture of the Indian Sub-Continent before the Coming of the Muslims*, 2nd edn, London, 1967.

A. P. de Zoysa, *Indian Culture in the Days of the Buddha*, Colombo, 1955.

M. Edwardes, *Everyday Life in Early India*, London, 1969.

D. D. Kosambi, *Ancient India. A History of its Culture and Civilization*, New York, 1965.

G. S. P. Misra, *The Age of Vinaya. A Historical and Cultural Study*, New Delhi, 1972.

T. W. Rhys Davids, *Buddhist India*, London, 1903; 7th edn, Calcutta, 1957.

N. Wagle, *Society at the Time of the Buddha*, Bombay, 1963.

POLITICS IN THE TIME OF THE BUDDHA

B. C. Law, *The Magadhas in Ancient India*, 2nd edn, Delhi, 1976.

Y. Mishra, *An Early History of Vaiśālī*, Delhi, 1962.

V. Pathak, *History of Kośala up to the Rise of the Mauryas*, Delhi, 1963.

B. C. Sen, *Studies in the Buddhist Jātakas*, Calcutta, 1974.

J. P. Sharma, *Republics in Ancient India c. 1500 B.C. – 500 A.D.*, Leiden, 1968.

THE SAṄGHA, CULTURAL INFLUENCE OF BUDDHISM, COUNCILS

D. K. Barua, *Vihāras in Ancient India. A Survey of Buddhist Monasteries*, Calcutta, 1969.

H. Bechert and R. Gombrich (eds), *The World of Buddhism. Buddhist Monks and Nuns in Society and Culture*, London, 1984.

B. N. Chaudhury, *Buddhist Centres in Ancient India*, Calcutta, 1969.

N. Dutt, *Buddhist Sects in India*, Calcutta, 1970.

N. Dutt, *Early Monastic Buddhism*, 2nd edn, Calcutta, 1960.

S. Dutt, *The Buddha and Five After Centuries*, London, 1957.

S. Dutt, *Buddhist Monks and Monasteries of India. Their History and their Contribution to Indian Culture*, London, 1962.

M. Edwardes, *In the Blowing Out of a Flame. The World of the Buddha and the World of Man*, London, 1976.

I. B. Horner, *Women under Primitive Buddhism. Laywomen and Almswomen*, 2nd edn, Delhi, 1975.

T. Ling, *The Buddha. Buddhist Civilization in India and Ceylon*, London, 1973.

P. Olivelle, *The Origin and the Early Development of Buddhist Monachism*, Colombo, 1974.

L. de la Vallée Poussin, *The Buddhist Councils*, 2nd edn, Calcutta, 1976.

BUDDHIST LAW AND DISCIPLINE

D. N. Bhagvat, *Early Buddhist Jurisprudence. Theravāda Vinaya-Laws*

(Studies in Indian History of the Indian Historical Research Institute 13), Bombay, 1939.

S. Dutt, *Early Buddhist Monachism*, 2nd edn, Bombay, 1960.

The Pāṭimokkha. 227 Fundamental Rules of a Bhikkhu, trans. Ven. Ñāṇamoli, Bangkok, 1966.

LEXICAL WORKS

T. O. Ling, *A Dictionary of Buddhism. A Guide through Thought and Tradition*, New York, 1972.

G. P. Malalasekera, *Dictionary of Pāli Proper Names*, 2 vols, 2nd edn, London, 1960.

G. P. Malalasekera, (ed.), *Encyclopaedia of Buddhism*, Colombo, 1961– (to date: *A-Cittavisuddhi*).

Nyānatiloka Thera, *Buddhist Dictionary*, 3rd edn, Colombo, 1972.

C. S. Upasak, *Dictionary of Early Buddhist Monastic Terms. Based on Pāli Literature*, Varanasi, 1975.

DOCTRINES

S. Collins, *Selfless Persons. Imagery and Thought in Theravāda Buddhism*, Cambridge, 1982.

E. Conze, *Buddhist Thought in India*, London, 1962.

R. A. Gard (ed.), *Buddhism*, New York and London, 1961.

H. von Glasenapp, *Buddhism – A Non-Theistic Religion*, London, 1970.

Lama Anagarika Govinda, *The Psychological Attitude of Early Buddhist Philosophy*, London, 1961.

K. N. Jayatilleke, *The Early Buddhist Theory of Knowledge*, 2nd edn, Delhi, 1980.

N. Katz, *Buddhist Images of Human Perfection. The Arahant of the Sutta Piṭaka compared with the Bodhisattva and the Mahāsiddha*, Delhi, 1982.

É. Lamotte, *History of Indian Buddhism* (English trans.), London, 1987.

W. Rahula, *What the Buddha Taught*, Bedford, 1959.

H. W. Schumann, *Buddhism, an Outline of its Teachings and Schools*, London, 1973.

A. K. Warder, *Indian Buddhism*, 2nd edn, Delhi, 1980.

MONOGRAPHS AND HANDBOOKS ON OTHER RELIGIONS IN THE BUDDHA'S TIME

A. L. Basham, *The Ājīvikas. A Vanished Indian Religion*, London, 1951.

K. K. Dixit, *Early Jainism*, Ahmedabad, 1978.

J. Dowson, *A Classical Dictionary of Hindu Mythology and Religion, Geography, History and Literature*, 8th edn, London, 1953.

P. S. Jaini, *The Jain Path of Purification*, Delhi-Varanasi-Patna, 1979.

G. Liebert, *Iconographic Dictionary of the Indian Religions, Hinduism-Buddhism-Jainism*, Leiden, 1976.

W. Schubring, *The Doctrine of the Jainas Described after the Old Sources*, 2nd edn, Delhi, 1978.

M. and J. Stutley, *A Dictionary of Hinduism – its Mythology, Folklore and Development*, Bombay-Delhi, 1977.

B. Walker, *Hindu World – An Encyclopaedic Survey of Hinduism*, 2 vols, London, 1968.

ARCHAEOLOGY OF BUDDHISM

D. Mitra, *Buddhist Monuments*, Calcutta, 1971.

B. K. Rijal, *Archaeological Remains of Kapilavastu, Lumbini and Devadaha*, Kathmandu, 1979.

D. Valisinha, *Buddhist Shrines in India*, Colombo, 1948.

FLORA AND FAUNA OF INDIA

S. Ali, *The Book of Indian Birds*, 6th edn, Bombay, 1961.

E. Blatter and W. S. Millard, *Some Beautiful Indian Trees*, 4th edn, Bombay, 1977.

D. V. Cowen, *Flowering Trees and Shrubs of India*, 6th edn, Bombay, 1970.

C. McCann, *100 Beautiful Trees of India*, 3rd edn, Bombay, 1966.

S. H. Prater, *The Book of Indian Animals*, 3rd edn, Bombay, 1971.

Index

Buddhism has for its main subjects the *Buddha*, the *Dhamma*, and the *Saṅgha*. The headwords Buddha (also Siddhattha), Dhamma, and Order have, therefore, been treated more in detail than the rest.